public enterprise economics

London School of Economics handbooks in economic analysis

EDITORS: S. G. B. Henry *Lecturer in Economics, University College London* and A. A. Walters *Cassel Professor of Money and Banking, London School of Economics and Political Science*

public enterprise economics

Ray Rees

Lecturer in Economics, Queen Mary College, London

Weidenfeld and Nicolson   **London**

Weidenfeld and Nicolson
11 St. John's Hill London SW11 1XA

ISBN 0 297 77170 1 cased
ISBN 0 297 77219 8 paperback

Filmset
by Willmer Brothers Limited, Birkenhead.

Printed in Great Britain by
Morrison & Gibb Ltd, Edinburgh and London

contents

preface

The aim of this book is to provide a systematic exposition of public enterprise economics, which goes beyond the analysis of marginal cost pricing and its applications, and incorporates the important theoretical developments of the last ten years or so. Roughly half the book is taken up with the discussion of public enterprise objectives and control, the meaning and validity of marginal cost pricing and problems of its application. In the remainder, I go on to analyse pricing and investment problems in a variety of second-best situations; consider the way in which taxation and income-distributional objectives can be incorporated into pricing policies; and conclude with an analysis of price and capacity determination under uncertainty.

The first two chapters, though more descriptive than the rest, play an essential part in placing the later economic analysis in context. In them, I have tried to set out the several objectives which public enterprises are expected to pursue, discuss the conflicts between them, and suggest how economic analysis may contribute to solutions of the problems of control. This analysis can appear metaphysical unless it is understood that the essence of the economist's approach is the search for *decentralized* procedures, which allow the several conflicting objectives to be pursued with a minimum cost of control. The continued controversy over the problems caused by excessive centralization and 'ministerial intervention' suggests that an analysis of the possibility of decentralization through the use of a pricing mechanism has much to contribute.

It will probably be clear by now that the analysis takes place mainly at the general theoretical level. I certainly share the view that the real problems of specific industries can only be solved by detailed numerical models, which represent adequately the particularities of technologies, distribution systems, etc. However, many things are taken as parameters in these models, for example prices and discount rates, which are really variables from the point of view of the industry or sector as a whole. The principles on which they should be determined can only be discussed at the more general level, in the context of theories about the working of the economy, and of explicit value judgements with respect to which optimality is defined. Subject to this, I have tried to choose problems for their relevance rather than their theoretical interest. Although the models in this book are usually simplified for expositional reasons, they are intended to capture the main features of the real problems.

The level of exposition is, in general, meant to be appropriate for second and third year economics undergraduates. I have assumed that the student has had a reasonably rigorous course in microeconomics, at about the level of Ferguson (1972), Baumol (1965), Stigler (1966), or Gravelle and Rees (1977), which will have included some welfare economics. This assumption relieved me of the need to provide expositions of economic theory as such, except when I wanted to suggest a specific emphasis or line of development for the purpose of analysing public enterprise problems. This is true for example of the discussions of welfare economics in chapter 3, cost curves in chapter 4, and intertemporal resource allocation in chapter 8.

The technical aspects of the book should be within reach of second or third-year students, with the possible exception of parts of the last chapter, which will in any case be of interest mainly to the more advanced reader. I have, without apology, used some algebra and a little calculus to sharpen up the statement of results, but there is ample verbal and geometric translation. Matters of purely theoretical concern are usually dealt with in the notes. The chief prerequisite for this book is a good understanding of economic theory.

The constraint on the length of this book was certainly binding, and its shadow price derives from three major omissions. Given the emphasis on analysis, it was not possible to include descriptive material on the nationalized industries – their histories, internal problems, significance to the economy, etc. This omission does not reflect the view that such material is unimportant: I have always felt happier with generalizations, when I have some knowledge of what is being generalized about. Fortunately, there have recently appeared a number of books – for example, Reid and Allen (1970), Reid, Allen, and Harris (1973), and Thomson and Hunter (1973), – which could be used to complement the theoretical approach adopted here.

A second omission was a 'positive' analysis of public enterprise policy. A marked characteristic of the European approach to public enterprise economics is its normative character. It is implicitly assumed that public enterprises will conform to the optimality rules, once they can be found. The North American literature, on the other hand, tends to be largely positive in approach: public utilities are regarded as firms with their own goals, which they pursue subject to externally imposed constraints. This difference of course reflects the different institutional forms of state control in Europe and North America. However, it is hard to ignore the fact that, quite naturally, public enterprise managers develop their own goals. The closest broad characterization of these would appear to be in terms of growth maximization, or rate of decline minimization, but it may be that a more subtle characterization than that would be required. The relevance of positive theories of public enterprise behaviour would mainly be to the problems of decentralization and control. Why *is* such detailed scrutiny of public enterprise plans thought necessary? What *would* happen if control were very much more decentralized, allowing public enterprises, for example, to determine their own prices according to some general pricing rules? Answers to such questions, which are close to the centre of policy debate, require some theory of the objectives of public enterprises as autonomous organizations. Unfortunately, it is not possible to present one here.

Finally, the analysis in the book is entirely in equilibrium and comparative statics terms, and no attempt has been made to provide a dynamic analysis of any problem. There are several problems, particularly to do with extractive industries such as gas, oil, and coal, in which a dynamic analysis has much to contribute. When time must enter in an essential way however, the more mundane approach of two-period analysis has been adopted here. The usual procedure is to reason from necessary conditions for a static constrained maximum, to optimal policies. In doing this, the emphasis has been on providing the student with a good understanding of the reasoning which underlies the analysis, at the expense, usually, of generality and rigour.

I would like to express my thanks to my colleague, Hugh Gravelle, who read and commented most helpfully on the entire manuscript. He is not of course responsible for the ways in which I have used and misused his comments, nor for the errors which may have escaped even his attention. When writing several chapters, I also had the benefit of Mr H. Levene's views on government economic policy. The book was completed during a year spent as a visiting professor at the University of Guelph, Ontario, Canada, and I should like to thank Chairman John Vanderkamp and colleagues for the friendly and stimulating atmosphere in which I found myself. I am especially grateful to Maria Larsen, Carmelina Ridi and Irene Pereira, who deciphered and typed the manuscript. And thanks go as always to Deni, for her charm, tolerance and support.

Ray Rees

July 1975
Guelph, Ontario

chapter 1
public enterprise objectives

A requirement for rational decision-taking, as it is usually defined in economics, is a well-defined and consistent scale of preferences over the outcomes of alternative choices. In the case where a decision-taker is to choose entirely in his own interests, it is quite reasonable to assume that a scale of preference exists and is known to him. There is a wide class of situations, however, in which a decision-taker is actually making choices on behalf of someone else, and the presumption is that he will choose in the other's best interests. We could call these *delegated choice* situations. There are two major problems common to such situations: the first concerns the transmission of information to the decision-taker, about the preferences of the individual or group whose interests he is supposed to be pursuing; the second is the problem of ensuring that the decision-taker's choices do in fact conform to these preferences. Accepting that public enterprise decision-takers are essentially in a delegated choice situation, we shall, in this chapter, consider the first of these problems, and in the next chapter, the second.

To confirm that the public enterprise decision situation is one of delegated choice, we can turn to the formula usually contained in the statute or nationalization act which, by vesting ownership of certain sets of industrial assets in a legal entity called a board, establishes a public enterprise. The board are given responsibility for the 'day-to-day management' of the enterprise, subject to directions [from a specified government minister] of a general character, as to the exercise and performance of their functions in relation to matters appearing to the minister to affect the national interest'. It has been said many times that this formula provides no clear cut distinction between the set of decisions to be taken by the board, and that to be taken by the minister. The ambiguity arises because of the imprecision of the terms 'day-to-day management', 'directions of a general character', and the 'national interest'. However, it is probably asking too much for clear lines to be drawn at the inception of a public enterprise, when nothing is known, although something may be guessed, about the kinds of problems which will arise. For our present purposes, it is enough to note that a delegated choice situation *is* established, and that it takes the following form. The board are, in *the first instance*, responsible for taking all decisions involved in operating the enterprise: they arrange matters so that inputs are bought, and outputs are produced and sold, and this requires choice of prices, outputs, investments, wage rates, manpower policies, etc. The preference ordering which applies to these decisions is to be a representation of the 'national interest', and is thought to differ from that applying to private enterprises, where shareholders' concern for profitability dominates. There is however a very large gap between the general term 'the national interest', and an operational evaluation of the outcomes of decisions. This gap is to be bridged by the minister. He is responsible for defining the 'national interest', identifying those aspects of the board's decisions which impinge upon it, and evaluating the outcomes of decisions in the light of his definition. The 'directions of a general character' are the means by which he informs the board of his interpretations and evaluations of the 'national interest', and implicit in the formula is the expectation that the board will make (or amend) decisions accordingly. Thus, in terms of our delegated choice concept, the minister is responsible for formulating the social preference ordering which should apply to public enterprise decisions, and informing decision-takers of it.

This conceptually neat picture of a minister specifying to decision-takers a preference ordering, which they can then apply to actual choices, does not of course describe the reality. There have been very few general statements defining those aspects of public enterprise decisions which are regarded as important from the view point of the 'national interest', and even these do not give precise descriptions of all such aspects. To learn how ministers have interpreted 'the national interest', we must examine what is in effect a body of case law. General concerns have usually become apparent through ministerial intervention to change specific decisions and to influence plans, rationalized in statements to Parliament and press, and perhaps, subsequently, in White Papers and memoranda. From all of this, we can deduce what ministers have taken to be the aspects of public enterprise decisions which affect the 'national interest', and the general nature of their preferences over these. We can distinguish four such aspects:
1. economic efficiency;
2. profitability;
3. effects on income distribution; and
4. relationship with macroeconomic policy.
We now discuss each of these in turn.

1.1 Economic efficiency
This aspect of public enterprise operations is the one whose desirability is most frequently stressed in formal statements of ministerial preferences, for example in the two White Papers on *Financial and Economic Obligations of the Nationalized Industries*, (Cmnds 1337 and 3437). It can be separated into two concepts of efficiency which are closely related.

1.1.1 *Managerial and technological efficiency*
This concerns the relationship between inputs and outputs. One production method is technologically more efficient than another if, for a given level of output, it absorbs less of at least one input and no more of any other; or alternatively if, with the same input levels, it produces more output. Similarly, one group of managers is more efficient than another, in a static sense, if they carry out a given set of managerial tasks with a smaller absorption of resources. In a dynamic sense, managerial efficiency is concerned also with readiness and ability to eliminate waste and exploit new technological and market opportunities. Other things being equal, ministers appear to prefer more technological and managerial efficiency to less. This is usually expressed in terms of the encouragement to adopt 'commercial' attitudes and methods, which is to be found in most White Papers concerned with nationalized industries.

1.1.2 *Allocative efficiency*
This concept is derived from the theory of welfare economics, and is concerned, at the most general level, with the entire allocation of resources in an economy. An inefficient resource allocation is one which can be changed in such a way as to make some people better off, and no one worse off, in terms of their own preferences. An efficient resource allocation is then one for which no such change is possible. The pursuit of allocative efficiency has many implications for public enterprise policies and, since most of the rest of this book is concerned with the analysis of these, little more needs to be said at this stage. We recognize the concern for allocative efficiency by ministerial statements which stress that prices paid by consumers should be related to the costs of supply; that important divergences between social costs and benefits on the one hand, and market prices on the other (due for example to external effects) should be taken into account; and that public enterprise investments should be evaluated in the light of the consumption and investment elsewhere in the economy which they may displace. These, and similar propositions, follow from the application of concepts of allocative efficiency to public enterprise decisions.

These two concepts of efficiency are related in the following way: allocative efficiency implies managerial and technological efficiency, but the converse does not hold, so that the existence of the latter type of efficiency is a necessary but not sufficient condition for the former. Thus, suppose an enterprise is using a technologically inefficient process which involves over-manning, so that the same amount of output could be produced with less labour and the same amounts of other inputs. Then in general, by reallocating the excess labour, it is possible to produce more of some outputs with no less of any other. As a result, everyone in the economy (including the reallocated workers) can be made better off. The technologically inefficient resource allocation was not therefore allocatively efficient.

An allocatively efficient resource allocation *must* be such that no technological inefficiencies exist, by its definition. On the other hand, allocative inefficiency may coexist with technological efficiency: for example, a public enterprise may be using efficient production methods, and may be producing its output at minimum cost, but, because of an inappropriate pricing policy, its output may be 'too large'. By this we mean that at the margin, the resources used in producing the output are worth more in other uses – the value of the output to its consumers is not as great as its opportunity cost. In this case, it will again be possible to find a way to reallocate resources and make everyone (including the consumers of the over-expanded public enterprise output) better off, and so the resource allocation is not allocatively efficient. Since the two types of efficiency, though related, are not equivalent, it is worth while to maintain the distinction between them.

1.2   Profitability
We define the *gross trading surplus* of a public enterprise as the excess of its total revenue over its operating costs. Its *profit* is defined as the excess of its gross trading surplus over interest and depreciation provisions. This would, in a private enterprise, correspond to the amount available for distribution to shareholders (after taxes, which public enterprises in general do not pay), and so would be the object of prime concern to management. It will soon become clear, however, that it is more useful to focus on the gross trading surplus of a public enterprise, and so 'profitability' will in this context refer to the size of this surplus. There are two main reasons for ministerial concern with the profitability of a public enterprise.

(a) Finance – the net contribution the enterprise makes to the public exchequer depends, given its investment spending, entirely on its surplus. The funds for the investment spending of the enterprise have two sources, i.e. its own reserves, consisting essentially of depreciation provisions, and loans made to it by the exchequer. The exchequer in turn obtains its funds largely from public enterprise gross trading surpluses, taxation and borrowing. These funds must also finance expenditure by: (i) other public enterprises; (ii) agencies supplying public services such as health, education and defence; and (iii) agencies paying subsidies to individuals (unemployment benefit, family allowances, pensions) and to firms (investment grants, agricultural support). Given the planned investment expenditure of the enterprise, the smaller is its surplus, the greater must be taxation and/or borrowing, and the smaller must be other forms of expenditure. It does not matter therefore how this surplus is divided into 'interest', 'depreciation' and 'profit'; all that matters is its total size. This is of course in contrast to a private enterprise, where failure to meet interest payments would probably result in bankruptcy and dissolution of the company, while inadequate depreciation provisions would force the company to contract. The creditor of a public enterprise, the exchequer, will not normally declare it bankrupt, and is prepared to capitalize interest payments, or waive them altogether, and even to cover operating deficits (negative gross trading surplus) with grants and loans. The total size of the surplus is what counts to ministers, since this determines the flow of funds into the exchequer, and the extent of increased taxation, increased borrowing, and reductions in other forms of public expenditure required to finance an investment programme.

(b) Motivation – the pursuit of profitability by a public enterprise is also seen as a means of stimulating managerial and technological efficiency. Thus, we know that if a firm seeks to maximize its profit, this requires it to minimize costs at every level of output. However, the objective of profit maximization has been explicitly rejected for public enterprises because in general they have monopoly power in at least some of the markets they supply, and so profit maximization would result in policies which nationalization was expressly intended to avoid. The problem is, however, that if profitability becomes irrelevant, the incentive to hold down costs may be weakened, if not removed. By reintroducing profitability as something which must be taken into account in decision-taking, though not as something the maximization of which is the overriding goal, it is hoped to stimulate public enterprise managers to pursue efficiency, and also to provide a yardstick by which their efficiency can be measured. Of course, the argument for rejecting profit maximization as a goal also implies that a profitable public (or private) enterprise need not be an efficient one: as long as the enterprise possesses a high degree of monopoly power in at least some of its markets, satisfactory profits can be generated by raising prices rather than by increasing efficiency. This implies that 'profit targets' need not stimulate efficiency if they are unaccompanied by some monitoring of pricing policy. This point has important implications which will be discussed in later chapters.

1.3   Effects on income distribution

A government will generally have specific views about the distribution of real income among households in the economy. These will be reflected in the policies it adopts towards the pattern of public expenditure and taxation. Its taxation policies, and many of its expenditure policies, can be regarded as instruments through which it tries to bring about the changes it desires in the distribution of real income (subject always to the constraint that a government inherits a particular taxation – expenditure pattern and may be able to make only marginal changes in it). A major way in which income is redistributed is through the system of transfer payments: money is paid directly to the old, the sick, the unemployed, victims of criminal assaults, those with incomes below a certain level, and those with children. At least as important, however, is the provision of goods and services at subsidized prices,[1] permitting greater consumption by certain groups of people than would be possible if they had to pay the full costs of supply. Most health and education services are of this kind, as are public housing and road use. In some cases, the prices are actually zero (state-provided education, road use, certain kinds of medical care), while in others, prices are to varying degrees below the costs of supply (public housing, prescription drugs, dental treatment). Note also that since a lower price will (in the absence of quantity rationing) lead to a larger scale of output, the suppliers of inputs used to produce these goods and services may benefit. In particular, the suppliers of labour specific to a good being sold at a subsidized price may gain, perhaps from being employed rather than unemployed, or from having a higher wage or salary than would otherwise be the case (this assumes of course that government does not use its monopsony power as an employer to hold down these wages and so lessen the cost of subsidization). Finally, real incomes are redistributed through policies operating directly on input markets rather than output markets. Regional policy is a good example of this: constraints are placed on the availability of particular inputs, usually land, in some areas of the country, and subsidies are paid to reduce the prices of other inputs – land, labour and capital – in other areas. The object is to change the spatial distribution of real income by changing the spatial distribution of economic activity. Thus, in summary, the instruments by which a government redistributes real income are direct money transfers, subsidized supply of outputs, and constraints and subsidies in supply of inputs, all in conjunction with the system of taxation.

Since public enterprise decisions will often have significant effects on income distribution, they impinge upon a government's income distribution policies, and so these effects will be a relevant attribute of those decisions. Indeed, more positively, public enterprise operations may be used as policy instruments, since they may appear to provide means of redistributing incomes in desired directions more cheaply and effectively than other instruments of public policy. Examples of this abound, and some will be presented and discussed in this and later chapters.

1.4 Macroeconomic effects

A major concern of government is macroeconomic policy, and again, since public enterprise decisions may appear to impinge on this, their potential macroeconomic effects become a matter of concern. Again, certain variables under public enterprise control may actually be viewed positively as instruments of macroeconomic policy. In formulating macroeconomic policies, attention is generally focused on four target variables: the level of unemployment; the rate of inflation; the surplus/deficit on the balance of payments; and the rate of growth of potential national output. The instruments by which the values of these variables are influenced are primarily those of monetary and fiscal policy, although such measures as direct administrative intervention in markets ('prices and incomes policy') have also been adopted from time to time. Several aspects of the operations of public enterprises, and in particular their investment, price and wage policies, appear to affect the values of the target variables. The investment expenditures may, through the usual multiplier effects, influence the aggregate level of economic activity in the short run, and in the longer run help determine the rate of growth of productive potential. Also these investment expenditures, in conjunction with gross trading surpluses, affect the government's financial requirement and so its need for borrowing and taxation, which in turn affect fiscal and monetary policy. Since public enterprises supply goods and services which account for a significant proportion of household expenditures and industrial costs, increases in their wages and prices may be thought to have correspondingly significant effects on the rate of inflation. The balance of payments may be affected both directly and indirectly by public enterprise policies. Public enterprises provide most of the basic infrastructure of the economy – energy, steel, transportation, and communications – and so the efficiency with which they operate will determine in part the international competitiveness of the economy. More directly, several public enterprises are extensively engaged in export markets – for example, British Airways and the British Steel Corporation – and their purchasing decisions may also have important balance-of-payments repercussions, a good example being the aircraft procurement policies of British Airways. Given the many instances in which ministers have intervened in public enterprise pricing and investment decisions, in the interests of prevailing macroeconomic policies, we conclude that the definition of 'the national interest' extends to these macroeconomic effects.

This fairly brief discussion has tried to provide a precise interpretation of the vague term 'the national interest', by classifying under four headings the aspects of public enterprise decisions which ministers have appeared to regard as matters of concern. We now go on to consider how this interpretation of 'the national interest' relates to public enterprise decision-taking.

1.5   Conflicts and objectives
The concept of a preference ordering is neat and powerful. In the present context, it would mean that all possible combinations of four magnitudes – economic efficiency, profitability, distributional equity, and macroeconomic impact – could be ordered in a complete, consistent way, according to ministerial preference. Armed with this ordering, public enterprise managers need only measure, for each decision alternative, the value of each of these magnitudes, and then use the ordering to find the preferred alternative. Simply to describe this ideal establishes its distance from reality.

In practice, discussion of the means of evaluating alternative decisions takes place in terms of a set of 'objectives' for public enterprises, which is at the same time less general and more vague a concept than that of a preference ordering. At its least helpful, specification of public enterprise objectives consists simply of naming the broad kinds of goals which the public enterprises should pursue. More concretely, there have been attempts to set quantitative targets and numerical parameters – for example the financial targets, and the test discount rate, discussed in some detail in the next chapter – which try to operationalize the goals, so that they may actually be used in planning. As a result of the interpretation of 'the national interest' just given, it is clear that to be complete, a specification of objectives must encompass the four relevant aspects of public enterprise decisions: economic efficiency, profitability, effect on income distribution, and macroeconomic effects. There are two major problems in this respect, however. The first is that conflicts exist among the four policy concerns, in the sense that attempts to increase the level of achievement of one of them may have what would be regarded as adverse effects on the others. Hence, a satisfactory statement of objectives must resolve these conflicts by attaching relative weights to each of the four. This is of course another way of saying that some kind of preference ordering must be constructed, since only in the simplest possible circumstances (where only one goal, say profit or growth, is being pursued) can rational decision-taking exist without one.

The second problem is that the way in which public enterprise control is exercised has so far appeared to be incompatible with specification of a consistent, stable, and comprehensive set of objectives. The first of these problems will be discussed in the remainder of this chapter. The second problem will be considered in the next chapter, when we shall have examined the organizational system through which public enterprise control is exercised.

The conflicts which arise among the four areas of policy concern are best discussed in terms of a number of examples. We shall take five main types of conflict in turn.

1. *Economic efficiency and income distribution.* There are several instances in which efficiency has been sacrificed in the interests of increasing or maintaining incomes of particular groups. For example, the decision taken by the Macmillan Government to divide a proposed new steel complex in two, locating one part at Ravenscraig in Scotland, and the other at Llanwern in Wales, sacrificed economies of scale in the interests of increasing Scottish income. The various measures of support for the coal industry throughout the 1960s – including a tax on fuel oil and 'compulsory coal-burn' by the electricity industry – raised energy costs in the UK economy generally, in the interests of slowing the rate of decline of the coal industry, and thus making the real incomes of coal-miners higher than they would otherwise have been. The persistence of over-manning in several public enterprises can be viewed as a tacit decision to distribute real income to particular groups of workers at the expense of economic efficiency.

2. *Profitability and income distribution.* In general, reduced technological efficiency implies lower profitability, and so the foregoing examples are also relevant here. Some examples which do not appear to imply technological efficiency losses (but which may imply allocative efficiency losses) can also be given. The supply of public enterprise outputs to particular groups of consumers at prices below cost increases their real incomes but reduces profitability. For example, many rural and commuter rail services incur a loss, as does the air service to the Scottish Highlands and Islands. The overall nature of the income redistribution implied by such policies depends on the way in which the below-cost provision of services is financed. If an enterprise must meet an overall target surplus, and receives no government subsidy to compensate for loss of profitability on below-cost operations, its prices on profitable services must be correspondingly higher. Hence, real income is distributed away from consumers of profitable services, to those benefiting from services provided at a loss. If this 'cross-subsidization' exists to any large extent, it must be assumed that the Minister accepts it as a form of income redistribution which is consistent with his government's policies. On the other hand, the losses may be subsidized by an *actual* or *implicit* payment from the exchequer, in which case the income is redistributed away from taxpayers in general (or from those who would have benefited from forms of public expenditure which have had to be reduced to finance the subsidies) and towards those benefiting from the below-cost services. An *actual* payment is a sum credited to the accounts of the enterprise by the exchequer: the enterprise can be thought of as acting as a 'contractor' for the government, supplying the services and presenting two bills for their cost, one to the government and the other to the consumers. An *implicit* payment is made if the government reduces the target surplus which the enterprise is expected to achieve, by an amount corresponding to the loss it sustains on the services provided at the government's request. Clearly, in terms of the net contribution which the enterprise makes to the exchequer, it makes no difference *in principle* whether the subsidy is implicit or actual – the financial effects of providing the below-cost services are precisely the same. However, recalling the motivational aspect of the concern with profitability of a public enterprise, there may be in practice a difference in terms of the effects on motivation of managers, and of the ability to use profitability as a yardstick of performance. This point will be further discussed in the next chapter.

3. *Profitability and macroeconomic policies.* The pursuit of profitability may also conflict with macroeconomic policies, the most striking example being the use of public enterprise price and wage policies as instruments in a formal or informal prices and incomes policy. The policy of the government in 1972 and 1973, which involved resistance to trades union wage demands at the cost of strikes, reduced the profitability of the coal and electricity industries in those years, because the losses

incurred during the strikes were not made up by cost savings from wage settlements lower than would have been achieved without the strikes. Similarly, the policy of restricting price increases of public enterprise outputs throughout 1972 and 1973, at a time when costs were rising sharply, actually led to operating deficits for hitherto profitable enterprises. Constraints which have been placed on aircraft purchasing of the air corporations, forcing purchase of British aircraft when American aircraft would have been cheaper, provide an example of the conflict between profitability and balance-of-payments support.

4. *Economic efficiency and profitability.* Although increases in *managerial and technological* efficiency will, other things being equal, increase profitability, so that no conflict exists in that respect, there may be a conflict between *allocative* efficiency and profitability. There is first the point that allocatively efficient pricing and investment policies will *imply* a particular surplus for the enterprise, which may be greater or less than that considered desirable. Turning the point around, if the enterprise is required to earn a specific surplus, then there is nothing to guarantee that the implied prices and outputs will be allocatively efficient. A particular instance of this, much discussed in the literature, is the case where marginal cost pricing is allocatively efficient, and is applied in an industry subject to increasing returns to scale, thus leading to a loss.[2] It may also occur, however, where there is thought to be a divergence between social costs and benefits on the one hand, and revenues and costs calculated at market prices on the other, so that optimization in terms of the former may lead to a loss. For example, it is argued that reductions in traffic congestion, and consequent time savings to travellers justify loss-making public transport systems, because of the overall excess of social benefits over social costs.

5. *Economic efficiency and macroeconomic policy.* The two most important examples of this type of policy conflict are provided by short-term cuts in public enterprise investment expenditure, and restraint of price increases. The first tend to be imposed when efforts are being made to contain total government expenditure, as for example in the late 1960s. The major problem is that by the nature of the investment programmes of public enterprises, a very high proportion of expenditure in the current and following year is committed to projects already in progress. Hence, significant cuts in expenditure for those years disrupts project planning, causes completion delays, and ultimately raises capital costs. Within a time horizon of at least two years, public enterprise investment is neither a cheap nor flexible instrument of short-term control of aggregate demand. The policy of public enterprise price restraint, which was applied, with varying degrees of stringency, from the late 1960s up to 1974, can be expected to distort the pattern of resource allocation. It implies falls in public enterprise prices relative to other prices in

the economy, which have usually not been subject to similar controls. Thus, demands and outputs will tend to be higher than would otherwise be the case, implying that, at the margin, resources absorbed by public enterprises would have a greater value in other uses. Closely related is the fact that since public enterprise gross trading surpluses have been lower than they would have been in the absence of the policy, outputs such as health and education, which are also financed by public expenditure, may have been correspondingly smaller.

1.6   Conclusions

This chapter has been chiefly concerned with the interpretation of the term 'the national interest', as it relates to public enterprise decisions, since such an interpretation is necessary for a clear statement of public enterprise objectives. By examining on the one hand general statements of policy, and on the other specific concerns which have prompted ministerial intervention in decision-taking, 'the national interest' appears to require that four aspects of public enterprise decisions be taken into account. These are: economic efficiency; profitability; effects on income distribution; and macroeconomic effects. Thus, any set of public enterprise objectives must allow boards to appraise alternatives in the light of their consequences for each of these, and to choose that alternative which is the 'best' in terms of its consequences for all four. But, given that conflicts exist among these four aspects of decisions, it is necessary that some set of relative weights be assigned, if the 'policy trade-offs' are to be taken into account in *a decentralized way*. In other words, the statement of objectives must consist of at least some kind of preference ordering, which as we began the chapter by noting, is a requirement for rational decision-taking. If this requirement is not met, then decision-taking cannot satisfactorily be decentralized. In its place, there would have to be continual intervention in the decision process by ministers and their departments, in order to ensure that the deficiencies in the statement of objectives do not result in decisions which run counter to the underlying policy aims. But such intervention blurs the lines of authority and responsibility, duplicates decision-taking, absorbs scarce resources, leads to delay in implementing decisions, and breeds dissatisfaction among public enterprise executives, who feel their discretionary powers sharply constrained. This is of course a description of what many regard as the actual experience of the relationship between ministers and boards.[3] We now turn to a more detailed examination of this relationship.

chapter 2

the system of control of public enterprise

In any situation of delegated choice, the problem exists of ensuring that decisions actually are consistent with the preference ordering of the individual or group in whose interests they are being taken. The problem of ensuring this consistency is the problem of *control*. *A system of control* is a set of rules and procedures, the object of which is to achieve consistency between decisions and preferences in a delegated choice situation.

There are two sets of costs which have to be weighed in the balance, when a system of control is being designed. The first consists of those costs associated with the operation of the system itself. Resources will be absorbed in monitoring decisions, collecting and transmitting information, and examining alternatives. Delays in the implementation of decisions, which the control system might cause, also impose costs. The second set consists of the costs which arise out of non-correspondence between decisions and preferences: if the choices actually made by the decision-taker are not the 'best', from the point of view of the preference ordering which is supposed to regulate decisions, then a cost is imposed, which could be measured by the difference between the 'value' of the outcome of the optimal decision, and that of the decision actually taken. This is, therefore, essentially an opportunity cost.

To see how these two sets of costs are related, let us take two extreme types of control system. In the first, the preference ordering over the outcomes of decisions in general[1] is transmitted to the decision-taker, who is then left entirely alone to apply this to specific decisions, with no further control activity. This is then a completely *decentralized* control system, with minimal costs of operation. On the other hand, the *risk* that decisions will not be taken in conformity with the preference ordering is at its greatest. It is worth stressing that it is a risk, and not a certainty, that costs of this kind will be incurred, and the *a priori* perception of this risk will depend, among other things, on the view taken of the tendency of the decision-taker to develop his own preference ordering over the outcomes of decision, which differs from that he is supposed to adopt.

At the opposite extreme, a control system might exist in which the decision-taker must justify every decision, by presenting information on the choices he has made, and the alternatives which were available. This appraisal procedure is conducted after the decision-taker has made his choice, but before it is implemented. The only risk that decisions will not conform to the preference ordering arises from the possibility that the decision-taker will present biased information. On the other hand, the costs of operating the control system are maximal, since effectively there is duplication of decision-taking, with the 'decision-taker' acting essentially as a preliminary organizer of information. Any actual system of control, in trading-off the two kinds of costs, will end up somewhere between these two extremes.

In the development of the system of control of public enterprise, there have been two contradictory tendencies, one of which lies closer to the first extreme system just described, the other to the second. Given the difficulty of arriving at a clear statement of the 'preference ordering' relating to public enterprise decisions, which we discuss later in this chapter, it is improbable that the system of public enterprise control could be completely decentralized. However, the proposals[2] to establish a set of quantitative objectives for public enterprises, together with pricing and investment 'rules' and appropriate shadow prices (e.g. the cost of public sector capital) represent an attempt to achieve a fairly decentralized system. Monitoring of decisions would take the form of comparing outcomes with objectives, and public enterprise managers are left with complete discretion to take specific decisions, which are not subjected to individual scrutiny prior to implementation. This type of system reflects quite closely the 'formula' for relations between ministers and boards, stated in the Nationalization Acts, and in the previous chapter.

The second tendency in the control system, which in practice has generally dominated, operates essentially by *sampling* from the set of decisions taken by public enterprises, and examining specific plans and projects, and their alternatives, before they are implemented. This results in larger information flows, and longer implementation delays, than in the more decentralized system, as well as to duplication of decision-taking, and a greater absorption of resources in the decision-taking process. The benefits arise presumably from the reduced risk that decisions will not be made 'in the national interest', as defined by ministers.

This brief discussion of the costs and design of control systems will prove useful, when we later come to place in context the contribution which economic theory can make to the problems of public enterprise control. First, we examine the system of control as it actually exists.

2.1   The system of public enterprise control

Control of public enterprises is exercised through a fairly complex administrative system, which is best described by taking separately each of its four components. These are:

1. the obligations and responsibilities associated with the status of *the public corporation*;

2. financial control and accountability;
3. economic 'ground rules'; and
4. specific inquiries by 'outside' bodies.

We now discuss each of these components in turn.

2.1.1   *The public corporation*

At the time of nationalization of a number of major industries in the late 1940s, a choice had to be made of the legal and organizational form of the bodies in which ownership of the industries' assets would be vested. At one extreme would be the Department of State, staffed by civil servants, and at its head a minister directly responsible to Parliament for all of the industry's operations. At the other extreme was the concept of a state holding company, the board of which would supervise the separate boards of the individual industries. The holding company would allocate investment funds, set profit targets and assess performance, and would be responsible to some Department of State, probably the Treasury, for the overall performance of the public enterprise sector. In the event, a compromise between these extremes was chosen: the assets of each industry were vested in a public corporation staffed as would be any other industrial concern, and headed by a board appointed by and directly responsible to a minister. We have already discussed the fairly imprecise formula which delimits the responsibilities and powers of board and minister: the minister is empowered to give general directions which effectively interpret the 'national interest' to the boards, and provide them with the framework of objectives within which to take decisions. The board is in turn accountable to the minister for its performance; i.e., the minister has a right to information on the operations of the enterprise, must appraise its performance, and respond, presumably with comments and 'directions of a general nature' to indicate the ways in which improvements might be made. We should note the way in which this arrangement related to the existing apparatus of economic policy. The ministers concerned already had responsibility for formulating policies for broad sectors of economic activity, particularly energy and transport, and so oversight of one or more public enterprises became a part of a minister's responsibility for a particular sector. In a sense, therefore, the public corporations controlling coal, gas, electricity, and railways were simply additions to the list of industrial concerns for which a minister had a responsibility of general oversight, and formulation of public policy. However, the public ownership of major parts of a sector made, at least potentially, a significant difference to the instruments available to a minister for implementing sectoral policies.

The reason for choice of the public corporation as the legal form for the public enterprise, rather than a Department of State, has been expressed by Professor Robson[3] as the 'need for a high degree of freedom, boldness, and enterprise in management' in contrast to the 'caution and circumspection . . . typical of Government departments'. The industrial enterprises, which were the new public corporations, should be operated by industrialists rather than civil servants. However, the nature of the industries was not thought to justify the degree of insulation from ministerial control represented by the holding company form of organization: the board of each industry was made directly accountable to a minister, who, moreover, had the responsibility for sanctioning investment and borrowing plans. In the event, ministers have been able to exercise powers not given them by statute.[4] The nationalization acts do not empower ministers to intervene to make or amend specific decisions, for example on a projected price increase or redundancy programme. In practice however the minister is able to persuade, cajole, and ultimately coerce a board to accept his view of the way in which a specific decision should be taken or policy formulated. The basis for this does not appear to lie in the minister's formal powers. Ultimately, of course, the minister could use his powers of appointment and dismissal, and of sanction of investment and borrowing, to bring pressure on the board. However, it is hard to find instances where resort to such pressure was necessary. In general, ministers have been able directly to influence and alter public enterprise decisions because of the tacit recognition of the realities of the situation of delegated choice: the public enterprises are state-owned and so are expected to operate in the national interest, and the boards appear to accept that the national interest is what the minister defines it to be. Hence the minister is able directly to influence decisions which he is not strictly empowered to take.

It is also important to note that the relation between a public enterprise and its 'sponsoring' department does not consist only of the accountability of the board to the minister: of a link, as it were, at the heads of the two organizations. Rather, there is continual contact and exchange of information and advice at various levels throughout the organizations, and it is this, rather than the occasional contact with the minister, which is the mainspring of 'ministerial control'. In formulating its own policies, the department will have groups of engineers, economists, accountants, statisticians, and other experts, working on specific plans and projects, often requesting information from an enterprise, and possibly duplicating similar work being done by it. Recalling the discussion in the previous section, on types of control system, and in particular on the properties of decentralization which each possessed, this suggests that the interpretation of 'accountability', and of the status of the public corporation, is such as to have led to a relatively centralized control procedure.

2.1.2   *Financial control and accountability*
Since the finance of public enterprise investment expenditure is provided by the exchequer, loans for this purpose can only be made with approval of the Treasury. Although in principle one could imagine this as a routine procedure, with funds

automatically being made available once the minister of the relevant department has accepted the investment plans of the enterprise, in practice it has become a substantive form of control, and one which introduces a new element in the situation of delegated choice. The straightforward minister–board relationship envisaged in the statutes has become a tripartite relationship, with the Treasury playing an active role. Treasury control over public enterprise investment is exercised in the following way. Each year there is an 'investment review', the purpose of which is to approve totals for the capital expenditure of each enterprise in each of the following five years. The spending totals for the first two of these years have largely been determined by past decisions, while the estimates for the last two years tend to be relatively uncertain, so that most attention is focused on the third year ahead. Each enterprise is required to present estimates of its projected capital expenditures, together with an account of the demand forecasts, technological and price assumptions, and policy considerations which underlie them. These plans are reviewed initially by the sponsoring department, which, as a result of its own analyses, should be able to form a view on their acceptability. From discussions between the enterprise and the Department, an agreed memorandum emerges setting out in fairly aggregative form the investment proposals of the enterprise. This is then put up to the Treasury for consideration. A series of meetings is held on these memoranda, attended by Treasury officials and officials of the sponsoring department, and in some cases by representatives of the enterprise itself, the outcome of which is that spending totals are agreed. The essential role of the investment reviews is to provide an opportunity to examine and discuss the underlying assumptions and policy choices of both the enterprise and the 'government side' – the sponsoring department and the Treasury – so that there is a two-way exchange of information. The formal requirement that all expenditure plans must be approved by the Treasury therefore provides an important opportunity to appraise, evaluate, discuss, and influence. Moreover, since the Treasury is the Department of State responsible for the formulation and implementation of macroeconomic policy, review procedure provides an opportunity for aspects of this policy to be introduced into the longer-term planning of the enterprises, e.g. in the phasing of investments over time. Thus, the investment review procedure is an instrument of long-term planning and control, the importance of which reflects the crucial role that investment plays in the development of an enterprise. At the same time, its effectiveness should not be exaggerated. The information received by the Treasury is in a highly abstracted and condensed form, and the Treasury has insufficient resources to enable it to provide a detailed evaluation of the investment plans. It can examine the general procedures by which capital budgets are formulated, the general assumptions used, and, in particular, the overall consistency of the plans of different enterprises in a given sector. However, it is rarely able to break down and evaluate specific aspects of an investment plan. Hence, if it is forced to make cuts in proposed investment expenditures, in order to accommodate them all within some given total, it usually has to resort to making roughly equal percentage cuts all round, leaving individual enterprises to decide on the precise parts of their programmes which must be abandoned or delayed. There is therefore no guarantee that investments which are dropped in one programme may not generate greater social benefits than those which continue to be undertaken in another.

In addition to control over the finance of investment plans, the Treasury also sets a limit on the amount which an enterprise may borrow short term to finance current operations, and an enterprise which wants to exceed this must seek Treasury authorization. This control is useful in giving advance warning of deteriorating operating results, possibly soon enough for quick remedial action to be taken.

2.1.3   *Economic ground rules*
In the mid-1960s an attempt was made to formulate pricing and investment rules, concerned essentially with profitability and economic efficiency, which would allow greater decentralization of decision-taking. There are three of these ground rules.

(*a*) *Marginal cost pricing.* As we shall see in the next chapter, it can be shown that, under certain conditions, allocative efficiency requires that a public enterprise should produce an output level such that the price which then clears the market is equal to its marginal cost. As we shall also see, there are several important practical and conceptual difficulties with this 'pricing rule'. For the moment, however, we note only that it has had little actual impact: the great majority of public enterprise prices are not set in relation to marginal costs. Reasons for this will be considered in a moment.

(*b*)*Financial targets.* Each enterprise is required to earn at least a minimum surplus of revenue over costs, expressed as a rate of return on gross assets. The size of this 'target' rate of return varies from one enterprise to another: for electricity, gas, and British Airways, for example, the rates of return lie in the range 8–12 per cent on gross assets (where the surplus is calculated after interest payments have been deducted, but inclusive of depreciation, and the asset values also include depreciation), while for the National Coal Board and British Rail, they correspond simply to the objective of breaking even. The size of the target set for an enterprise first of all reflects its basic viability; the extent to which it can set prices which generate the required surpluses, without pricing itself out of its markets; and some concession seems to be made for the extent to which the enterprise carries out loss-making activities in pursuit of the other objectives of government policy (primarily income redistribution), though it is doubtful that this concession always results from a careful costing of the losses due to these activities. It is accepted, of course, that circumstances in a particular year may cause the target to be under-achieved, but the enterprise is expected over a period of five years to make an *average* annual surplus at least equal to the target. These targets are essentially the form in which the goal of profitability is made operational for public enterprises: they reflect both the government's concern with revenue, and the attempt to stimulate efficiency and provide a yardstick of performance. We also see the conflict between profitability and macroeconomic policy objectives evidenced in the fact that, due to counter-inflationary 'price restraint', public enterprises have often failed to meet their targets even over a period of years. Indeed, in the years from 1972 to 1974, the targets have had to be ignored, since any degree of profitability proved to be incompatible with the extent of the price restraint to which the enterprises were subjected.

(*c*) *Investment criteria.* This ground rule requires an enterprise to appraise its planned investments on the basis of discounted cash-flow techniques. This first requires it to set out the time stream of revenues and costs associated with an investment, which in turn requires explicit assumptions to be made about demand, technology, input supplies, and prices well into the future. The time stream must then be discounted to a net present value, using a discount rate (known as the test discount rate, or TDR) specified by the Treasury for use in the entire public sector. The conceptual basis for this procedure will be analysed in chapter 8. Here we note only one important point: in practice it is not the case that public enterprise investment is to any significant extent determined by the TDR. Each enterprise determines its total scale of investment by forecasting future demand, on the basis (in the more sophisticated cases) of assumptions about future incomes, prices, technology, etc. It then finds the capacity corresponding to its 'adopted' demand forecast, and plans the investment expenditure required to bring installed capacity up to this level. In no part of this procedure does the TDR play a role (this is closely related to the fact that public enterprises do not base prices on marginal cost, since, as we show in chapter 4, there is an equivalence between choice of scale of output by a discounted cash flow procedure, and marginal cost pricing). Given the requirement for increased capacity, the TDR is then used in discounted cash flow procedures designed to find the least-cost ways of making this increase in capacity, for example in optimizing the mix of coal-fired, nuclear, gas turbine, and oil-fired electricity generating plant. Since the capital expenditure on different types of capital equipment may differ, this does exert a marginal influence on the total capital expenditure plan, but it is relatively slight. It follows that even quite significant changes in the TDR would have only slight effects on the total of public enterprise investment procedure, which in turn must imply that this rate cannot be viewed as an *instrument* by which public enterprise investment funds are allocated, under present practice. If changes in a variable leave the allocation virtually unchanged, it cannot be regarded as an instrument of that allocation. This is not to say that the level of the TDR is a matter of irrelevance: it is of considerable general importance whether the bulk of electricity generating plant is nuclear or coal-powered, and significant changes in the TDR could certainly influence this kind of allocation. Rather, the point is that, under present practice, the TDR plays virtually no role in the allocation of investment funds to the public enterprise sector in total, and as between individual enterprises.

These three 'economic ground rules' can be viewed as an attempt to induce public enterprises to increase their levels of achievement of economic efficiency and profitability, first by improvements in the procedures by which pricing and investment policies are formulated, and secondly by clarifying the objectives of these policies. The most important general feature of the rules is that they are intended to operate in a *decentralized way*: they represent a movement towards the type of control system in which decision-takers are left to implement particular rules and pursue specified objectives, subject only to *ex post* checks on performance. If the rules had been successfully introduced, they would have implied less ministerial intervention in specific decisions and in the decision-taking process. Thus not only would performance have improved, but there would also have been a reduction in the costs of operating the control system itself.

The attempt to introduce these decentralized rules and procedures has apparently failed, at least up to the present time.[5] One set of explanations might run in terms of reluctance to innovate, lack of economic understanding and expertise, reluctance by ministers and departments to relinquish control, lack of 'follow through', and so on. In the author's view, whether or not such factors operated, there are two more fundamental reasons why the ground rules could not be successfully implemented. The first is that the three rules are mutually inconsistent, and cannot be implemented simultaneously, so that at least one of them would have to be discarded. This is because, as suggested in the previous chapter, a 'rule' for achieving allocative efficiency, for example marginal cost pricing, need not be consistent with an *independently* chosen profit target. The statement of the ground rules (in the White Paper *Financial and Economic Obligations of the Nationalized Industries*, 1967, Cmnd 3437) did not suggest how the inconsistency could be resolved, and so gave no indication of how the rules could be operationalized.[6]

The second reason for the lack of success of the ground rules is that they dealt with only two out of the four aspects of public enterprise decisions which, as we have seen, are considered to be important. In particular, they ignored the question of the macroeconomic effects of public enterprise pricing decisions, and this meant that the policy was overtaken by events. Throughout the period from 1967 to 1974, public enterprise pricing was dominated by macroeconomic considerations, and since the 'rules' made no analysis of or provision for these, they did not survive. The main implication is that any system of decentralized rules, as well as being internally consistent, must take account of the full set of policy concerns. We discuss these issues further when we have completed the description of the system of control.

2.1.4   *Specific intervention by outside bodies*

An 'outside body' is an investigatory committee or commission external to the basic triplet of enterprise, sponsoring department, and Treasury. The three most important of these are:

(a) The Royal Commission or Committee of Enquiry. These are *ad hoc* bodies set up by the government and given quite far-reaching powers of investigation, often in response to an accumulation of poor financial results, dissatisfaction from consumers, and criticism from both outside and within government. Their role has been to collect and organize information and opinion, and to make recommendations. Their importance is demonstrated by the fact that most major structural reforms of public enterprises were preceded by such Committees and were influenced strongly by their recommendations.

(b) Select Committee on Nationalized Industries (SCNI). This is a Parliamentary Committee, composed of a small number of non-ministerial Members of Parliament of all parties, and sitting regularly through the lifetime of each Parliament. Its purpose is to examine in depth any particular issue in the entire public enterprise sector. Its reports have considered the structure, organization, and performance of specific enterprises, as well as more general subjects, such as the whole question of ministerial control and intervention. It is able to question executives of the enterprises, civil servants in sponsoring departments and the Treasury, and ministers themselves. It is able also to question 'witnesses' from outside the public sector. Its enquiries are taken seriously by those called to give evidence, and its reports, which give not only summaries of the information presented and the conclusions of the Committee, but also complete transcripts of the proceedings of the hearings, are both informative and influential. It has been suggested that one of the Select Committee's most important functions is to act as a kind of 'court of appeal' for public enterprise executives, and as a forum in which they can air their grievances.

(c) Other statutory bodies. The public enterprise sector has usually been, and continues to be, subject to scrutiny by those bodies responsible for the oversight of private industry, chief among which is the Monopolies Commission. Until its demise, the National Board for Prices and Incomes (NBPI) was also empowered to report on specific aspects of public enterprise pricing and productivity, and these reports make useful case studies.

2.2   A critique of the system of control

We can now pull together the strands of the argument of this and the previous chapter. No clear statement exists of the objectives which a public enterprise should pursue, and, in particular, none which reconciles the conflicts among the four main policy concerns, in a way which gives public enterprise executives a stable, consistent, operational set of goals. In place of this, there is a control system the main elements of which are the accountability of boards to ministers, and procedures for control of investment expenditure. These operate in a way which leads to examination of specific decisions and a substantial degree of participation by civil servants in the decision-making process, which is far greater than was envisaged at the time of nationalization. The system is relatively centralized.

It cannot be claimed that the system has worked especially well. Because of the degree of centralization, it is relatively costly in resources and time, and appears to have generated a good deal of friction, which cannot help the performance of the sector in the long run. At the end of 1974, the financial performance of the public enterprises was as poor as at any time in the history of nationalization, a situation which is directly traceable to ministerial intervention in price and wage determination. It is also not at all clear that the system of control has stimulated significant improvements in economic efficiency[7]: a system which examines individual decisions perhaps may succeed in preventing 'mistakes', but does nothing to stimulate general improvements in performance. This is much more a matter of the ability and motivation of management and the overall framework of incentives within which they operate, and a centralized system is more likely to inhibit than to stimulate.

It is also possible to argue that there are many instances in which ministerial intervention has worsened the performance of public enterprise without any apparent gains to the 'national interest', and in so far as the degree of centralization of the control system facilitates such intervention, this is a contributory factor. The argument starts from the deficiencies of general economic policy over the past two decades. This policy has not been notable for its stability, and, because of the ease with which ministers can intervene in the affairs of public enterprises, instability has been imported into this sector. Thus the 'stop-go' cycle has been made to bear particularly heavily on public enterprise pricing and investment policies, because of the nature of the system of control. Associated with this is the tendency towards 'politicization' of resource allocation: politicians try to win support, or buy off opposition, by diverting the allocation of resources in particular directions. To use a phrase of D. Coombes,[8] 'political judgement based on electoral advantage, party ideology, patronage, or bargaining' becomes a stronger determinant of resource allocation, the more direct is the control which politicians have over the resource allocation process.

However, it is possible to go too far in the direction suggested by this argument. To quote Professor Robson:[9] 'Efficiency does not determine the ends an industry seeks to attain, but only the effectiveness and economy with which given ends are pursued. Determination of ends involves value judgements of a political, social, or economic character.' Thus, discussion and formulation of the 'right' economic policies necessarily involves political activity, since 'rightness' is not only a matter of technical means but of ends. The problem of ensuring the 'right' public enterprise policies is part of the general problem of economic policy formulation, and cannot be divorced from politics. In criticizing specific policies, we have to distinguish between two sets of issues. The first is concerned with the definition of 'the national interest.' We can clarify this ambiguous term by noting that a particular statement of what is in the national interest implies a specific preference ordering over alternative social states or what may be called a 'social welfare function'. One may disagree with a minister's interpretation of the national interest, perhaps because it appears to place too much weight on his own career interests or the political expediency of the moment, but also because one has in any case a different social welfare function. The checks to major divergences between the social welfare function which ministers formulate and those held by individuals in the society, are provided through political activity: Parliamentary debate, and the force of public opinion, brought to bear in whatever ways the political system allows. This applies directly to public enterprise policies. Persistent divergences between Ministerial policies and what is thought to be the 'real' national interest indicate a failure of the political system, and, in particular, Parliamentary control. It follows that the correction of such divergences is a matter for the political system in general, rather than for the system of public enterprise control, although, as we shall see in a moment, the design of the latter may have implications for the broader question of control over Ministers' interpretation of 'the national interest'.

The second set of issues relates to the design of optimal policies *given* the preference ordering which has been defined. We may criticize policies not because we disagree with the underlying preference ordering, but rather because the policies are not the best means of achieving the objectives out of all those available. The position adopted here is that the centralized system of control described earlier can be criticized on these grounds. It is a costly control system, which has proved relatively ineffective in stimulating economic efficiency and profitability. A more decentralized system, in which public enterprises would operate within a framework of quantitative objectives and prescribed *decision rules* with no direct Ministerial intervention in decision-taking, appears to be a better alternative. It would also have an important indirect benefit: the policies by which Ministers would seek to influence outcomes, *via* the objectives and decision rules, would have to be more open and explicit. This would allow greater public and Parliamentary scrutiny, and so reduce the susceptibility of public enterprises to policies which do not lie within most people's definitions of the 'national interest'.

This position defines the orientation of the rest of this book. We have earlier argued that the attempt made by the Treasury to introduce a set of decentralized procedures was bound to fail. However, it *is* possible to devise pricing and investment policies which are internally consistent, and which can take account of trade-offs among the several aims of policy. Taking these policy aims as given and outside the scope of the discussion, we shall be concerned in the remainder of this book with an economic analysis of some elements of such pricing and investment policies.

chapter 3

welfare economics and public enterprise policy

3.1 Welfare economics

Most of what economists have written about public enterprise pricing and investment policies has been concerned with allocative efficiency, and so can be regarded as an application of welfare economics. In this chapter, we examine some basic propositions of welfare economics, and consider their main implications for public enterprise policies. Of course, no attempt will be made to provide a complete exposition: we shall simply set out as clearly as possible those propositions relevant to our purposes.

We can best begin with a definition due to Dr E. J. Mishan:[1] welfare economics is that branch of study which tries to formulate propositions by which we may *rank on a scale of better or worse, alternative situations* open to the *economy*. The key words in the definition are italicized, and we shall expand upon the definition by interpreting them.

The choice of a *scale of better or worse* requires a set of ethical or value judgements, which are necessarily subjective. In trying to formulate propositions which will be applicable *in general*, economists have tended to adopt a set of value judgements which appear to be mild and generally acceptable. We call these the *Paretian* value judgements.[2] They take the following form:

1. Individuals are held to be the best judges of their own welfare, so that we accept that a person is better off in situation A than in situation B if he prefers A to B.

2. Situation A is better than situation B, if at least one individual in the economy is better off at A than at B, and no one is worse off.

The property of the first value judgement is that it avoids paternalism, while that of the second is that it avoids the need to make *interpersonal comparisons*, i.e. to evaluate against each other the well-being of different individuals. These properties confer a particular kind of generality on the propositions which can be derived from the value judgements, since to incorporate specific paternalistic judgements and interpersonal comparisons into the analysis would limit its scope.[3] This generality is, however, bought at a cost: if, in situation A, some individuals are worse off, while others are better off, than in situation B, we cannot say whether A is better or worse than *B*. *A* and *B* are in this case *non-comparable*, and so the ranking of 'alternative situations' may be incomplete.

A criticism which could be levelled at the Paretian value judgements is that although they may be general in a logical sense, they do not describe the kinds of value judgements which are in fact generally held, particularly by policy-makers. The most important difference is that people generally do have ethical or political views which lead them to make interpersonal comparisons. These may be based on a comparison of the intensities or magnitudes of gain and losses, or on some views about the individuals or groups who deserve to gain or lose, related to the levels of welfare they already enjoy. For example, given some initial state of the economy, *B*, suppose that we generate a new state, *A*, by taxing the very rich and giving the proceeds to the very poor. Many people would say that *A* is better than *B*, perhaps because they think the gain in well-being to the poor exceeds the loss to the rich, or because in any case they think the poor more deserving than the rich, since they are absolutely worse off. On Paretian grounds, on the other hand, *A* is neither better nor worse than *B*: they are not comparable.

Although accepting the validity of this criticism, we find it most useful to proceed *initially* on the basis of the Paretian value judgements; we shall, however, subsequently give careful attention to the consequences of assuming that a policy-maker does make explicit interpersonal comparisons.

The *alternative situations* referred to in the definition depend on the problem under study. Most generally, we take the 'alternative situations' to be the entire resource allocations available to the economy, where a resource allocation can be thought of as a set of quantities of goods consumed and inputs supplied by all households, and goods produced and inputs used by all firms. However, in specific contexts, we may define the alternatives quite narrowly: for example, cost–benefit analysis is usually concerned with applying welfare propositions to situations with and without some specific investment project. In this book, the alternative situations consist generally of different levels of outputs, prices, inputs, and investment of public enterprises. The propositions we shall develop are designed to answer such questions as: How should the energy market be divided among coal, gas, electricity and oil? Should the price of rail transport be higher or lower in peak hours than at other times of day? Should public enterprises be allowed to undertake investments with lower rates of return than would be acceptable in the private sector? What is the appropriate size of labour force for the steel industry? Often, we shall analyse such questions at the level of the individual enterprise, but sometimes more general, and hence more complex, models will have to be constructed.

The word *economy* does not require a definition, but it is italicized in order to stress the following: the propositions we derive are not *initially* about some real-world economy 'out there', with its actual prices, outputs, buyers and sellers.

Analysis can only take place in terms of a *model* of the economy, i.e. an abstract system of variables and relationships which, it is hypothesized, capture certain elements of the real economy. In formulating a model, we necessarily have to make simplifications and abstractions, which render tractable the complex reality. It follows that different models may be good or bad representations of reality. Propositions are first formulated in the context of some model of the economy. If we then apply a proposition to the real economy, we would have more confidence in its correctness, the better the representation of reality its associated model appears to be.[4] Thus, we can distinguish between the *validity* and the *relevance* of a proposition.

A proposition is *valid* if it is correctly deduced, without logical error, from its premises. A proposition is *relevant* if it is not only valid, but also likely to be helpful and correct in its application to reality. This point is worth making because, as we shall see, much of the theoretical discussion in public enterprise economics has centred on the validity of propositions whose relevance was small, which was in turn due to the fact that they were derived from a model of the economy which is a poor approximation to reality. For example, the following two propositions are valid but not very relevant:

(a) allocative efficiency is achieved (in a *first-best* model of the economy) if prices are equated to marginal costs; and

(b) allocative efficiency is achieved (in a first-best model of the economy) if public sector investments are discounted at a rate equal to the marginal rate of return in the private sector.

These propositions have been much debated in the literature, and, as we saw in chapter 2, formed a large part of the basis of the Treasury's attempts to decentralize public enterprise control. The debate often tended to confuse their validity with their relevance. The critical phrase is the one in parentheses: its presence establishes both the validity and the irrelevance of the propositions. The fact that it is usually omitted from statements of these propositions has been responsible for much fruitless debate. We now consider what exactly is meant by a first-best economy.

3.2   The first-best economy

The inelegant term 'first-best' is chosen to contrast with the concept of the 'second-best'. A first-best economy is defined as follows:

1. There is a given population of individuals, with given tastes, which do not change.[5]

2. Time is divided into equal discrete periods, indexed $t = 0, 1, 2, \ldots$, where $t = 0$ is the present. Within each time period, production and exchange take place, exchange being organized through a system of markets. This establishes a complete resource allocation, and a system of relative prices,[6] within each period.

3. In addition to the markets for goods and services, a capital market is held at

each period, in which are exchanged dated claims to future wealth called *bonds*. Borrowing is the act of selling bonds; to lend is to buy bonds. The price in the capital market is expressed in terms of an interest rate r: a claim to one unit of wealth today exchanges for a claim to $1 + r$ units in one period's time.

4. All markets, including the capital market, are perfectly competitive.

5. At any point in time, all economic agents (consumers and firms) know the prices which will be established on markets at all future dates.[7] Consumers know their tastes over all future consumptions, and the endowments of goods and services they will have in each future period. Firms know with certainty all future technological possibilities.

6. There are no external effects in any period, i.e. there are no direct interdependences external to the price mechanism between economic agents.

In this first-best economy, consumers can at $t = 0$ draw up a plan specifying their net consumptions of every good in every time period, and their borrowing or lending (bond sale or purchase) in each period. Firms can draw up a plan specifying net productions, investment, and finance in every time period. Because of assumption 5, all such plans are consistent, in the sense that planned demands for any one good equal planned supplies for any one good at the price which everyone expects to prevail.[8]

A rather simpler version of the model is obtained if we take only $t = 0$, and ignore all subsequent time periods. We could then analyse the price system and resource allocation on the basis only of assumptions 1, 4 and 6. Such an *atemporal* model would be useful for certain purposes, particularly for deriving some 'short-run' welfare propositions, and for examining in the simplest context the consequences of relaxing the assumptions of perfect markets and no externalities. If we wanted to say anything about investment and 'long-run' pricing problems, however, we would have to consider more than one time period, and this in turn requires assumptions to be made about the structure of the capital market, and about knowledge of future prices, tastes and technology.

The first-best economy is obviously a highly abstract model of the real economy. However, it has, in one form or another, been the basic model of microeconomic analysis. Here, we are concerned with the welfare propositions derived from this model.

3.3. Some welfare propositions

Recall the Paretian value judgements, which hold one 'situation' to be better than another if at least one person regards himself as better off, in terms of his own preferences, and no one regards himself as worse off. Let us define 'situation' as a resource allocation in the first-best economy. Suppose, given some initial resource allocation B, it is possible to find another allocation A at which someone is made better off and no one worse off. Then *A* is called *Pareto preferred* to *B*. Suppose we make the change to *A*, and then find that there is no other resource allocation which is Pareto-preferred to *A*; in other words, we cannot find a way to make someone better off and no one worse off, by moving to another attainable resource allocation. Then, *A* is called a *Pareto-optimal* resource allocation, since, according to the Paretian value judgements, we have achieved the best resource allocation we can. The following propositions[9] can be shown to be valid:

I. In a first-best economy, a market equilibrium resource allocation is always also a Pareto-optimal resource allocation.

II. Any resource allocation which is Pareto optimal can be attained as a market equilibrium resource allocation by choosing an appropriate initial distribution of wealth.

A diagram will help illustrate these propositions. Suppose there are only two individuals[10] in the economy. Let the well-being or *utility* which the first receives from any given resource allocation be denoted by u_1, and that received by the second by u_2. Then, values[11] u_1 and u_2 can be plotted along the axes of figure 3.1, as shown, so that any point within the axes represents a pair of values $(u_1 u_2)$.

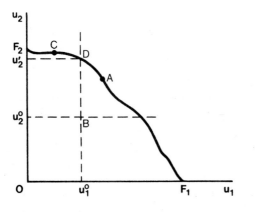

Figure 3.1

The line $F_1 F_2$ in the figure has the following interpretation: given the resources which are available to the first-best economy, it shows, for any given value of u_1, the greatest value of u_2 which can be achieved. To find any one point on the line, set u_1 equal to some value, say u_1^0, then choose that resource allocation which maximizes u_2 out of the set of all resource allocations which generates u_1^0, and finally find that value of u_2 implied by this resource allocation. The whole line is obtained by repeating this procedure for all values of u_1 in the interval $[OF_1]$. The line will be called the *utility possibility frontier*, since it shows the 'outermost' values of utilities which can be obtained in this economy. It can be shown, using 'standard' assumptions, that the frontier *must* have a negative slope: in moving along it, we can only make one individual better off by making the other worse off. Also, using these same assumptions, it can be shown that each point on or below the line corresponds to one and only one resource allocation, so that although strictly speaking such points are pairs of numbers $(u_1 u_2)$, we will often refer to them as 'resource allocations'.

We first can show that the set of points on the line $F_1 F_2$ correspond to Pareto-optimal resource allocations, while the set of points below the line correspond to Pareto non-optimal allocations (the points above the line are of course unattainable). Thus, consider point B in the figure. This cannot be Pareto optimal since, holding u_1 at u_1^0, we can, by changing the resource allocation, increase u_2 from u_2^0 to u_2'. Thus, we make the second individual better off and the first no worse off. Alternatively, we could make them *both* better off by changing the resource allocation so as to move to some point north-east of B, such as A. This clearly holds for all points below the line $F_1 F_2$. Therefore, no such point can be Pareto optimal. However, given any point on the line, such as D, no other point is attainable at which one individual is made better and the other no worse off. Changes can only be made which make both worse off, or one better off at the other's expense. Since this is true of *all* points on the line $F_1 F_2$ they all correspond to Pareto-optimal resource allocations.

Propositions I and II above can now be expressed in terms of figure 3.1 as follows: in a first-best economy, an equilibrium resource allocation corresponds to a point on the line $F_1 F_2$, such as A, D or C; while any point on the line can be attained as an equilibrium resource allocation given an appropriate initial distribution of wealth. Thus the line $F_1 F_2$ corresponds to *both* the set of Pareto-optimal allocations *and* the set of possible market equilibrium resource allocations.

Since our main concern is with questions of economic policy, we can now derive some policy implications from these propositions. The first of these is as follows: if a policy-maker in a first-best economy holds the Paretian value judgements and is content to achieve any Pareto-optimal resource allocation, then his best policy is simply to leave the market mechanism entirely alone – he is in fact redundant. The reason is of course that left to itself the market mechanism will produce an equilibrium which is a Pareto optimum.

Suppose, however, that included among the firms in the economy are some which are public enterprises.[12] The policy-maker will have to formulate specific policies to determine their pricing and investment decisions. What should these be? First we note the following: in order to be Pareto optimal, a resource allocation must satisfy certain necessary conditions.[13] The necessary conditions will be satisfied in a market economy if the following conditions are in turn satisfied:

(a) all consumers and firms face the same price for each good, borrow or lend at the same interest rate, and always act as price-takers; and

(b) all firms set output levels so as to equate marginal cost to market price (which is the same for all producers of the same good), and set input levels so as to equate the marginal value product to price.

In a first-best economy without public enterprises, these conditions are satisfied. They will be satisfied in a first-best economy *with* public enterprises if the policy-maker instructs the enterprises to adopt rule (b): they should adopt marginal cost pricing policies and employ inputs, including capital goods, up to the point at which their marginal value products equal market price.[14] In this way, given that the necessary conditions are also *sufficient*, a Pareto-optimal resource allocation on the boundary of F_1F_2 will be achieved.

We can note here an important point. Suppose that 'initially', i.e. before he has received the advice of his economists, the policy-maker has instructed public enterprises simply to 'break even', which implies that they would equate prices to average costs. Assuming non-constant returns to scale, it can be shown[15] that the necessary conditions for a Pareto optimum are then violated, which in turn implies that the economy will be at some point such as B in figure 3.1. Hence, his economists will advise the policy-maker that he can make everyone in the economy better off by instructing the public enterprises to adopt the new rules of marginal cost pricing and net present value maximization. If they were to do so, we would get a change in resource allocation, with prices rising in diminishing returns industries, and falling in increasing returns industries, and with corresponding changes in investment expenditures. *There is no guarantee, however, that the economy will thereby move* from B to A or D. All we know is that once the necessary conditions are satisfied, the economy will be at some point on F_1F_2 (assuming those conditions are also sufficient). The economy could very well have moved in fact to C, at which someone is worse off and someone is better off. It follows in this case that the decision *to implement* the pricing and investment rules can not be justified on Paretian grounds, since B and C are non-comparable on the Paretian value judgements. It is important to make the distinction between *being* at a resource allocation which satisfies the necessary conditions, and *having to move* from a resource allocation at which the conditions are not satisfied, to one at which they are. In the latter case, a specific move which follows from implementation of the rules may not be justified on Paretian grounds; rather, the valid proposition is that given the initial allocation, there exists *some* way of changing the allocation which makes everyone better off. However, more may be involved in this change than a simple instruction to implement certain general rules which are known to hold at an optimum. This important question of the *transition* to an optimum will be considered further below. There we will show how the apparent paradox – that a move to a Pareto-optimal resource allocation may not be justifiable on Paretian grounds – can be resolved.

To return to the basic policy implications: we have so far asserted and illustrated the validity of the propositions on which they are based; what now of their relevance? The propositions follow from the premises first, that the policy maker is a Paretian, and second, that the economy is first-best. The realism of these premises determines the relevance of the propositions. Let us examine them in turn.

3.4 The distribution of welfare

The policy-maker is likely to have specific value judgements which lead him to make interpersonal comparisons of utility. To put this another way, he will be prepared to compare situations in which some individuals lose and some gain, and the basis of his comparison will be ethical or political views he holds about who *should* lose and who should gain. However, given that these views meet a certain fairly plausible condition, this observation does not lead to a rejection of our earlier Paretian analysis, but rather to an extension of it. This condition takes the following form: an increase in any one individual's utility, all other individuals' utilities remaining unchanged, must always be regarded by the policy-maker as a good thing. Note that satisfaction of this condition does not rule out the possibility that the policy-maker would be prepared to make someone worse off *in order to* make someone else better off (soak the rich to help the poor); but it does rule out the possibility that he would want to make someone worse off for *its own sake*, with no corresponding improvement for anyone else. The condition is obviously satisfied if the policy-maker is a Paretian, but we assume it also to be satisfied by the value judgements of a policy-maker who is prepared to make interpersonal comparisons, and consequently explicit choices of who should gain and who should lose. We immediately can draw an important conclusion: an optimal (from the point of view of the policy maker's value judgements) resource allocation must still correspond to a point on the line F_1F_2 in figure 3.1, and so must still satisfy the necessary conditions for a Pareto optimum. To see this, we note that our policy-maker will always approve of a move which makes at least one individual better off and none worse off, just as if he were Paretian, and so he would always favour a move from any point below the line, such as B in figure 3.1, to an *appropriately chosen* point on the line, such as D or A. We can now say something more. Because of his readiness to make explicit interpersonal comparisons, the policy-maker is able to rank resource allocations which a Paretian would find non-comparable; in particular he is able to choose among different points on the line F_1F_2, and identify that or those he prefers. Thus, the policy-maker might *reject* the move from B to C on the grounds that he prefers the utility pair at B to that at C. He would *accept* the move from B to D, but he might well *prefer* the move from *B* to *A* on the grounds that it produces a 'better' distribution of utilities between the two individuals.[16]

What are the policy implications of this analysis? The answer hinges upon the assumption we make about the means available to the policy-maker for bringing about redistributions of wealth and therefore utility. The crucial question is whether or not he can make *lump-sum redistributions of wealth* to any required extent. A lump-sum redistribution consists of a set of payments to some individuals, financed by taxes on others, where these payments and taxes are not regarded by households and firms as being affected by any decisions they may take. This rules out income-related taxes and payments, as well as indirect taxes and subsidies, since these affect the prices which households and firms face on markets, and cause them to adjust accordingly. An example of a lump-sum tax would be a tax on pure economic rent, earned by a good or service in perfectly inelastic supply, while a lump-sum payment would simply be an outright gift to specified individuals, where the gift must not depend on some activity within the individuals' control. The important feature of lump-sum redistribution is that it does not lead to violation of the necessary conditions for a Pareto optimum. In the case of taxes on incomes or outputs, the price a buyer pays will differ from the price a seller receives, and so the Pareto-optimum conditions will not be fulfilled.

Let us suppose, therefore, that by lump-sum redistribution the policy-maker can achieve any desired distribution of wealth. In addition, recall that the resource allocation which he regards as optimal will be in the set of Pareto-optimal allocations. We can then apply proposition II given earlier, which stated that any Pareto-optimal allocation can be attained as a market equilibrium, given a choice of the appropriate wealth distribution. The planner can allow the market mechanism to determine an allocation of resources, while he uses a system of lump-sum redistribution to bring about the distribution of utilities he prefers. This can be explained in terms of figure 3.1 as follows: suppose the market mechanism initially establishes a resource allocation corresponding to point *C*. The policy-maker finds this outcome unattractive, and so redistributes wealth in a lump-sum way, away from individual 2 and towards individual 1. This will, of course, cause a change in the pattern of market demands and supplies and so a change in resource allocation. But, given that the market determines the new equilibrium, this must be on the line F_1F_2 to the right of point *C*. By a sequence of such redistributions, the policy-maker could arrive at his preferred utility distribution. We conclude that in a first-best economy, if lump-sum redistribution is possible, then even when the policy-maker has explicit views about the distribution of welfare, the market mechanism is allowed to operate with only minimal intervention in the form of lump-sum redistribution.

We can immediately draw a similar conclusion for the case in which some firms in the economy are public enterprises: by introducing the marginal cost pricing and net present value maximization rules, the policy-maker ensures that a Pareto optimum is achieved. He then achieves his preferred welfare distribution by lump-sum redistribution. This also allows us to resolve the paradox suggested earlier to the effect that a move from a Pareto-non-optimal to a Pareto-optimal resource allocation may not be justifiable on Paretian grounds. Thus, suppose as before that the implementation of the rules moves the economy from point *B* to point *C* in figure 3.1. The policy-maker may prefer *B* to *C*, but by lump-sum redistribution he is able to move to point *A*, which he prefers to both. Hence, *if it can always be accompanied by appropriate lump-sum redistribution*, introducing the first-best pricing and investment rules will always be an optimal policy.

3.5.   The second best
When we review the assumptions which define the first-best economy, it is clear that they abstract from important features of the real world. It is the unrealism of the first-best economy which leads us *a priori* to doubt the relevance of the propositions on policy derived so far. There is a need for further analysis to establish the extent to which the propositions so far derived retain their optimality properties in more realistic models of the economy. This analysis should also suggest how, if at all, we may extend these propositions so as to give them a higher degree of relevance. The term 'second best' is applied to an economy in which at least one of the assumptions defining the first-best economy is violated. The result of this violation is to invalidate proposition I given above: the market mechanism will not in general achieve a Pareto-optimal resource allocation, implying that given the technological possibilities and resource availabilities in the economy it would be possible to make some people better off and no one worse off than in the market allocation. Since the policy propositions so far derived depend heavily on proposition I, we would expect significant differences in economic policy in a second-best economy. We now go on to consider these differences, particularly as they relate to public enterprises.

To begin with, let us consider the divergences between the first-best model and reality. The most important of these are: market imperfections arising from monopoly and oligopoly; widespread external effects; and uncertainty, in that all economic agents must take current decisions in the light of incomplete information about future prices, tastes and technology.[17] A somewhat separate but closely related set of issues concerns the policy-makers' involvement in the economy. State economic activity does not consist only of wealth redistribution. The state provides public goods, such as defence and 'law and order', as well as many goods of a 'social service' character, for example medical care and education. In financing the provision of such goods, and also in pursuing its policies towards wealth redistribution, the government imposes taxes and pays subsidies which are *not* lump-sum. It does not appear to be feasible to design a system of lump-sum taxes and subsidies on the scale required to meet the government's redistributive policies, and needs for finance. The income and output taxes which are in fact used, in themselves lead to violations of the conditions for a first-best optimum. As a result, the separation between the achievement of an optimum resource allocation by the market mechanism and of a desired distribution of welfare by wealth redistribution breaks down. There is now an interdependence between the redistribution policies and the necessary conditions for an optimum, in the sense that the latter cannot be defined independently of the policy-maker's preferences over alternative distributions of welfare.

Thus we have the problem of deriving propositions which can form the basis for economic policy in a second-best economy. In chapters 6 to 9 below, we carry out some detailed analyses aimed at solving this problem. To illustrate the general nature of the analysis of the second best, we consider here a simple model of an economy which contains a number of monopolies. As a mnemonic, we call it the M-economy. The purpose of the following discussion is to bring out certain important general features of second-best problems, which should not be lost sight of in the later, more detailed analysis, easy though it is to do so.

The M-economy
Suppose that the policy-maker in this economy is able to identify the set of *first-best* Pareto-optimal resource allocations,[18] and that these correspond to the line F_1F_2 in

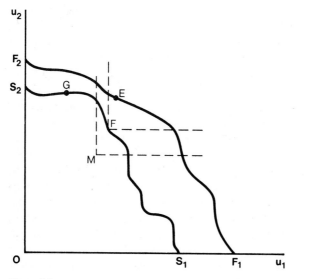

Figure 3.2

figure 3.2. We would generate this line essentially in the same way as before. Taking as constraints *only* the technological possibilities and resource availabilities in the economy, and ignoring its institutional structure (in particular that some firms are monopolies), we could find the resource allocations which maximized u_2 for each given value of u_1 in the interval $[OF_1]$. As proposition I previously stated, a *first-best* economy would achieve a market equilibrium resource allocation on the line F_1F_2. However, the M-economy contains 'deviant sectors', in the form of profit-maximizing monopolies, and the result is that the necessary conditions for a first-best Pareto-optimal resource allocation are not satisfied. Hence, the economy is at some point below F_1F_2, such as M in the figure. Can a policy be devised which will improve the situation? The answer depends crucially on the assumption we make about the *policy instruments* open to the policy-maker. Two cases can be distinguished:

(a) The policy-maker is able to influence directly the price-output decisions of the monopolists. Then, in this case, it is possible to define a subsidy policy, or a policy of price regulation, which will actually lead the economy to achieve a *first-best* Pareto optimum, and hence a resource allocation on the line F_1F_2 in figure 3.2. In this case, it can also be shown that the first-best rules for public enterprise pricing and investment are *still valid*. The direct correction of the behaviour of the deviants means that the rest of the economy can be treated as if the M-economy were in fact first best. This can be illustrated with a simple model. In figure 3.3(a) and (b) we show demand, marginal revenue, and marginal cost curves[19] of two private sector industries, and in figure 3.3(c) we show the demand and marginal cost curves of a public enterprise. Suppose that initially the economy is in a first-best equilibrium,

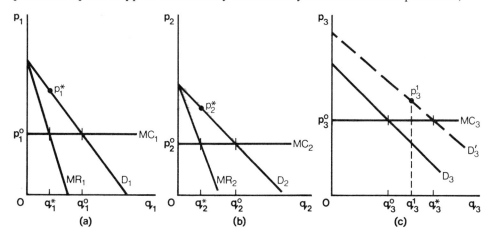

Figure 3.3

with prices (p_1^0, p_2^0, p_3^0), and outputs (q_1^0, q_2^0, q_3^0). Now suppose that industries 1 and 2 become monopolized, with no change in marginal costs. To maximize profits, the monopolists raise price to p_1^* and p_2^*, respectively, and outputs correspondingly fall to q_1^* and q_2^*. For simplicity, we assume that cross-elasticities of demand between the first two industries' outputs are zero, so the price increases have no effects on the positions of the first two demand curves. Suppose, however, that both goods are substitutes for good 3, the public enterprise output. Then, the increase in p_1 and p_2 will cause increased demand for good 3, so that the demand curve shifts upward, say to D_3'. If the public enterprise continues to set price equal to marginal cost, its output will be q_3^*. Assuming continued full employment in the economy, the effect of the monopolization has been to release from the first two industries the resources which were required to produce outputs $(q_1^0 - q_1^*)$, and $(q_2^0 - q_2^*)$, respectively, and these are then absorbed into industry 3 to produce the output increase $(q_3^* - q_3^0)$. The resulting set of outputs (q_1^*, q_2^*, q_3^*) and the associated resource allocation is not Pareto optimal; it corresponds to a point such as M in figure 3.2. The reason is, of course, that price ratios are unequal to marginal cost ratios, and, in particular

$$\frac{p_1^*}{p_3^0} > \frac{MC_1}{MC_3} \quad \text{and} \quad \frac{p_2^*}{p_3^0} > \frac{MC_2}{MC_3}. \tag{3.1}$$

We know, therefore, that it is possible to make everyone better off in this economy by reallocating resources out of industry 3 and into industries 1 and 2. One way of putting this is to say that consumers of goods 1 and 2 would be prepared to bribe consumers of good 3 to release resources; the former consumers could fully compensate the latter for their loss of consumption, and still have a gain in utility. The market mechanism fails to organize such exchanges, however, because of the intervention of the monopolists who control industries 1 and 2. This is the situation which confronts the policy-maker in the M-economy. Since we assume that he can act directly on the monopolies, we have the result that by a suitable choice of policy he can attain a first-best resource allocation. Thus, suppose the policy-maker can enforce on the monopolists a marginal cost pricing policy. Their prices fall to p_1^0 and p_2^0, respectively, demand for good 3 falls to D_3, and the initial first-best situation is reattained. In effect, we have an economy consisting of two regulated monopolies and a public enterprise, with marginal cost pricing as the optimal policy for each of them. An alternative policy to regulation would be the subsidization of consumption of goods 1 and 2 by just enough to make the price which consumers pay (= market price *minus* subsidy) equal to marginal cost in each industry. This again would cause increases in demand for goods 1 and 2, a reduction of demand for good 3, and a reallocation of resources in the desired direction. With the appropriately chosen subsidies, a resource allocation which satisfies first-best Pareto-optimality conditions would be achieved, and so once again marginal cost pricing would be appropriate for the public enterprise. Note that the two policies described here have the effect of moving the economy from a point such as M in figure 3.2, to (probably different) points on F_1F_2. These movements will involve changes in the distribution of welfare as compared to point M. Therefore, the comments made earlier in relation to the *transition* to a point on F_1F_2 still apply. Such a transition can only be justified on Paretian grounds if it represents a move to a point north-east of M, such as E in figure 3.2; on the other hand, if lump-sum redistributions are possible, some way can always be found of making a transition which makes everyone better off.

(b) Suppose now that the policy-maker in the M-economy cannot influence the price-output decisions of the monopolies directly, but can *only* do so through the policies of the public enterprises under his control. Thus, the pricing policies of the enterprises are the *only available instruments* of second-best policy. He will want to choose these policies in such a way as to achieve a Pareto optimum, but *subject to the constraint* that the monopolists are free to determine their own behaviour. A detailed analysis of this problem is given in chapter 6. Here we note and illustrate two important results:

(i) For any one public enterprise, the second-best Pareto-optimal pricing rules will differ from the first-best (marginal cost pricing) rule, *except* in the case where changes in its prices do not affect the price-output policy of any monopolist.[20]

(ii) The Pareto-optimal second-best resource allocation will be inferior to first-best resource allocations, and hence the policy of indirectly influencing monopolies through public enterprise policies is inferior to that of direct regulation of monopolies. Thus, in figure 3.2, let the line S_1S_2 correspond to the set of resource allocations which can be achieved by an *indirect* policy. It is possible to make everyone better off, moving from point M to a point such as F on S_1S_2, by adopting the appropriate second-best public enterprise policy. It would be possible to do better still, however, for example achieving the move to E, if a *direct* policy of regulation could be adopted.

Propositions (i) and (ii) can be further illustrated by figure 3.3. Given the resource allocation with prices (p_1^*, p_2^*, p_3^*) and outputs (q_1^*, q_2^*, q_3^*), the planner is aware that welfare gains can be made by reallocating resources from industry 3 to industries 1 and 2. Since he is constrained to act only on good 3, he can instruct the public enterprise to raise its price, say to p_3^1. This will cause demand to fall along D_3' to q_3'. Since goods 1 and 2 are substitutes for 3, their demands will increase, and resources will be diverted into their production. The problem of determining the final optimal position in the three industries is quite a complex one and will be analysed further in chapter 6: it cannot be usefully handled with figure 3.3. However, the figure should give the flavour of the result: by varying the price of good 3, the planner is able to cause demand variations and price changes (as the monopolists adjust their profit-maximizing positions to the changes in demands) in the other markets, until finally a resource allocation is achieved, such that no consumer can be made better off without making another worse off, *given* the policy instrument (public enterprise price) available to the policy-makers. This, then, is the second-best Pareto optimum.

3.6   Conclusions

In this chapter we have examined the welfare economics foundations of public enterprise pricing and investment policies. Assuming a Paretian policy-maker, and a first-best economy, we have the proposition that optimal rules for a public enterprise involve marginal cost pricing and net present value maximization, using as discount rate the market interest rate. Where a policy-maker is prepared to make explicit interpersonal comparisons of welfare, these rules are still applicable, *provided that* his value judgements satisfy the 'Paretian condition', *and* that lump-sum wealth redistribution is possible. When we allow the existence of monopolies, we find that the set of first-best Pareto optimal resource allocations is in principle still attainable, if the policy-maker is able to adopt appropriate policies. These involve direct intervention in monopolized markets, or subsidies, to ensure that prices equal marginal costs. If these policies are adopted, then public enterprises can be treated *as if* they were part of a first-best economy, and therefore the rules already described apply. If the possibility of such policies exists, then the economy is in a sense only *weakly* second best: the market system alone would not achieve a first-best optimum, but the system, reinforced with the appropriate corrective policies, could. A *strictly* second-best situation arises when there exist constraints on the set of policy instruments the planner may use, which preclude or inhibit direct intervention in monopolized markets. In that case, we can speak of 'uncorrected' sectors of the economy. The problem is to define optimal public enterprise policies given such uncorrected sectors. The first conclusion is that the optimal second-best policy for a public enterprise is the same as in the first-best, if price and output decisions for the public enterprise do not affect the equilibrium position of *any* decision-taker in an uncorrected sector. If this condition is not met, then in general the second-best policy will differ from the first-best, so that marginal cost pricing rules are inapplicable. Also, in general, the welfare position reached by the optimal second-best policies will be inferior to those of the first-best. An obvious question therefore concerns the constraints on policy instruments: why is it the case that public enterprise policies are taken to be the only policy instruments in the second-best economy? This question is taken up in chapter 6, where, after the analysis of the intervening chapters, we shall be in a better position to answer it. We note here only the general point: the strictly second-best situation arises out of the constraint on policy instruments, and, in analysing second-best problems, it is essential to specify the policy instruments which we take to be available.[21]

chapter 4
marginal cost pricing and partial equilibrium

The discussion in the previous chapter took place mainly at the level of the entire economy, that is, at the general equilibrium level. It was concerned with the relation between some general propositions of welfare economics, developed essentially for entire resource allocations, and public enterprise pricing and investment policies. However, when we come to consider the implementation of optimal policies, the general equilibrium level of analysis is rather *too* general and abstract. We encounter problems concerned with the particular features of products, technology and demand, which are much more fruitfully handled at the partial equilibrium level, the level of the individual enterprise or market. In chapter 5 we shall examine in a partial equilibrium context some problems which arise when the attempt is made to apply marginal cost principles to the pricing policies of public enterprises. First, however, it will be useful to clarify the meaning of marginal cost pricing, within the neat and simple framework of the standard textbook analysis.

In the light of the remarks in the previous chapter it may seem surprising that we should now be concerned with marginal cost pricing, since in general this rule is not very relevant to a strictly second-best economy, which is what we take the real economy to be. However, there are two strong arguments for examining the attempts to apply marginal cost pricing: the first is that it constitutes much of the core of what is currently 'public enterprise economics', and it is worth while to know this core before one tries to extend it; the second is that although second-best optimality generally requires departures from marginal cost pricing, the optimal prices will usually be related in some way to marginal costs, and hence the problems of the determination of marginal costs will still remain. One way of viewing the attempts to apply marginal cost pricing is as an elucidation, in various situations, of the structure of marginal costs, and as such they are relevant to second-best rules.

4.1. The derivation of marginal costs
We assume we are in a first-best economy, with no market imperfections or externalities and, of particular importance in this partial equilibrium analysis, complete certainty about future demand and technological conditions. Recall that time is divided into equal discrete periods which we can conveniently call 'years'. We

shall consider the application of marginal cost pricing policies, beginning at the first instant of the year 0, and continuing indefinitely. For simplicity, we assume there are only two inputs, L and K. The first can be varied at will, while the second takes time to vary: an order is placed, the required quantity is delivered, installed, and then can be brought into production. It is convenient to assume that all this takes one 'year': a decision taken at the first instant of year 0, to add a certain increment ΔK to the amount of K available for production, will result in that increment's availability at the first instant of year 1. K can be thought of as capital, and L any variable input.

Output is a flow, and so must always have a time dimension: we can only speak of production at a rate of so many units *per unit time*. Here, it will be convenient to define the time unit as the period already identified, the year, which is also the time it takes to expand input K.

In relating costs to output, we make a distinction between the characteristics of L and K. The inputs of L required for production throughout the 'year' are paid for as they are used up: they are labour services supplied to, or raw materials consumed by, the enterprise, for which immediate payments are made. K, on the other hand, is a durable input, which is owned by the enterprise. It yields productive services over a number of years, but no direct payment is made for them. Rather, its cost has two components: first, in supplying productive services through the year, it undergoes wear and tear which reduces its productivity, and which represents a cost. The value of this cost is reckoned as follows: at the beginning of the year t, the market value[1] of one unit of K will be some number denoted by V_t. At the end of the period (beginning of the next) this value will be V_{t+1}. The difference $\delta_t = (V_t - V_{t+1})$ which can be called 'depreciation', gives the first component[2] of the cost of using one unit of K over the period t. Secondly, in acquiring one unit of K, the enterprise will borrow to finance the cost of acquisition, or use funds which it could otherwise lend. Given a perfect capital market, the yearly interest *cost* of these funds, from whatever source, will be rP_t given by the market interest rate r times the price of one unit of K in the year in which K is installed. The annual cost of one unit of K is then $rP_t + \delta_t$, the annual interest cost involved in its acquisition, plus the fall in value resulting from its use in one year's production. Much complexity is avoided if we assume δ_t and P_t invariant both with respect to t and to scale of K.[3] Hence, we can define the *annual rental, n* $= rP + \delta$, as the price of one unit of K in each year.

The decision situation which we shall analyse is this: the enterprise is located in time at the first instant of year 0. It must take two kinds of decisions: it must set a price for year 0, which will determine actual sales, costs, profits, etc. in that year, and it must form a *plan* which specifies the price it will set in year 1, and the amount of the inputs L and K it will require to produce the resulting output.[4] If the implied amount of K differs from that currently available, it must institute an 'investment programme', which will be carried out in the course of year 0, and result in the desired amount of K being available at the first instant of year 1. Thus, it actually *implements* in year 0 an investment programme and a pricing policy for that year, and the former is based on a *plan* it makes about price and output in year 1.

The crucial difference between the problem of setting price for year 0, and the problem of choosing a planned price for year 1, is that in the former the enterprise must take the quantity of K as fixed, while in planning for year 1 it can regard K as variable. This has an important effect on the way in which costs will vary with output in each year. Given the prices of the two inputs, n for K and, say, w for L, total costs C are computed as $C = nK + wL$, for any input quantities K and L. Now when planning for year 1, K is variable, and so the enterprise can proceed in the following way: for some given rate of output in year 1, it can find those quantities of K and L which produce it at the lowest possible cost.[5] Valuing these cost-minimizing input quantities at their respective prices, and adding, gives the total cost of producing this rate of output *when both inputs are variable*. Performing this computation at each possible rate of output leads to a relationship between total costs and output in year 1. When planning for year 0, however, K is fixed at some level K_0 in which case its associated costs are also fixed[6] at nK_0. Variations in output can only be achieved by varying L, and likewise cost variations only arise from changes in L. Within this constraint, it will be possible to find the least-cost amount of L with which to produce each rate of output in year 0, and the corresponding total cost can then be calculated.

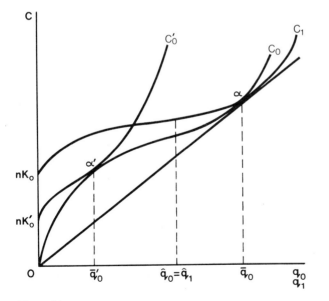

Figure 4.1

Because of the different circumstances, we would expect the cost–output relationship or *cost function* in year 0 to differ from that defined on outputs planned for year 1. However, these two cost functions will be related in a specific way. Figure 4.1 analyses this relationship.

In the figure, the curve OC_1 shows the relation between rate of output in year 1 and total costs, given that both inputs can be varied. Its shape is determined by technological assumptions commonly made in economics: as the rate of output q_1 in year 1 is increased from a value of 0, costs first rise less than proportionately with output, reach a point of inflexion, and then rise more than proportionately with output. The initial stage is said to correspond to 'increasing returns to scale', and the latter stage to 'diminishing returns to scale'. By its derivation, the curve shows the lowest possible total cost, given the state of technology and input prices,[7] n and w, at which each rate of output q_1 can be produced.

Let output $\bar{q}_0$ in the figure have the following property: it is that rate of output for which the fixed amount of K, K_0, is in fact the cost-minimizing amount. Told the year before that $\bar{q}_0$ was to be produced in year 0, the enterprise would have chosen K_0 as the appropriate value for that output. It follows that the cost of producing $\bar{q}_0$ in year 0 is the same[8] as it would be in year 1, and is shown by the vertical distance $\bar{q}_0 a$. Suppose, however, that the enterprise considers producing other rates of output in year 0. This can only be done by varying L, with K_0 fixed, and so deviations from the least-cost input combinations must result.

It follows that the cost of producing some rate of output $\hat{q}_0 \neq \bar{q}_0$ in year 0 must be greater than the cost of producing an equal rate of output $\hat{q}_1 = \hat{q}_0$ in year 1. Hence the curve relating total costs in year 0 to output in year 0 must lie above curve C_1 at all points except a, as shown by the curve C_0 in the figure. Moreover, the greater the difference between $\hat{q}_0$ and $\bar{q}_0$, the greater will be the divergence from the optimal input proportions (the less appropriate will K_0 be). This explains why C_0 diverges steadily from C_1 as we move rightwards or leftwards from point a in the figure. At zero output in year 0, no L would be used, and so costs would consist only of nK_0,[9] as the figure shows.

We can generalize this argument: assume a different level of fixed K, say K_0', implying a different level of output $\bar{q}_0'$, for which capacity in year 0 is optimally adjusted. By repeating the argument we could generate a second year 0 cost curve, which would have the same general properties as C_0. An example is shown in the figure as C_0'. By choosing every possible output, $\bar{q}_0, \bar{q}_0', \bar{q}_0'', \ldots$, we could generate an infinity of such curves, each lying above the curve C_1 except at just one point. The year 1 cost curve C_1 would then be *the envelope* of the year 0 cost curves C_0, C_0', $C_0'', \ldots$.

We now use these total cost curves to derive the marginal cost curves which are used in the analysis of pricing. Marginal cost is defined as the derivative of total cost with respect to output. In year 1, the cost function which relates to output variations is C_1 and hence we have

$$MC_1 = \frac{dC_1}{dq_1} = C_1'(q_1). \tag{4.1}$$

Given the assumed shape of the total cost curve C_1, the marginal cost curve will have the shape of the curve drawn in figure 4.2 as MC_1. We define average cost in year 1 as

$$AC_1 = \frac{C_1}{q_1} \tag{4.2}$$

and this is also graphed in figure 4.2.

To define average and marginal costs for year 0 is not quite so straightforward, since in principle we have an infinity of different cost curves. However, if we assume that capacity output in year 0 is given by $\bar{q}_0$, this defines C_0 as the relevant total cost curve for year 0. It follows that marginal cost in year 0 is given by

$$MC_0 = \frac{dC_0}{dq_0} = C_0'(q_0) \tag{4.3}$$

and average cost by

$$AC_0 = \frac{C_0}{q_0} \tag{4.4}$$

and these are also graphed in figure 4.2.

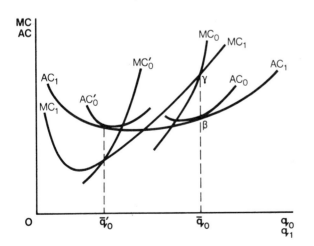

Figure 4.2

The relationship between these four curves is important for a proper understanding of the real meaning of 'marginal cost pricing'. The most important feature of this relationship is that, at capacity output $\bar{q}_0$, and *only* at that output, we have simultaneously that:

$$MC_0 = MC_1 \quad and \quad AC_0 = AC_1 \tag{4.5}$$

as shown at points γ and β in the figure. The proof of these equalities can be given by referring back to figure 4.1. As we showed there, at and only at point a, the C_0 and C_1 curves must touch: the curves meet in the same point at output $\bar{q}_0$. Moreover, this point is a *point of tangency* of the two curves, since they are converging up to that point and diverging after it. Hence, at point a the *slopes* of the curves are the same. But these slopes are measured respectively by MC_0 and MC_1, and so these are equal at that point. The equality of average costs can also easily be shown. Consider, in figure 4.1, the ray $0a$. The slope of this ray is $a\bar{q}_0/0\bar{q}_0$. When referred to the C_0 curve, this slope is therefore $C_0/\bar{q}_0 = AC_0$ at $\bar{q}_0$. Since the point a is common to the two curves, these two average costs are equal. Hence we have the important proposition:

when output is at the rate for which the fixed amount of K is optimal,[10] *the marginal and average costs for output variations with K fixed are equal to the marginal and average costs for output variations with K variable.*

By selecting a different output, say $\bar{q}_0'$ in figure 4.1, we could use similar reasoning to show that the marginal and average cost curves MC_0' and AC_0' corresponding to capacity fixed at K_0', derived from the total cost curve C_0', will also have this property. At output $\bar{q}_0'$, and only at output $\bar{q}_0'$, the marginal cost curve MC_0' will intersect MC_1, and the average cost curve AC_0' will just touch AC_1, so that at that output $MC_0' = MC_1$ and $AC_0' = AC_1$. Extending this to each possible output level, and its corresponding appropriate value of K, leads to the well-known result that AC_1 is the *envelope* of the average cost curves $AC_0', AC_0', AC_0'', \ldots$ (see Viner (1931)).

4.2   Marginal cost pricing

We can now apply this analysis of cost curves to the question of 'marginal cost pricing' in a partial equilibrium context. Recall that the problem really has two aspects:

(a) to set at the beginning of year 0 a price which will prevail in that year; and

(b) to choose at the beginning of year 0 an investment programme, based on *planned* price and output in year 1.

We now see how these problems are solved.

To be able to discuss pricing policies at all, we must assume that the enterprise has some knowledge of demand curves. Our assumption of the first-best economy allows us to take it that the enterprise knows the demand curves which will exist in years 0 and 1. These are graphed, along with the marginal cost curves from figure 4.2, in figure 4.3(a) and (b).

Consider first the analysis for year 1. In figure 4.3(b), D_1 is the demand curve which will prevail in that year, and MC_1 is the relevant marginal cost curve, since it is based on the assumption that both K and L are variable. The principle of marginal cost pricing implies that planned output should be q_1^* and planned price p_1^*, since then the market-clearing price equals marginal cost. Corresponding to planned output q_1^* will be cost-minimizing input quantities K_1^* and L_1^*. Since K_0 is the amount of K available at the beginning of year 0, the enterprise must carry out investment[11] in year 0 of the amount $K_1^* - K_0$.

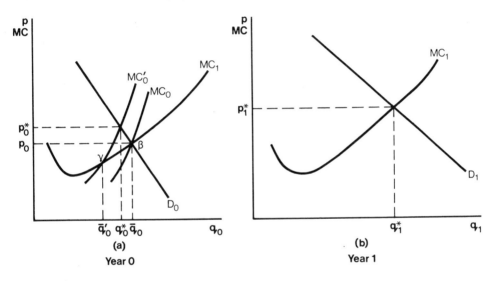

Figure 4.3

Consider now the choice of price and output in year 0, shown in figure 4.3(a). Given the demand curve D_0, does marginal cost pricing imply choice of the price and output pair $(p_0 \bar{q}_0)$, at the intersection of D_0 and MC_1? The first step in the answer is to note that the MC_1 curve is irrelevant for year 0 decisions. It relates to the possibility of varying *both* K and L, but K is fixed in year 0. Given that the output which has been planned for this year, back in year $t = -1$, was in fact $\bar{q}_0$, then, *because the relevant curve, MC_0, must pass through point β*, the pair $(p_0 \bar{q}_0)$ *is* appropriate. Suppose, however, that the output $\bar{q}_0'$ had been planned: the demand curve D_0 has turned out to be higher than expected. The installed K will be at the level K_0' appropriate to $\bar{q}_0'$. Hence, the relevant marginal cost curve, given that K is fixed at K_0' in year 0, must be that passing through point γ in figure 4.3(a), since this is the point on the MC_1 curve corresponding to output $\bar{q}_0'$. This marginal cost curve is denoted by MC_0' in the figure. It follows that the appropriate price and output for year 0 are p_0^* and q_0^*, since these correspond to the intersection of the demand curve with *that marginal cost curve which relates to variations in year 0 output*.

This discussion can be summarized as follows: marginal cost pricing requires that the price which will prevail over a particular period be equal to the marginal cost of varying output *within that period*. Output variations within the current year are constrained by fixed K; variations within future years are not. At a given point of time, two sets of decisions are being taken. Given the demand curve prevailing in the current year, a price–output pair has to be set. Given the demand curve expected to exist in the future year, future price and output have to be planned, and the corresponding investment programme determined and set in motion. The planned price and output will actually be implemented in the future year, if the assumptions about demand and costs upon which they are based turn out to be correct. Otherwise not.

The analysis of this section has been concerned with the meaning of 'marginal cost pricing' in a partial equilibrium context. We have not so far tried to justify or rationalize it in partial equilibrium terms: the validity of marginal cost pricing was considered in the previous chapter in terms of a general equilibrium analysis, and this is always the most appropriate framework for such questions. Illustrations and explanations can conveniently be given in partial equilibrium terms, but they are not rigorous and may mislead because we are not forced to make explicit the full set of assumptions and postulates on which the analysis is based. It is hard to avoid such explicitness at the general equilibrium level, as we saw in the previous chapter. The basis economists have for advocating marginal cost pricing is that provided by the necessary conditions[12] for a Pareto optimum in a first-best economy. These conditions are *derived* from a general equilibrium analysis, as should be any other sets of conditions which try to deal with the inadequacies of the first-best model.

Bearing all this in mind, we now translate the rationale for marginal cost pricing into partial equilibrium terms. We assume that there is some unit of account, or 'money'[13] in which prices of all goods are measured. Now, from consumer theory, we have the important result that the price of a good gives a money measure of the subjective value, to each consumer, of the marginal unit of consumption of that good.[14] In addition, marginal cost gives a money measure of the value of the output sacrificed by supplying the marginal unit of the good.[15] Now suppose that output were set at a level at which price exceeded marginal cost. This implies that consumers value the marginal unit more than the sacrifice involved in producing it, and hence are prepared to bid resources away from other uses in order to expand production of the good concerned. If, on the other hand, output were at such a level that marginal cost exceeded price, the value of the resources used in producing the marginal unit exceeds the value of that unit to consumers. In that case, there exist consumers of other goods prepared to bid away resources. Only if price just equals marginal cost, is the value of the marginal unit to consumers just equal to the value of what has to be sacrificed to provide it. In that case only, will it not be possible to move resources about and (provided appropriate lump-sum compensations are paid) make some people better off and no one worse off. To reduce the argument almost to a slogan: the intention of marginal cost pricing is to impose on the consumer the cost of providing his marginal unit of consumption, so as to cause him to adjust his total consumption to the point at which the value of the marginal unit to him is just equal to its cost.

The argument could be restated rather more formally as follows: suppose that there exists some function $B(q_1, q_2, q_3, \ldots, q_J)$, defined on J goods and services, and giving a money measure of the total satisfactions or benefits which consumers derive from consumption of these goods and services. We do not know this function,[16] but we do know that in the first-best economy, in which we adopt the Paretian value judgements, the following holds:

$$\frac{\partial B}{\partial q_j} = p_j, \qquad j = 1, 2, \ldots, J, \tag{4.6}$$

i.e. the price of the jth good measures its marginal social benefit. Likewise, there exists a total cost function $C(q_1, q_2, \ldots, q_J)$, such that

$$\frac{\partial C}{\partial q_j} = MC_j, \qquad j = 1, 2, \ldots, J. \tag{4.7}$$

Suppose we now define aggregate net social benefit as

$$S \equiv B(q_1, q_2, \ldots, q_J) - C(q_1, q_2, \ldots, q_J) \tag{4.8}$$

and maximize this over the q_j. Then the necessary condition with respect to the jth output is

$$\frac{\partial S}{\partial q_j} = \left[\frac{\partial B}{\partial q_j} - \frac{\partial C}{\partial q_j} \right] = 0, \quad \text{or } p_j = MC_j. \quad j = 1, 2, \ldots J \tag{4.9}$$

Note that we may call the term in square brackets in the first equality the 'marginal net social benefit' of q_j equal also to $p_j - MC_j$. At a maximum of net social benefit it must be zero, for otherwise it would be possible to reallocate outputs in such a way as to increase net social benefit.

This kind of reasoning is persuasive, and incorporates at least two important ideas which are often not perceived by those who determine resource allocation in reality. First, there is the significance of a market price as a measure of marginal valuations, as a device for transmitting information on marginal costs, and as a means of determining consumption; and secondly there is the idea of opportunity cost. It is the latter which gives the answer to the question of 'which' marginal cost is relevant for pricing. As we have already seen, the answer is found by defining appropriate time periods over which prices are to be set, and asking, how exactly do total costs vary with output within each period, given the possibilities of input variation? Using this procedure, no confusion should result.

However, in some ways the reasoning is *too* persuasive. It does not make clear the welfare value judgements on which it is based; the implicit assumptions about compensation which must be made; and the fact that its validity is totally dependent on the existence of a first-best economy. In a second-best economy, one or both of the equalities in (4.6) and (4.7) no longer hold: the marginal social benefit of an output may no longer be measured by its market price, and the marginal social cost may no longer equal the marginal cost incurred by the enterprise or firm. Thus, the intuitively appealing argument just set out becomes invalid.

There is a history of criticism of the marginal cost pricing 'doctrine' almost as long as that of the doctrine itself. Before considering briefly the main strands of this criticism, we complete the exposition by examining the relation between pricing and investment 'rules'.

4.3 Marginal cost pricing and investment appraisal

In the previous section, we saw that investment took place in order to increase output to the rate implied by marginal cost pricing in year 1. Given a marginal cost curve relating to output variations in every future year $t = 1, 2, 3, \ldots$, and a demand curve for each year, it is possible to determine the sequence of annual rates of output implied by marginal cost pricing. This in turn determines a sequence of required levels of K (based on cost minimization), and hence a time stream of investments. However, in discussions of investment planning, or 'capital budgeting' as it is sometimes called, a different kind of procedure is suggested for determining an investment programme. This is based on the discounted cash flow concept. The net present value (NPV) of investment is found by estimating the time stream of net social benefits generated by it, discounting this at a particular rate, and subtracting from the result the initial investment expenditure.[17] An investment is accepted if its NPV is positive, and rejected if negative. Formally, we have

$$\text{NPV} = \sum_{t=0}^{\infty} \frac{S_t}{(1+r)^t} - I_0, \tag{4.10}$$

where S_t is net social benefit in year t; r is the interest rate; and I_0 is the investment expenditure in year 0.

There is no apparent connection between this kind of investment planning and that associated with marginal cost pricing. However, the two can be shown to be exactly equivalent ways of formulating the investment programme of a public enterprise. We can state this in a formal proposition:

choosing an investment programme by maximization of net present value of social benefits is, in a first-best economy, exactly equivalent to choosing an investment programme by marginal cost pricing.

In this proposition, we specify the existence of a first-best economy because, as the previous chapter suggested, the existence of external effects and market imperfections makes marginal cost pricing no longer the necessary condition for a social optimum.

First we prove the proposition, then discuss its implications. For simplicity, we assume the following: there is no wear and tear on capital equipment – it lasts forever, and there is a known demand curve for each future period, which is the same in each period (though higher than the demand curve at $t = 0$). One result of these assumptions is that only a once and for all investment expenditure is required in year 0.

The NPV of social benefit is maximized in two steps. We first find the level of output which maximizes net social benefit in each period taken separately, with the value of K taken as fixed and predetermined. Call this value K_1. This then gives us a time-stream of net social benefits which depend only on the level K_1 we choose. We then choose K_1 (thus implying an investment $K_1 - K_0$), in such a way as to maximize the net present value of the stream of net social benefits.

Ignoring all other goods but that with which we are specifically concerned, the total benefits consumers will receive from output q_t in year t can be denoted by $B_t(q_t)$, $t = 1, 2, \ldots$. We take the equality in (4.6) above to hold for every t, and so

$$\frac{dB_t}{dq_t} = p_t, \qquad t = 1, 2, \ldots . \tag{4.11}$$

The net social benefit of output in year t, *given* the value of K_1, is:[18]

$$S_t \equiv B_t(q_t) - wL_t, \qquad t = 1, 2, \ldots \tag{4.12}$$

We maximize S_t with respect to output and L in each period t, taking account of the production function holding for period t, given by[19]

$$q_t = f(L_t, K_1), \tag{4.13}$$

where K_1 is fixed. Hence, the necessary condition for a maximum of S_t can be written as [20]

$$p_t \frac{\partial q_t}{\partial L_t}\bigg|_{K_1 \,=\, \text{constant}} - w = 0, \qquad t = 1, 2, \ldots , \tag{4.14}$$

which can be solved for optimal q^*_t and L^*_t. But given that the demand and production functions are the same in every period, as is K_1, the optimal values q^*_t and L^*_t will also be the same in each period. We can write the *optimized S_t*, denoted S^*_t, as

$$S^*_t = B_t(q^*_t) - wL^*_t, \qquad t = 1, 2, \ldots, \tag{4.15}$$

which is the same in each period.

The expression for NPV of the S^*_t time-stream can be written

$$\text{NPV} = \sum_{t=0}^{\infty} \frac{[B_t(q^*_t) - wL^*_t]}{(1+r)^t} - P(K_1 - K_0). \tag{4.16}$$

where $P(K_1 - K_0)$ is the value of investment expenditure. We now have to choose K_1 in such a way as to maximize this, again given the production function in each period:

$$q_t = f(L^*_t, K_1). \tag{4.17}$$

However, the optimal values L^*_t are each functions of K_1, since K_1 was held constant in the previous maximization, so we can replace L^*_t in (4.17) by the function $L^*_t(K_1)$. In maximizing NPV with respect to K_1, we note first that we can express the term under the summation sign in (4.16) in a more convenient way. S^*_t in each year is a constant, and we are discounting over an infinite horizon; hence, we are concerned with the present value of a perpetual annuity, which can be written[21]

$$\frac{B(q^*_t) - wL^*}{r}, \tag{4.18}$$

where the t subscript is dropped because constancy of the variables makes it unnecessary.

Then maximizing (4.16) with respect to K_1 gives the necessary condition

$$\left\{ \frac{dB}{dq} \left[\frac{\partial q}{\partial L} \frac{dL^*}{dK_1} + \frac{\partial q}{\partial K_1} \right] - \frac{wdL^*}{dK_1} \right\} \frac{1}{r} - P = 0, \tag{4.19}$$

which, on substitution and rearranging, gives

$$\frac{1}{r} \left[p \frac{\partial q}{\partial L} - w \right] \frac{dL^*}{dK_1} + p \frac{\partial q}{\partial K_1} \frac{1}{r} - P = 0. \tag{4.20}$$

But the term in brackets on the left-hand side is, by (4.14), zero. Hence, rearranging (4.20) gives

$$p = \frac{\partial K_1}{\partial q} \cdot rP. \tag{4.21}$$

But the right-hand side of (4.21) is marginal cost[22] in each future year, and so maximizing the NPV of the net social benefits of output in each period is equivalent to the marginal cost pricing rule set out earlier.

This result suggests an alternative way of expressing the pricing rule previously derived. We could say that optimality is achieved by (a) setting price equal to marginal cost within each period, taking K as predetermined, and (b) determining investment (and therefore future K) so as to maximize the NPV of net social benefits resulting from the prices set under (a). The important point is that (a) and (b) are interdependent, since future marginal costs depend on current investment.

Note that from (4.14) and (4.21), we have

$$p_t = w \frac{\partial L_t}{\partial q_t}\bigg|_{K_1 = \text{constant}} = \frac{\partial K_1}{\partial q_t} \cdot rP. \tag{4.22}$$

This can be read as price in year t is set equal to marginal cost with K fixed, which in turn is equal to marginal cost with K variable, at the optimal point. Thus, we have derived the counterpart in algebra of the earlier geometric analysis.

In this analysis, we have used some clearly unrealistic assumptions: effectively, input prices, technology, and demands in every future year are known in year 0, and are assumed not to change. Moreover, technological possibilities were assumed to be capable of being represented by a differentiable production function, and there was no depreciation. These assumptions define the simplest possible case, for which it is relatively easy to demonstrate the equivalence of marginal cost pricing and net present value maximization rules. As long as we continue to assume complete certainty, it is possible to relax the assumptions of constancy of input prices, technology and demands, and to introduce plant rigidities and depreciation with no fundamental changes in this result: such generalizations are important for practical planning but not for the conceptual analysis.[23] We now turn to the general criticisms of the marginal cost pricing principle.

4.4   Criticisms of marginal cost pricing
There have been many criticisms of marginal cost pricing, some of which have been trivial or wrong, but some of which have been valid and important. These latter emanate from a set of problems which can be grouped under three main headings.

4.4.1   *Problems of application*
The neatness and simplicity of the textbook analysis, so necessary for clear discussion at the conceptual level, is seldom encountered in reality. We often find, for example, discontinuities arising from capacity restrictions, indivisibilities, and jointness of production and costs, which present difficulties to the definition of

marginal cost. As we would expect, discontinuities in relevant functions mean that concepts based on derivatives of those functions have to be applied with some care. This has been a fruitful area for the generation of paradoxes and conundrums, for example, what is the marginal cost of the $N + 1$st rail passenger when the capacity of a train is exactly N? And the following 'paradox': 'once a bridge has been constructed, its capital costs are bygones, and marginal cost pricing requires a price of (virtually) zero (since the costs imposed by one trip across a bridge are very small); hence, the marginal cost price *before* the event, when capital costs are variable, must differ from that *after* the event, when it is fixed; moreover, the capital costs will never actually be recovered in revenues, given the marginal cost price which will be charged once the bridge is built, even though before the event it appears that they will be.' Such riddles are useful to solve, since we invariably learn something about both the theory and the world in doing so. They also make good examination questions. It cannot be said, however, that the problems of application of marginal cost pricing invalidate the principle: rather, they preclude unthinking application of the textbook model, and require the results to be worked out again from first principles in the context of an appropriate model. These results can not really be viewed as departures from the marginal cost principle, but rather as extensions of it. We see this in the next chapter.

4.4.2   *Objections arising from the theory of second-best*
These were introduced in the previous chapter, and will be extensively discussed in chapters 6, 7 and 8. They stem essentially from the non-correspondence of the first-best economy with the real world, and establish the irrelevance of the marginal cost pricing principle under a wide range of circumstances. Criticisms based on second-best theory are therefore fundamentally damaging to the principle.

4.4.3   *Objections to the assumption of certainty*
Common to the analysis of marginal cost pricing in this chapter, and the later second-best analysis, is the assumption that future demands, technology and prices are known with certainty at the point in time at which decisions and plans are made. In a sense, relaxation of this assumption is the most fundamental step of all, since it requires us to reformulate our theories of the consumer and the firm; consider institutions such as insurance and stock markets, which have no place in a world of certainty; and change the conceptual framework around which both first and second-best theories are constructed. Thus, criticisms of the assumptions of perfect knowledge in our earlier analysis are quite far-reaching, since they require a major change in the model before we can even begin to assess their importance for the results. Some aspects of the problems presented by uncertainty are considered in chapter 9.

The extensions to the analysis necessitated by each of these sets of criticisms are considered in subsequent chapters. Some examples of the criticisms which are here called 'trivial or invalid' are:

1. marginal cost pricing invariably implies that the enterprise operates at a loss, and so is unacceptable;

2. the marginal cost pricing principle is ambiguous, since there exists more than one marginal cost, each corresponding to some particular group of inputs which are being held fixed, and price cannot be equal to all of them at once;[24]

3. the analysis of marginal cost pricing cannot handle changes in future demands, prices and technology (assuming these are known with certainty);

4. the analysis assumes unrealistically that the enterprise is starting up from scratch, and does not have a hodge podge of plant and equipment inherited from past decisions;

and so on. Proofs of the triviality or invalidity of these propositions should be quite possible with the help of the principles set out in this chapter and the next, and are left to the reader as an exercise.

chapter 5

marginal cost pricing in practice

When the attempt is made to apply marginal cost pricing principles to some particular enterprise it is usually necessary to extend the structure of the theory, in order to deal with specific features of outputs, demands and costs. In this chapter, we consider the major kinds of extensions to the theory which have been made. It is most useful to do this in a general, theoretical and somewhat simplified way. Rather than choosing a specific enterprise, and discussing it in some detail, we shall set up general models which incorporate the essential features of the practical problems. This will give more insight into the general nature of the problems and their solutions.

We shall consider three main sets of problems. First, we take the situation in which the technology of an enterprise is such that, once capacity is installed, a maximum output level is defined, which cannot be exceeded at any cost. This is the 'fixed-capacity case', which appears to be typical of most public enterprises. The central problem is that of the indeterminacy of marginal cost at capacity output, but we also encounter the important issue of the relative desirability of rationing by price as opposed to rationing by non-price methods. In considering this issue we are led to extend the principle of marginal cost pricing to incorporate the principle of rationing by price. Secondly, we take the situation in which demand on an enterprise may vary from minute to minute in a systematic way over a given time period – the so-called 'peak-load pricing problem'. There are really two interdependent problems here: that of determining the optimum number and lengths of sub-periods into which to divide the whole period, such that price within each period is uniform, while prices between periods differ; and that of determining optimal prices for these periods. An analysis is presented which, while not giving the general solution to the problem, makes clear the essential elements of this solution. Finally, we consider the problem of plant indivisibilities, which again make marginal costs indeterminate in certain respects. We see that 'marginal cost pricing rules' can still be defined and implemented, the main difference to other cases being that marginal calculations cannot be used to define optimal investment programmes: we become involved in comparisons of total benefits with total costs which, as cost–benefit analysis has shown, are much more difficult to make than marginal calculations based on market prices.

These problems are considered *seriatim*, even though in practice most public enterprises[1] encounter them simultaneously. Far more success will be achieved in solving the real problems, if a firm grasp of basic principles is first obtained, and the theoretical approach of this chapter will try to impart this.

5.1   Fixed-capacity plant

The theoretical model of the previous chapter assumed what is called *flexible capacity*. There was a particular rate of output for which capacity was optimally adjusted (e.g. $\bar{q}_0$ in figures 4.1 and 4.2), but it was possible to increase output beyond this point by increasing the variable input. A situation which is often encountered, however, is that in which the installed plant has a given rate of capacity output which cannot be exceeded at any cost. We call this *fixed-capacity plant*. This situation should be distinguished from that of plant *indivisibilities*, which exists when increments to capacity can only be made in discrete finite amounts, rather than in infinitely divisible amounts. Indivisibilities are important in practice – indeed indivisibilities and fixed-capacity often occur together – and will be considered below. The analysis is helped by taking one problem at a time, however. We assume, given installed capacity, that although a particular rate of output cannot be exceeded in any one time-period (the 'year'), installed capacity can be expanded by any amount, however small, with a gestation period of a year.

Except for the fixed-capacity assumption, the basic situation is assumed the same as in the previous chapter. The enterprise is at the first instant of year 0, it must choose a price and output for that year, and also an investment plan. This investment plan is in turn derived from the planned price–output pair for year 1. The important difference between years 0 and 1 is that in the former output variations can be made only within the limitations of fixed capacity, whereas in the latter output variations can be planned allowing all inputs to vary. The cost parameters are also the same. One unit of L costs w; one unit of K costs the interest cost, plus δ, the annual 'wear and tear' cost, or depreciation, so that the annual capital rental is again n. Hence annual costs are $C = wL + nK$, where the first component varies with output in a given year, while the second is fixed within a year but variable between years.

Let us first consider the total costs associated with variations in output in year 0. The curve C_0 in figure 5.1 embodies the assumption we shall make: at zero output, variable costs are also zero, so that total costs in year 0 are nK_0, with K_0 again the value of installed K at year 0. The segment ab of C_0 shows how total costs increase as L and output are increased up to the capacity limit $\bar{q}_0$. It is assumed that variable costs rise proportionately with output: a given increment in output always requires the same increment in L, and since w is constant, always causes the same increment in cost.[2] At the capacity output rate, C_0 becomes vertical; costs go to infinity, which is another way of saying that more output cannot be obtained at any cost. Note that

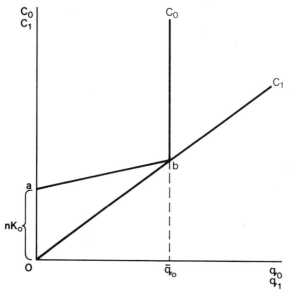

Figure 5.1

the slope of C_0, given by the derivative dC_0/dq_0, is well defined, and is in fact constant, over the interval $0 \leq q < \bar{q}_0$. However, at $q = \bar{q}_0$, there is a kink in the curve, which implies that the slope of C_0 is not defined at that point.

Now consider the line OC_1. This is the total cost curve which relates to output variations in year 1, when K can be regarded as variable. Hence, at zero output, zero costs are incurred, and, as output increases, total costs are assumed to increase proportionately, i.e. there are constant returns to scale. The OC_1 line is smooth and continuous because it is assumed that there are no indivisibilities – capacity can be planned in quantities which can be written out to as many decimal places as we like. Hence, at every point on the line, the slope or derivative dC_1/dq_1 is well defined and constant. C_0 and C_1 must meet at $\bar{q}_0$.[3] Choice of output $\bar{q}_0$ to be produced in year 1 would imply total costs given by point b on C_1. If, once the corresponding capacity is installed, output falls from $\bar{q}_0$ this will cause costs to fall but at a slower rate than along C_1 since *only* the input L can be reduced. Hence, the curve for year 0 output variations corresponding to capacity $\bar{q}_0$ must meet C_1 at point b and must also meet the vertical axis at the point a, as shown, where total costs are nK_0.

To discuss pricing policy, we translate the total cost curves of figure 5.1 into the marginal cost curves of figure 5.2. The slope of the line OC_1 in figure 5.1, which is a constant, is shown as MC_1, and the slope of the segment ab of C_0, also a constant, is shown as MC_0. The vertical segment of MC_0 at $\bar{q}_0$ indicates that marginal cost is undefined at that point. Note that since OC_1 is steeper than the segment ab of C_0, MC_1 exceeds MC_0. Given the installed capacity, an increment in output can be achieved only with an increment in L, and, as long as $q < \bar{q}_0$, this increment costs less than it would if capacity had also to be expanded. However, it still remains true, as figure 5.1 shows, that the *total* cost of producing outputs below q_0 is less when it is possible to vary both inputs, than when it is possible to vary only one of them.

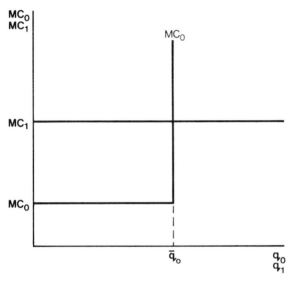

Figure 5.2

Before introducing the demand curves necessary for discussion of pricing policy, let us make some minor assumptions which will allow us to express these cost functions in a simple form. One unit of K will be capable of producing a certain number of units of output per year, and it is consistent with the assumption of linearity of OC_1 in figure 5.1 to assume that this is the same whatever the value of K. Thus, let the output produced by one unit of K be equal to $\tilde{q} = \bar{q}_0/K_0$. It follows that we can express the annual rental n as a cost per unit of capacity *output*, simply by dividing $\tilde{q}$ into n. Thus, we define the capacity cost per unit of annual output β as[4]

$$\beta \equiv \frac{n}{\tilde{q}} = \frac{rP + \delta}{\bar{q}_0/K_0}$$

so that $\beta \bar{q}_0$ gives the total annual interest and depreciation costs associated with capacity output $\bar{q}_0$.

In addition, let v be the cost resulting from increasing annual output by one unit when capacity is fixed, i.e. $v = w\Delta L$, where ΔL is chosen so that the corresponding $\Delta q = 1$ unit. We can then write the total cost functions[5] for years 0 and 1, respectively, as

$$C_0 = vq_0 + \beta\bar{q}_0 \quad \text{for} \quad 0 \le \bar{q}_0 \le q_0, \quad \text{and} \quad C_1 = (v + \beta)\,q_1. \tag{5.1}$$

It follows then that, in figure 5.2,

$$MC_0 = v \quad \text{for} \quad 0 \le q_0 < \bar{q}_0 \quad \text{and} \quad MC_1 = v + \beta. \tag{5.2}$$

We can call v 'running costs', and $v + \beta$, 'running costs plus capital charges'. Note that this formulation also assumes that changing the level of fixed capacity output does not affect the 'running cost' v; i.e. 'plants' of different capacity have identical running costs. These assumptions and simplifications are made because they provide us with a convenient and intuitively appealing specification of the cost structure, and one which is often used in the literature. It should always be remembered that it *is* only a convenience, however, and the essential nature of the results does not depend on it. This can always be shown by returning to more general specifications of the total cost curves.

In figure 5.3 we analyse the determination of marginal cost prices. In (a) and (b) are shown alternative possibilities for year 0. In (a), the demand curve in year 0 is D_0, and, since the relevant marginal cost for output variations in year 0 is $MC_0 = v$, price will be set equal to v, on marginal cost pricing principles. Note that this implies a

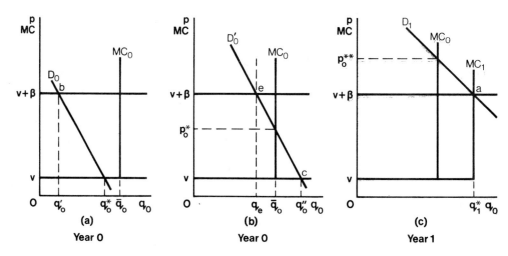

Figure 5.3

large loss for the enterprise. At a price of v, actual output is q_0^*, and so the loss, revenue *minus* total costs, is

$$vq_0^* - [vq_0^* + \beta \bar{q}_0] = -\beta \bar{q}_0 \tag{5.3}$$

or the whole of capital costs. In this case this is an unavoidable consequence of marginal cost pricing. The justification of this policy in partial equilibrium terms is as follows: suppose that in year 0 the enterprise were to set price greater than v, for example equal to $v + \beta$ (at which, however, it would still make a loss). At such a price, the quantity demanded will be q_0' in the figure implying an excess capacity of ($\bar{q}_0 - q_0'$). The marginal social cost of increased output, v, is below the value which consumers place on the marginal unit of consumption, which is measured by the price. Hence, net social benefits are increased by increasing output, and utilizing otherwise idle capacity; the capital costs β are 'bygones', they do not vary with output in year 0 and so should be ignored.

This argument, although perfectly acceptable in a first-best economy, ignores the fact that the 'policy-maker' may not be indifferent to the amount of net revenue accruing to the exchequer from the public enterprise. The fact that no interest payments are being made by the enterprise implies that (since the government must itself service the debt it issued to finance the investment of the enterprise) the policy-maker must increase taxes or borrowing, or reduce other public expenditure. In a first-best economy, the finance could be raised by lump-sum taxation, and so (provided the policy-maker does not dislike the resulting change in wealth distribution), the deficit could be met in this way. This would imply no loss of allocative efficiency elsewhere in the economy. However, in a second-best economy financing the deficit may have welfare effects which need to be taken into account in the pricing decision. Hence, the straightforward and appealing marginal cost pricing argument may not apply. This criticism raises in a partial equilibrium context the issues of wealth distribution, indirect taxation, and the second best, discussed earlier in chapter 3.

Figure 5.3(b) also relates to year 0, and differs from (a) in the assumption that the demand curve D_0' intersects the 'vertical portion' of the MC_0 curve.[6] A price set at v would now imply excess demand of the amount $q_0'' - \bar{q}_0$, since maximum output is fixed at $\bar{q}_0$. If excess demand is to be avoided, price must be set at p_0^*, since then demand exactly equals $\bar{q}_0$. This suggests the important point that whether price is set at v, p_0^*, or indeed some intermediate level, it does not affect total output and consumption, which cannot exceed $\bar{q}_0$. Rather, the choice between p_0^* and v determines the way in which available output will be rationed among consumers. If price is set at v (or any other value below p_0^*), the resulting excess demand necessitates some sort of non-price rationing system – queuing, points rationing, random allocation – which will in part depend on the nature of the good being produced.[7] Pricing at p_0^*, on the other hand, means that consumption is secured by those most willing to pay for it, i.e. those who value it most in money terms. There is a strong presumption among many economists that rationing by price is preferable, and this stems from two sets of arguments. First, non-price rationing is likely to lead to a loss of allocative efficiency, in that the resulting allocation of output among consumers will not be Pareto-optimal, and there would be scope for everyone to be made better off by further reallocation. To see this, note that under rationing by price, households choose their consumption in such a way that the money value of everyone's marginal unit of consumption is the same, being equal to the market price. Under a non-price rationing scheme, a different allocation of the given total output among households is likely to result. It follows in that case that some households will value their marginal consumption at more than the price, and some at less, so there is scope for 'gains from trade'; everyone can be made better off by appropriate exchanges of money for some quantities of the good. Thus, non-price rationing is allocatively inefficient, while price rationing is allocatively efficient. Secondly, as a mechanism for allocating output, a non-price rationing scheme is likely to absorb more resources than would rationing by price. If, by the 'costs of a non-price rationing scheme', we mean both the loss in allocative efficiency and the resource costs of the scheme, then the economists' conclusion is that non-price rationing is more costly than rationing by price.

Support for non-price rationing derives basically from the view that income is inequitably distributed: rationing by price implies consumption by those most *able* to pay for it, and so is an inequitable rationing device unless there is a 'fair' distribution of income. We have, in fact, a close parallel to the discussion of first- and second-best economic policies in chapter 3. If the policy-maker is neutral toward the distribution of welfare, or if he can achieve any desired distribution by lump-sum transfers, then rationing by price would be an optimal policy. In a second-best world, however, there may be circumstances in which allocative efficiency will be traded off for distributional equity, which in the present case might imply that price may not be used as a rationing device. Since the optimality of marginal cost pricing is conditional on the existence of a first-best economy in general, it seems appropriate to regard marginal cost pricing as being equivalent to rationing by price in the fixed capacity case. Hence, the price p_0^* in the figure is that which is consistent with the marginal cost pricing rule.

There is, for year 0, a third possibility, which is shown in figure 5.3(c). Suppose that in year 0, demand were as high a D_1. As we shall see, if demand were expected to continue at this level the enterprise would plan to expand capacity. However, in year 0 this is not possible. Then, if price is to be used to ration available output, it will have to rise to p_0^{**}, which also generates a profit for the enterprise, since $p_0^{**} \bar{q}_0 > (v + \beta).\bar{q}_0$. Thus, we can state the marginal cost pricing rule[8] for year 0:

when there is fixed capacity equate price to v *unless* there is excess demand at this price, in which case price should be raised to whatever level is necessary to restrain demand to capacity output. As was pointed out, however, there are issues concerned with profitability, rationing, and the distribution of welfare which may have to be resolved before this conclusion can be accepted.

Figure 5.3(c) can also be used to analyse the planned price–output decision for year 1. Assume now that D_1 is the demand curve which the enterprise expects to prevail in year 1 (it can be assumed that demand is expected to grow from D_0 or D_0', or that it will remain constant at D_1, depending on which of the three year 0 cases so far considered actually prevails). The relevant marginal cost curve for planning year 1 price and output decisions is MC_1, since K can be treated as a variable in planning one year ahead. It follows that the price planned for period 1 will be equal to $v + \beta$, and planned output will be q_1^*, since D_1 intersects MC_1 at a. It follows that in order to increase capacity from $\bar{q}_0$ to q_1^*, the enterprise will have to set in motion the required investment programme in year 0. Then, when a year has elapsed and the enterprise finds itself at the first instant of year 1, it will have a fixed capacity of q_1^*. It will then have to *set* a price for year 1, in the light of the demand which actually exists, and choose a *planned* price and output for year 2, which will imply a year 1 investment programme; and so the cycle repeats itself. If demand in year 1 turns out to be less than D_1, then we have similar results to those shown in figure 5.3(a) and (b); marginal cost pricing, or rationing by price, will imply that price in year 1 will actually be set below $v + \beta$, the planned level, and losses will be made. If demand turns out to be higher than D_1, the price which restrains consumption to equal capacity output must be above $v + \beta$, and profits will be made. Thus we have the result that when marginal cost pricing policies[9] are applied under fixed-capacity conditions with constant marginal costs, over-estimation of demand always leads to losses, and underestimation of demand always to profits. Correct estimation of demand leads to neither profit nor losses.

5.2   Peak-load pricing

In the analyses of this chapter and the last, we have worked with an arbitrarily chosen time-period, the 'year', over which a uniform price would be charged for all units bought in that period. The actual nature of the time-profiles of demands for many public enterprise outputs requires us now to examine more closely the question of defining the time-periods for which uniform prices are set.

It has been observed that for many outputs there is a systematic pattern of demand fluctuations within a given period, this pattern repeating itself from period to period. The duration of the fluctuations is too short to permit capacity to be varied to match them, while the high cost or technological infeasibility of storage rules out this way of reconciling fluctuating demand with smooth production. In effect, output can only be 'stored' in the form of capacity to produce it. Thus, we could think of the demand cycle as completing itself within a 'day', as compared to the 'year' it takes to vary installed capacity. Denote the demand in the mth minute of the day by D_m, where $m = 1, 2, \ldots, 1440$. If we were to plot demand, minute by minute, against each successive minute of the day, we would typically observe the kind of pattern of peaks and troughs shown in figure 5.4. Such a pattern characterizes daily demand for most energy supplies and transport services, especially rail and bus services and electricity and gas supply. The problem is that demands at all minutes are met from the same installed capacity, and so there are corresponding fluctuations in capacity utilization.[10] If sufficient capacity is provided to 'meet the peaks', then the rest of the time varying amounts of it are lying idle. On the other hand, since the demand at each minute will depend on the price which prevails in that minute (as well as those prices set in other minutes, in general), pricing policy could be used to 'flatten' the peaks and raise the troughs, so as to get a more even rate of capacity utilization with a lower overall level of capacity. The peak-load pricing problem is, then, in its most general form, that of determining optimal values for a sequence of prices $p_1, p_2, \ldots, p_m, \ldots, p_{1440}$, and an overall capacity level. It can be shown that in a first-best economy, necessary conditions for Pareto optimality in this case require marginal cost pricing. Hence, we can regard the problem as essentially one of applying marginal cost pricing to a system of fluctuating demand.

It is useful to have a general solution to this problem.[11] However, there are two reasons for not pursuing this general solution here: greater insights into the meaning

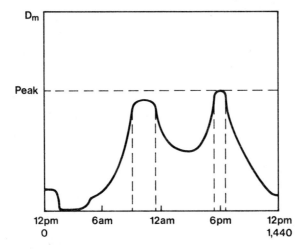

Figure 5.4

of the results are obtained by taking a simple case; and, in practice, it is not feasible to have a system of prices which change 'by the minute'. We have often ignored in economic theory the fact that operating a pricing mechanism incurs costs,[12] and in the present context this fact becomes very relevant. To have 1440 prices for electricity per day would require complex and costly metering equipment; a railway ticket office at which fares changed every minute has vast comic possibilities. In practice, the day is divided into relatively few time-periods, within which uniform prices are set. This suggests that the peak-load pricing problem consists of two interdependent parts: we have to find the optimal number of pricing periods, given the costs associated with pricing structures of varying complexity, and we have to determine optimal total capacity and uniform prices within these periods.

Although it is possible to solve this problem in one grand step,[13] again we will gain greater insight, as well as remaining within the constraints set for this book, by proceeding in a more pedestrian way. First, in this section we shall assume that the daily demand pattern is as shown in figure 5.5. The day can be divided into two 12-hourly periods, during each of which demand in each minute is the same. Assuming negligible costs of simple two-period price differentiation, there is then no need to worry about determining the optimal structure, since the demand pattern does this for us: we have only to determine the price to set in each period. Analysis of this problem will bring out the main elements of peak-load pricing problems, and suggest immediate applications. We then in the next section consider the problem of determining the number of pricing periods, and the optimum uniform price in a period, given that demand may actually not be constant within it.

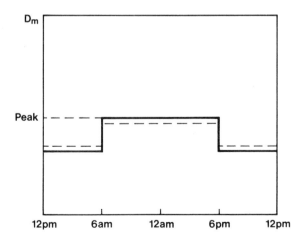

Figure 5.5

Let q_1 be total output produced in the 12-hour period[14] with lower demand in figure 5.5, and q_2 that produced in the 12-hour period with higher demand. We assume that we have fixed-capacity plant and, for simplicity, that all relevant marginal costs are constant. The key to the analysis is the appropriate definition of the units in which costs are measured. As before, we take the annual per unit interest cost as rP, and the annual 'wear and tear' or depreciation on a unit of K to be δ. We can express these in terms of 12-hourly periods as follows: since there are 8760 hours in the year, $\delta' = \delta \times 12/8760$ is the depreciation for one 12-hourly period. Likewise, let r' be the 12-hourly interest rate.[15] Then, the cost per 12-hourly period, of adding one unit of K, is $n' = \delta' + r'P$. If $\tilde{q}$ is the 12-hourly output of one unit of K, where $\tilde{q} = 12.\tilde{q}/8760$, then the 12-hourly capacity cost per unit of output is $\beta' = n'/\tilde{q}$. Likewise, let v' be the cost of the amount of L required to produce one unit of 12-hourly output. We assume v', the 12-hourly 'running cost', is the same in each period. We can then write the cost functions for periods 1 and 2, respectively, as

$$C_1 = v'q_1 + \beta'q_1^0 \quad \text{for} \quad O \le q_1 \le q_1^0 \tag{5.4}$$

and

$$C_2 = v'q_2 + \beta'q_2^0 \quad \text{for} \quad O \le q_2 \le q_2^0, \tag{5.5}$$

where q_1^0 and q_2^0 are, respectively, the 12-hourly capacity outputs in periods 1 and 2. But we must have that $q_1^0 = q_2^0$, since the installed capacity is the same in each period. We call this common 12-hourly capacity output q^0. The total *daily* costs of the enterprise are simply the sum of costs in each 12-hourly period, and so are given by

$$C = C_1 + C_2 = v'(q_1 + q_2) + 2\beta'q^0. \tag{5.6}$$

The problem faced by the enterprise is similar to that considered in the previous section, with the added dimensions of price differentiation between outputs q_1 and q_2. It must, at the first instant of year 0, set prices for q_1 and q_2 which will hold for each respective 12-hour period throughout that year, *given* the available 12-hourly capacity q^0. It must also plan the prices and outputs for year 1, in the light of its expectations about 12-hourly demands in that year, and given that it can regard capacity as a variable for that year. These planned prices and outputs will then determine an investment programme to be carried out in year 0. The analysis of this problem is set out in figure 5.6, which shows the situation in year 0.[16] Capacity is fixed at q^0, and D_1 and D_2 are the demand curves for output in the two periods. On marginal cost pricing principles, the price in period 1 will be set equal to v', implying an output of q_1^*, which is below capacity. If we accept that available output should be rationed by price, then price in period 2 will be set at p_2^*, since then demand, at point a on D_2, is equal to capacity q^0. The fact that D_2 is higher than D_1 implies that the price at peak demand is above that at off peak. However, if D_2 had intersected the

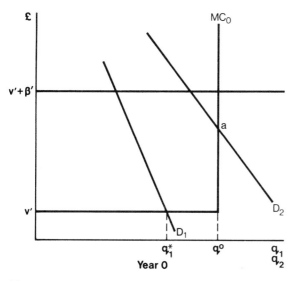

Figure 5.6

horizontal section of the MC_0 curve, *both* prices[17] would have been set at v'. The arguments here are precisely those set out in the previous section. In the case shown in figure 5.6, the enterprise makes a daily loss: its revenue each day is $v'q_1^* + p_2^*q^0$, so, given its daily cost as in equation (5.6), its net loss is

$$L = v'q_1^* + p_2^*q^0 - v'(q_1^* + q^0) - 2\beta'q^0 \tag{5.7}$$

$$= [p_2^* - (v' + 2\beta')]q^0. \tag{5.8}$$

The daily capacity cost is $2\beta'q^0$, since the 12-hourly capacity cost is $\beta'q^0$. Hence, this daily loss can be regarded as the daily capacity cost less the excess $(p_2^* - v')q^0$ of revenue over running cost made on peak output. Off-peak output simply covers running costs, and makes no contribution to capacity costs. The arguments set out in the previous section concerning finance of such losses are directly applicable here. Note again, however, that these losses are due to past over-estimation of demand. It is quite conceivable that demands could have been underestimated: for example the demand curves D_1 and D_2 could intersect the vertical portion of MC_0 at points above the line $v' + \beta'$ which implies that rationing by price would generate a profit. Thus, the losses or profits are attributable to marginal cost pricing in *the presence of incorrect demand estimation* in the past, rather than marginal cost pricing as such.

We now consider the problem of choice of planned prices and capacity for year 1. The analysis will be carried out with the help of figure 5.7, where D_1' and D_2' are the

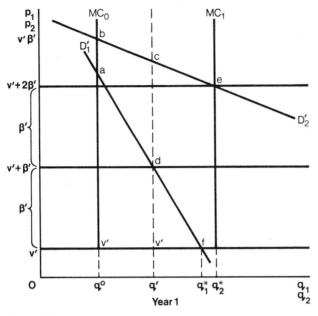

Figure 5.7

expected demand curves for period 1 and 2, respectively. First, recall that at any given output level in period 1, the price at the corresponding point on the demand curve D_1', measures the marginal value of output to period 1 consumers (in a first-best economy). Likewise, the price on the demand curve D_2' shows the marginal value of period 2 output. Thus, in the figure if output in each period were at the rate q^0, the marginal value of output to period 1 consumers is shown by the vertical distance aq^0, and that to period 2 consumers by bq^0. Now, v' shows the marginal 'running cost', the value of the *variable* input required to provide one extra unit of output. Consider therefore the difference between period 1 price and this marginal cost, $p_1 - v'$, and the similar difference for period 2, $p_2 - v'$. We can interpret these differences as measuring, in each respective period, consumers' *willingness to pay for an increment in capacity output*, or the *value to them of an increment in available capacity output*. This interpretation follows quite simply because the differences represent the excess of the value to consumers of a small increment in output over the cost of the variable, or non-capacity, inputs required to produce it. Now β' measures the cost, in each 12-hourly period, of an increment in capacity output. Hence, it seems reasonable to argue that if we have both

$$p_1 - v' > \beta' \quad \text{and} \quad p_2 - v' > \beta' \qquad (5.9)$$

then capacity should be expanded: its marginal value to consumers in each period exceeds its marginal cost in each period. With reference to figure 5.7, the condition in (5.9) is clearly satisfied at output q^0, and indeed at every output level up to q'. Thus, at q^0 the difference $p_1 - v'$ is given by av', and $p_2 - v'$ by bv', and each of these is clearly greater than β'. Taking each output between q^0 and q' as a possible capacity output and comparing the distances between v' and the respective demand curves, on the one hand, with β', on the other, would lead to the same conclusion: i.e. the value of an increment of capacity output to consumers, in each period, exceeds the cost of providing it, and so welfare is increased by expanding capacity. At output q', on the other hand, this is no longer so; the marginal value of capacity to period 1 consumers, dv', is just equal to β'. Therefore, is q' the optimal capacity level we are seeking? The following argument suggests that it is not. At output q', the marginal value to period 2 consumers of an increment in capacity output, cv' is actually greater than $2\beta'$, which is the cost of providing an increment of capacity output over the entire day. Hence, it is actually worthwhile to increase capacity output on the basis of its value to period 2 consumers alone, since they are more than prepared to pay the entire daily cost of installing the extra capacity. This again holds true for every level of output up to q_2^*. As long as the period 2 demand curve D_2' lies above the line $v' + 2\beta'$, we must have that $p_2 - v' > 2\beta'$, implying that an expansion in capacity is justified by its value to period 2 consumers alone. However, at output q_2^*, D_2' intersects the line $v' + 2\beta'$ at point e, indicating that the marginal value of a capacity increment to period 2 consumers is just equal to its marginal cost. If capacity q_2^* is provided, we see also that output in period 1 at q_1^* will be less than capacity since at this point the marginal value of output p_1 is just equal to v', the marginal cost of providing it, *given* capacity q_2^*. Hence, the marginal value to period 1 consumers of a capacity increment is zero, while that to period 2 consumers is just equal to its marginal cost $2\beta'$, and so we conclude that the optimal solution is at q_2^*. The optimal period 2 price, p_2^*, will equal $v' - 2\beta'$, while the optimal period 1 price, p_1^*, will equal v', and so the peak price carries the whole of capacity cost. Planned capacity will be fully utilized in the peak period and under-utilized off peak. Note also that the total revenues which will accrue from these planned prices will equal total costs, so that no losses are made, i.e. we have

$$p_1^* q_1^* + p_2^* q_2^* = v' q_1^* + (v' + 2\beta') q_2^*. \tag{5.10}$$

A convenient way of stating this result is as follows: when capacity is set at q_2^*, the marginal cost of period 1 consumption is v', and hence it is appropriate on marginal cost principles to equate p_1 to this. The marginal cost of peak output, however, is v', the marginal running cost, plus $2\beta'$, the marginal cost of providing capacity which must be available for the entire day. Hence, peak-time price should be equated to $v' + 2\beta'$.

The conclusion thus appears to be that optimal capacity is found by equating p_2 to $v' + 2\beta'$, while p_1 is set equal to v'. However, although this solution certainly holds in the case just analysed, it is not completely general, as figure 5.8 shows. This figure reproduces the cost and demand curves of figure 5.7, except that D_1' is replaced by D_1''.

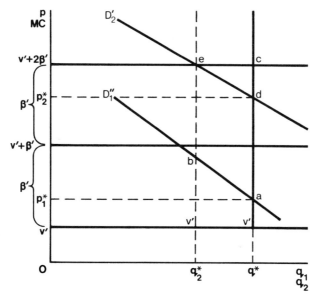

Figure 5.8

The result is that at output q_2^*, the period 1 demand curve is now such as to intersect the vertical line eq_2^*, implying that at output $q_2^*, p_1 > v'$. The economic significance of this is that the value to period 1 consumers of an increment in capacity at output q_2^* is now positive and measured by bv'. The marginal value of capacity to period 2 consumers is positive and measured by ev'. Together these marginal values sum to an amount greater than $2\beta'$, the cost per day of providing the increment in capacity, and so there is a welfare gain if the increment in capacity is made. In symbols, we have that at capacity output q_2^*

$$(p_1 - v') + (p_2 - v') > 2\beta', \tag{5.11}$$

which suggests that the increment in capacity should be made. In other words, we have introduced the idea that the relevant measure of the marginal benefit to consumers arising from an increment in capacity is the *sum* of marginal values of capacity to period 1 and period 2 consumers; this reflects the 'jointness' of the outputs – the increment to capacity generates outputs and therefore benefits in both periods, and it is the total of these which should be compared with its cost. This then suggests the condition for determination of the optimum capacity level, namely that the sum of the marginal values of capacity in the two periods at the optimal output be equal to its marginal cost, i.e. that

$$(p_1^* - v') + (p_2^* - v') = 2\beta'. \tag{5.12}$$

This condition is satisfied in the figure at output q^*, which is therefore the optimal capacity level. We see that the condition is satisfied by noting that the distance av' $= cd$, i.e. that

$$p_1^* - v' = v' + 2\beta' - p_2^* \tag{5.13}$$

which therefore implies the equality in (5.12).

The results for this case clearly differ in interesting ways from those derived earlier. Although there is still a peak–off price differential, it is smaller than in the previous case, and *both* prices p_1^* and p_2^* make a contribution to capital costs. In addition, the rate of output in each period is the same, implying 100 per cent 'round the clock' capacity utilization. Note also that the condition in (5.12) was satisfied in the previous case, since there $p_1 - v' = 0$, and so it can be regarded as the general necessary condition for determination of optimal planned prices and capacity.[18] Thus we have two solution possibilities:

(a) at the optimal point, we have equation (5.12) satisfied, with optimal output in period 1 *less than* capacity, and $p_1^* = v'$; and

(b) at the optimal point, we have equation (5.12) satisfied, with optimal output in period 1 *equal to* capacity, and so $p_1^* > v'$.

The essential difference between the two cases is that in the former, at the optimum, period 1 consumers derive no benefit from an increment of capacity, while in the latter case they do. Either case may occur in practice: it depends entirely on the relationship between the two demand curves, and their juxtaposition with the cost curves. An empirical test would be as follows: suppose we were to set p_2 at a level sufficient to cover all capacity costs, and p_1 at running costs. Would demand in the 'off-peak' period 1 then exceed that in period 2, so that the 'peak' apparently shifts from period 2 to period 1? If not, we have case (a), while if so, we have case (b) (confirm with reference to figures 5.7 and 5.8). For this reason, case (b) is often called the 'shifting peak case'.

5.3   Uniform pricing and the pricing structure

To restate the problem: if we take the minute as the smallest time unit in which to measure demand, and take as the most general case that in which demand varies from minute to minute, marginal costs may then vary accordingly. The 'peak-load pricing problem' now becomes that of determining a schedule of prices $p(m)$, $m = 1$,

2, ..., 1440, and a level of capacity. However, such a schedule of prices would be prohibitively costly to implement, and so we have to consider the problem: what is the optimal set of periods into which to sub-divide the 'day', such that within each period a single price prevails, whatever the consequent variations in output and marginal cost? We now turn to the problem of the 'decomposition of the load curve'.[19]

We could solve this problem in its full generality, but this involves some heavy mathematics. In the interests of maximizing insight rather than generality we take the following simple approach: our intuition tells us that the optimum pricing structure will have been found when the costs of adding one more pricing period exceed the benefits from doing so. We take the costs of operating the pricing structure as a straightforward function of the number of pricing periods: this will determine the costs of measuring (metering) consumption, providing information on prices, changing prices, computing bills, making mistakes, etc. Hence, the analysis resolves itself into an examination of the benefits of introducing $n + 1$ pricing periods where previously there were n. We take the simplest possible case, where $n = 1$. Then the problem becomes that of analysing the welfare losses arising from setting a uniform price over a period within which there are two levels of demand, since the elimination of these losses constitutes the benefit to introducing price differentiation. The essential results can be obtained most simply by taking the

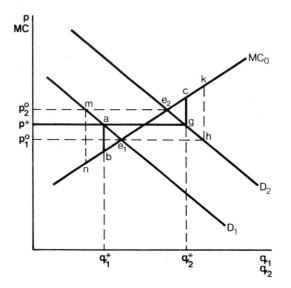

Figure 5.9

model of the previous section, with the added conditions that a uniform pricing constraint rules out the possibility of peak–off-peak differentiation.

We again have the type of load curve of figure 5.5, with the demand curves and cost structure exactly as shown in figure 5.6. However, we now have a uniform price constraint: only one price may be set over the entire period. The welfare loss arising from this constraint will be found by comparing the price–output solutions with and without it. We have already analysed the latter, so we now consider the former.

We want first to consider the problem of setting a price in year 0, with capacity output for each 12-hourly period in the year fixed at q^0. In this case, we can ignore capacity costs β', and consider only marginal running costs v'. As it turns out, however, we obtain some rather special, though interesting, results for the fixed-capacity case, and so to put them in context let us digress briefly to consider the (logically) more general flexible capacity case. In figure 5.9, the marginal cost curve MC_0 shows the 12-hourly marginal cost of outputs q_1 and q_2, respectively. The demand curves D_1 and D_2 relate to periods 1 and 2, respectively. The optimal uniform price over the two periods p^* is shown in the figure, implying an output of q_1^* in period 1 and q_2^* in period 2. The property of the optimal uniform price p^* and outputs q_1^* and q_2^* is that they satisfy the necessary condition[20]

$$p^* = W_1 MC_0(q_1^*) + W_2 MC_0(q_2^*), \tag{5.14}$$

where

$$W_1 = \frac{dp_1}{dq_1} \bigg/ \frac{dp_1}{dq_1} + \frac{dp_2}{dq_2} \quad \text{and} \quad W_2 = \frac{dp_2}{dq_2} \bigg/ \frac{dp_1}{dq_1} + \frac{dp_2}{dq^2}. \tag{5.15}$$

Hence, $W_1, W_2 > 0$, and $W_1 + W_2 = 1$. This condition says that the optimum uniform price p^* is set equal to a weighted average of marginal costs MC_0 in each period, where these marginal costs are calculated at the corresponding outputs in these periods. The weights are given respectively by the ratio of the slope of the demand curve in period i ($i = 1, 2$) to the sum of the two slopes. Before analysing the derivation of this relation, we note some straightforward implications:

1. If marginal costs in each period are constant at the same value $\overline{MC}_0$, then

$$p^* = (W_1 + W_2)\overline{MC}_0 = \overline{MC}_0. \tag{5.16}$$

In other words we have the intuitively obvious result that uniform pricing with fluctuating demand involves no departure from marginal cost principles when marginal costs are the same.

2. If the demand curves have the same slopes dp_i/dq_i, $i = 1, 2$, at the optimum point, then $W_1 = W_2 = \frac{1}{2}$, and so we have

$$p^* = \frac{MC_0(q_1^*) + MC_0(q_2^*)}{2}, \tag{5.17}$$

i.e. the optimal uniform price is simply the arithmetic mean of the two marginal costs.

3. If marginal cost increases with output, and $q_2^* > q_1^*$, then since $W_1 + W_2 = 1$, we have

$$MC_0(q_2^*) > p^* > MC_0(q_1^*),\tag{5.18}$$

i.e. the uniform price must lie between the two marginal costs. Moreover, we can rearrange (5.14) to obtain:

$$p^* - MC_0(q_1^*) = (-)\frac{W_1}{W_2}[p^* - MC_0(q_2^*)]\tag{5.19}$$

which implies that the period in which the demand curve's slope is greater (in absolute value) will have the higher divergence of price from marginal cost (again in absolute value).

The derivation of the uniform pricing condition in (5.14), and its implications, are illustrated in figure 5.9, where it has been assumed that the marginal cost curve in each 12-hour period MC_0 is linear, and that the demand curves D_1 and D_2 are parallel straight lines and therefore have everywhere the same slope. Now if peak–off-peak price differentiation could be practised, marginal cost pricing would imply prices p_1 and p_2, respectively, corresponding to intersection points e_1 and e_2. We can best see the effects of a uniform pricing constraint by supposing that initially these two prices did prevail, but then uniform pricing was imposed. Now, recall that the marginal value of output to consumers is measured by price, while its cost is measured by marginal cost. Then, the marginal net social benefit of output is measured by price *minus* marginal cost. Thus we can write:

$$\frac{\partial S}{\partial q_1} = p_1 - MC_0(q_1) \quad \text{and} \quad \frac{\partial S}{\partial q_2} = p_2 - MC_0(q_2),\tag{5.20}$$

where $\partial S/\partial q_1$ is the marginal net social benefit of output in period $i = 1, 2$.

Now suppose that the uniform price were set initially at p_2^0 in the figure, so that $p_2^0 - MC_0(q_2) = 0$, while $p_2^0 - MC_0(q_1)$ is given by the distance mn. This means that an increment in q_1 would yield a net gain in welfare. Thus the change should (on Paretian grounds) be made. This change can only be brought about by reducing the uniform price below its level p_2^0. Extending this reasoning, we can see that at any uniform price above p^* in the figure, the value of $(p_1 - MC_0(q_1))$ will be greater than the value of $(MC_0(q_2) - p_2)$, indicating that a further reduction in the price will generate a greater welfare gain in period 1 than the welfare loss in period 2. Hence, assuming appropriate compensation were paid, a Pareto-preferred position can always be reached. At p^*, on the other hand, we have that $ab = cg$, i.e. that

$$p^* - MC_0(q_2^*) = MC_0(q_2^*) - p^*\tag{5.21}$$

so that no net welfare gain would be made by a further price reduction.

Using similar reasoning, we could begin with a uniform price at p_1^0, and show that the marginal welfare gain from reducing q_2, measured approximately by kh, exceeds the marginal welfare loss from reducing q_1, which is zero, and so such a reduction would be Pareto optimal, again assuming appropriate redistribution. Extending this reasoning would again lead to p^* as the uniform price at which the marginal welfare gain in period 2 is just equal to the marginal welfare loss in period 1. Thus, we have that p^* is the Pareto-optimal uniform price, since any other price holds out the possibility of Pareto improvement.

Because of the assumption of parallel demand curves, we have in this case that the uniform price is the arithmetic mean of marginal costs in the two periods, as was earlier shown to be the case. The figure also enables us to show the welfare gains from introducing peak–off-peak price differentiation. If the uniform price p^* were replaced by the prices p_1^0 and p_2^0 in periods 1 and 2, respectively, then the welfare gain in period 1 is approximately[21] the area abe_1, while that in period 2 is approximated by the area cge_2. Hence the sum of these areas should be set against the cost (per day) of operating a pricing mechanism which would permit such price differentiation. Note that the sum of these areas will be greater: (a) the steeper the marginal cost curve MC_0, and (b) the greater the difference between the heights of the demand curves.

Moreover, as we would expect, the effect of a uniform pricing system is to lead peak output to be greater, and off-peak output to be less, than under a peak-load pricing system, as can be seen in figure 5.9.

Since period 2 consumers are better off at g than they would be at e_2, while period 1 consumers are worse off at a than they would be at e_1, the uniform pricing system could be thought of as 'discriminating' against off-peak consumers and in favour of peak consumers.

The notion that the uniform price should be set so that the marginal net social benefit, price *minus* marginal cost, is equal in absolute value in each period, is intuitively appealing. However, as equation (5.19) shows, this is not quite true in the general case, but rather only in the special case we have just examined. As (5.19) shows, in general the price–marginal cost divergences will be different in each period. The reason is that the instrument by which we adjust outputs and welfare losses in the two markets is the uniform price p and so the relevant optimality condition is that the marginal net welfare losses, *with respect to changes in the uniform price*, must be equal. Equality of marginal net welfare losses with respect to price is equivalent to that with respect to output if and only if the effect on output of a change in the uniform price is the same in each market. In the case we have just examined this was so, but in general it is not.

Thus, the condition for a maximum of net social benefit with respect to the optimal uniform price p is

$$dS/dp = 0. \tag{5.22}$$

The 'function of a function' rule of differentiation implies, since we have that $S = B(q_1 q_2) - C_0(q_1) - C_0(q_2)$, and since each quantity q_1, q_2 depends on the uniform price via the demand functions, that

$$\frac{dS}{dp} = \left[\frac{\partial B}{\partial q_1} - MC_0(q_1) \right] \frac{dq_1}{dp} + \left[\frac{\partial B}{\partial q_2} - MC_0(q_2) \right] \frac{dq_2}{dp}, \tag{5.23}$$

while from (5.20) we have that

$$\frac{\partial B}{\partial q_1} = p_1 \quad \text{and} \quad \frac{\partial B}{\partial q_2} = p_2. \tag{5.24}$$

Hence, substituting into (5.22) from (5.23) and (5.24) gives the optimality condition

$$[P_1 - MC_0(q_1)]\frac{dq_1}{dp} + [p_2 - MC_0(q_2)]\frac{dq_2}{dp} = 0 \tag{5.25}$$

from which, with $p_1 = p_2 = p^*$, we can derive the condition given in (5.14).

The foregoing discussion of optimum uniform pricing has prepared the way for analysis of the problem in the fixed-capacity case. We find in this case some results which differ in an interesting and empirically important way from those just derived. First, we analyse the problem of setting price in year 0, with capacity given. Figure 5.10 shows three logical possibilities. In (a) we have the case in which the demand curves in both periods intersect the horizontal portion of the MC_0 curve, i.e. there will be excess capacity in both periods. In that case, we can conclude immediately

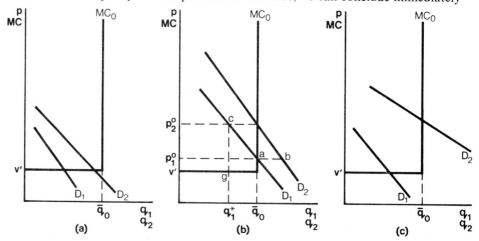

Figure 5.10

from the previous analysis that the uniform price will be set at v', since marginal cost is the same in each period. Hence, in this case, there is no departure from the principle of marginal cost pricing.

In figure 5.10(b) we have that both demand curves intersect the 'vertical portion' of MC_0. In this case, the following problem arises: if the uniform price is set below p_2^0 in the figure, there will be excess demand in period 2, while if it is set above p_2^0, there will be a welfare loss in period 1. In analysing the nature of an optimal choice, we must therefore take into account the costs and feasibility of using non-price rationing methods, and weigh these against period 1 welfare losses. Thus at one extreme, suppose that demand can be *costlessly* restricted to capacity in a way which ensures that units of output are acquired by the people who would be prepared to pay the most for them. In this case, the optimum solution is to set the uniform price *no higher than* p_1^0 in figure 5.10(b). The reason for this is that at any higher price, period 1 consumption would be less than capacity $\bar{q}_0$, and there would be a welfare loss measured at the margin by the excess of price over v'. Now if, on the other hand, price were set at p_1^0 (or indeed at any value down to v'), this welfare loss would be avoided. A price of p_1^0 would imply that in period 2, since output cannot exceed $\bar{q}_0$, there would be excess demand of the amount ab. The assumption of costless non-price rationing, however, implies that period 2 demand could be restricted to capacity $\bar{q}_0$ without cost. Hence, the policy of setting price at p_1^0 and restricting demand in period 2 to capacity would generate no welfare loss, as compared to a uniform price greater than p_2^0. Thus, we have the optimal uniform price[22] as p_1^0.

This conclusion obviously depended on an extreme and unrealistic assumption about non-price rationing. Let us now choose its opposite, and assume infinite costs of *any* amount of non-price rationing, however small. It follows that a uniform price at any value below p_2^0 in figure 5.10(b) would involve infinite costs arising out of the consequent need to restrict demand in period 2 to capacity $\bar{q}_0$. The conclusion must be that p_2^0 is the optimal price, since at that price no non-price rationing costs are incurred, while the total welfare loss (as compared to the previous case with price at p_2^0) is incurred by period 1 consumers, and is approximated by the area cga in the figure.

These two extreme cases serve to bring out the main issues. Any uniform price in the interval $p_2^0 > p^0 > p_1^0$ must involve welfare losses in period 1 and excess demand in period 2. Therefore, the optimal uniform price now depends on a comparison of the costs of non-price rationing on the one hand, with the period 1 welfare losses on the other. Thus, suppose that the costs of non-price rationing depend continuously upon the amount of period 2 excess demand $q_2 - \bar{q}_0$ so that we can write the 'rationing total cost function' as

$$R = R(q_2 - \bar{q}_0). \tag{5.26}$$

Then, it can be shown[23] that the optimal uniform price $p*$ must satisfy the condition

$$(p* - p_1^0)\frac{dq_1}{dp} = \frac{dR}{dq_2}\frac{dq_2}{dp}. \tag{5.27}$$

This condition has a straightforward interpretation. The term on the left-hand side is the marginal welfare loss in period 1 with respect to changes in the uniform price. The term on the right-hand side is the marginal rationing cost with respect to the uniform price. The optimal uniform price is such as to equate these. Only in the case in which this marginal rationing cost dR/dq_2 is zero, would the uniform price be set at p_1^0. In general it would not be, and so we would expect welfare losses in both periods. It follows from this that the introduction of peak–off-peak price differentiation will have two effects: it will, in allowing prices to be set at p_1^0 and p_2^0 in the respective periods, first eliminate the welfare losses of period 1 consumers, and secondly avoid the costs of non-price rationing in period 2. Thus, the sum of these savings should be set against the costs of operating the pricing mechanism.

The third case, shown in figure 5.10(c), has D_1 intersecting the horizontal portion of MC_0, and D_2 intersecting the vertical. Apart from a few details, this case leads to the same conclusions as that just considered. It is left to the reader to provide the analysis, and, in particular, to justify the conclusion that the optimal uniform price condition is now

$$(p* - v')\frac{dq_1}{dp} = \frac{dR}{dq_2}\frac{dq_2}{dp}. \tag{5.28}$$

We can now conclude this discussion of uniform pricing in the context of fixed capacity plant by examining the problem of planning price and capacity for year 1, when price differentiation for peak and off-peak demands cannot be made. Of particular interest will be the implications for the investment programme of the enterprise.

Here, we do not consider the 'shifting peak' case discussed in the previous section; instead we leave the reader to extend to this the analysis now given for the case in which off-peak output will be less than capacity. In figure 5.11, we again assume parallel demand curves, D_1 and D_2, respectively. Recalling our earlier solution for peak-load pricing, we know that if price differentiation were possible, planned capacity would be set at $\bar{q}_2$, with planned price in period 1 at v', and in period 2 at $v' + 2\beta'$. However, the uniform pricing constraint precludes this solution, but we find that the new solution resembles closely the results just derived for uniform pricing in year 0. Thus, first suppose that the costs of non-price rationing are infinite. Then, capacity *must* be made available to meet any given peak demand which may result from the uniform price. At the same time, in setting the uniform price we must take

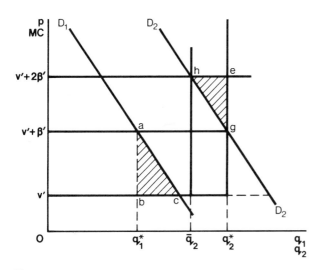

Figure 5.11

account of the variability of capacity. The optimal solution for the case in which demand curves are parallel is shown in figure 5.11, and requires that the uniform price p^* be set equal to $v' + \beta'$, with corresponding capacity at q_2^* in the figure. The argument runs as follows: at any uniform price p the marginal welfare loss in period 1, with respect to output, is measured by $p - v'$, price *minus* marginal cost. Likewise, the marginal welfare loss with respect to output in period 2 is also price *minus* marginal cost, which in this case is $p - (v' + 2\beta')$. Since the demand curves have equal slopes, we can ignore the dq_1/dp terms, and state the condition for optimal uniform price as the equality of marginal welfare losses in the two periods:

$$p^* - v' = v' + 2\beta' - p^*, \tag{5.29}$$

which on rearranging gives simply

$$p^* = v' + \beta'. \tag{5.30}$$

From figure 5.11, it can readily be confirmed that at this uniform price marginal welfare losses ab in period 1 and eg in period 2 are equal, as are total welfare losses, measured by areas abc and egh. Thus, in this case we note that the consequence of uniform pricing is to reduce the welfare of off-peak consumers, and to over-expand capacity. The total daily welfare gain from introducing price discrimination would in this case be the sum of the areas abc and egh, and this should be set against the daily cost of operating the system of price discrimination. Note also that under uniform pricing, the enterprise in this case makes a loss, since, with $p^* = v' + \beta'$ in each period, its 'profit' is

$$\Pi = (v' + \beta')q_1^* + (v' + \beta')q_2^* - vq_1^* - (v' + 2\beta')q_2^*, \tag{5.31}$$

$$= \beta'(q_1^* - q_2^*) < 0. \tag{5.32}$$

In other words, the profit the enterprise makes from charging off-peak consumers more than it costs to supply them, are more than offset by the loss made by *not* charging peak consumers what it costs to supply *them*. Any welfare losses associated with the financing of the deficit of the enterprise should be added into the other welfare losses already identified, in evaluating the net benefits of introducing off-peak price discrimination.

Using our earlier results, we can relax the assumption of parallel demand curves and write the general condition[24] for optimal uniform price as

$$[p^* - v']\frac{dq_1}{dp} = [v' + 2\beta' - p^*]\frac{dq_2}{dp}. \tag{5.31}$$

This can be rearranged to give simply

$$p^* = v' + K2\beta', \tag{5.32}$$

where

$$K = \frac{dq_2}{dp} \bigg/ \frac{dq_1}{dp} + \frac{dq_2}{dp}.$$

Thus, the point between v' and $v' + 2\beta'$ at which the uniform price falls depends on the relation between the slopes of the two demand curves. The general conclusions just set out for the case in which these slopes are equal still hold.

To complete the analysis, it would now be necessary to consider the cases in which non-price rationing has zero cost, and then positive but not infinite cost. The analysis essentially follows that given earlier for these cases, however, and so only the broad conclusions need be stated. If non-price rationing is completely costless, then the uniform price should be set at v', capacity should be set at $\bar{q}_2$, and period 2 demand restricted to this level. No welfare losses are thereby incurred, except for any associated with finance of the resulting deficit, which would be equal to the whole of the capacity costs, $2\beta\bar{q}_1$. Where rationing costs are positive but finite, the uniform price will lie somewhere between v' and $v' + \beta'$, the values defined by the extreme cases already considered, while capacity will be set between $\bar{q}_2$ and q_2^*, the precise point being determined, other things being equal, by the value of the 'marginal rationing cost'.[25]

To summarize the conclusions from the analysis of uniform pricing in a situation of fluctuating demand: except in the case of perfectly costless non-price rationing, there are invariably welfare losses arising from the deviations of price from marginal costs in each period. When capacity is fixed, the overall welfare loss is the sum of the loss of consumption benefits to off-peak consumers, and the costs of non-price rationing of peak demand (which may not all be borne by the enterprise).

When capacity is variable, the welfare loss is the sum of loss of consumption benefits to off-peak consumers, costs of over-expansion of capacity, and non-price rationing costs. All these losses would be avoided by a system of peak–off-peak price discrimination, and so should be compared with the costs of introducing and operating such a system. Note that we have been discussing an *optimal* uniform pricing system. It is possible to argue that any uniform pricing system in fact in use would not be optimal.[26] Then, this implies that the welfare losses set out above *understate* the true losses from uniform pricing, since they refer to the case in which these are minimized. This of course strengthens the case for price differentiation.

The main purpose of the analysis was to bring out the basic elements of a general solution to the problem of 'decomposition of the load curve'. If there were 1440 different demand curves, rather than just two, the analysis would be the same in kind. However, the simple analysis set out here probably has more practical relevance than the general one. It is unlikely that more than two or three pricing periods would in practice be justified, and so a simple analysis is adequate. Moreover, in many parts of the public sector the major gain would probably be realized by introducing just two pricing periods where currently there is one, with sharply diminishing returns accruing to further complexity. Hence, the analysis presented here is likely to be directly applicable.

Finally, the analysis of the optimal uniform price is itself of immediate relevance to the peak-load pricing problem. Once optimal pricing periods have been determined, it is probable that there will be some fluctuations of demand within them. Hence, the price set for each period will itself be a uniform price, and the present analysis has suggested how this could be determined.

5.4 Indivisibilities

The assumption of continuity, or infinite divisibility, which underlies most of economic analysis is always an approximation: everything in reality is measured in finite units. In many contexts, where the basic unit of measurement is small relative to the aggregate, this approximation is acceptable. However, it may happen that the aggregate is small relative to the unit, in which case marginal analysis based on the 'nicely calculated less or more' may not be applicable. Indivisibilities imply discontinuities and therefore the absence of well-defined derivatives on which marginal analysis is based. Here we consider the problems which arise when we try to apply marginal cost pricing rules to public enterprises whose capacity can only be increased in relatively large indivisible units. Examples abound: if the capacity of a railway coach is x passengers, to carry the $x + 1$st requires another coach; to increase the capacity of a cross-channel ferry service requires another ship; if existing airports are at capacity, expansion requires a new runway and terminal facilities; and so on. Note that two kinds of situation may exist here: there may be an absolute technological or physical barrier to relatively small capacity increments; or, though technically feasible, it may be extremely costly to make small increments. Many 'indivisibilities' are likely to be of the latter kind. It would be quite possible to design the one-man railway coach or to launch the one-passenger cross-channel ferry service, but they would be 'prohibitively' expensive ways of adding to capacity. The question of the appropriate scale of expansion therefore becomes an economic problem, with the technological indivisibility an extreme case, in which the costs of marginal increments are infinite. Here, however, we analyse only this extreme case.

We take the fixed-capacity situation of the first section of this chapter and assume that there are no peak-load problems: demand is uniform in every minute of the year, and so we again choose the year as the time unit in terms of which to express the rate of production. Again, it is assumed to take a year to expand capacity. Now, however, capacity can only be expanded in fixed, indivisible amounts $\bar{K}$. Thus, if the enterprise has at the beginning of year 0 a capacity of K_0, its capacity in year 1 can only take on the possible values K_0, $K_0 + \bar{K}$, $K_0 + 2\bar{K}$, ..., or in general $K_0 + \lambda \bar{K}$,

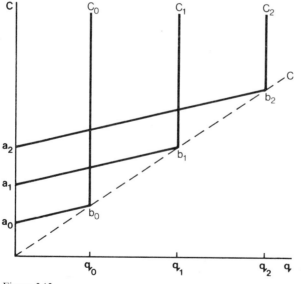

Figure 5.12

$\lambda = 0, 1, 2, \ldots$. We assume essentially the same cost conditions as in the first section of this chapter, except for the amendments made necessary by the existence of indivisibilities. The total cost curves for various levels of capacity will be as shown in figure 5.12. The output rates q_0, q_1 and q_2, represent the respective capacity levels K_0, $K_0 + \bar{K}$ and $K_0 + 2\bar{K}$. The dotted line C is hypothetical; the only points on it which are actually available are b_0, b_1 and b_2. The total cost curves become vertical at those points because of the rigid capacity assumption. The intercepts a_0, a_1 and a_2 represent capacity costs nK_0, $n(K_0 + \bar{K})$ and $n(K_0 + 2\bar{K})$, respectively. Segments, $a_0 b_0, a_1 b_1$ and $a_2 b_2$, reflect the assumption that total costs vary proportionately with output as output increases towards capacity.

To analyse the problem of setting price and output in year 0 would add nothing to the analysis in the first section, and so we consider only the planning problems of the enterprise. At the beginning of year 0 the enterprise must forecast a demand curve for year 1, choose planned price, output and capacity, and determine its investment programme. Clearly, at the root of the problem is the question of the *timing* of new investment: in what year is it optimal to make the great leap from one capacity level to another? We analyse the determinants of the answer[27] with the help of figure 5.13. Capacity output in year 0 is $\bar{q}_0$, and the marginal cost 'curves' take the now familiar form for the fixed-capacity case. Let D_1 be the estimated demand curve for year 1. In the light of this, the enterprise can adopt one of two alternative investment plans. It can choose not to invest, in which case capacity output remains at $\bar{q}_0$; or it can make the increment $\bar{K}$ to capacity so that capacity output increases to $\bar{q}_1$. Each of these

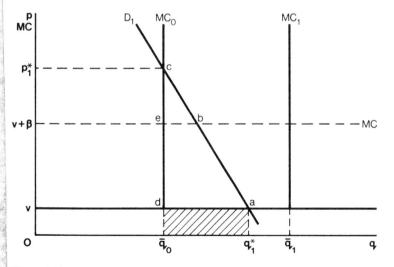

Figure 5.13

implies a corresponding pricing policy. In the first case, rationing available output by price implies that price should be set at p_1^*. In the second case, the principle of marginal cost pricing requires that price be set at v, equal to marginal running costs. Given that these pricing policies *would* accompany the corresponding investment choice, how do we determine which choice should be made?

First, consider the benefits to consumers arising from the expansion. As before, $B(q)$ measures the money value of benefits received by consumers from output q. Then, if capacity is expanded, the gain which consumers would receive from the output increase is given by

$$\Delta B = B(q_1^*) - B(\bar{q}_0). \tag{5.34}$$

The costs imposed by the increase are first the increase in variable costs, given simply as $v(q_1^* - q_0)$, which is the shaded area $aq_1^* q_0 d$ in the figure; and secondly the capacity costs, which depend *not* on the increase in output, $q_1^* - \bar{q}_0$, but the increase in *capacity*, $\bar{q}_1 - \bar{q}_0$, and so are given by $\beta(\bar{q}_1 - \bar{q}_0)$. Hence, the criterion for undertaking the capacity expansion, namely that consumer benefits exceed costs, could be written as

$$B(q_1^*) - B(q_0) > \beta(\bar{q}_1 - \bar{q}_0) + v(q_1^* - \bar{q}_0). \tag{5.35}$$

If this criterion is not satisfied, then no investment should be made in year 0, though of course the decision can be re-examined at the beginning of year 1 in relation to the demand estimate for year 2.

Take as an approximation to the value of the change in benefits ΔB the area $aq_1^* q_0 c$ under the demand curve. Then, netting out the increased variable costs ($=$additional total expenditure by buyers) gives the 'consumer surplus' adc as the benefit gain, to be compared to the increased capacity cost $\beta(\bar{q}_1 - \bar{q}_0)$. Assuming the former is greater, expansion would take place. Note in that case the enterprise would make losses, equal *not* to $\beta(\bar{q}_1 - \bar{q}_0)$, the *increment* in capital costs, but rather to $\beta\bar{q}_1$, the entire capital costs, since the price of *all* units of consumption must fall to v. This loss must be financed, and again, the welfare effects of this in a second-best world may not be neutral, and neither may be the effects on the distribution of welfare. Thus, satisfaction of the criterion in (5.35) above implies that the capacity expansion is only *potentially* Pareto optimal. If the losses resulting from the expansion are financed by making people other than the consumers worse off, the capacity expansion cannot be justified on grounds of Pareto optimality – the situation before and after the expansion are non-comparable. If, however, by lump-sum taxation (e.g. by 'scooping out' some of the consumers' surplus cda) the policy-maker can cover the deficit, then nobody loses and someone gains, so that the expansion is Pareto optimal. Alternatively, the policy-makers may approve of the distributional changes consequent upon the capacity expansion and its associated financing, in which case we do not require the situations to be Pareto comparable.

To summarize the results of this case: the decision on whether to undertake the given indivisible quantum of capacity expansion depends on a comparison of the increase in total net benefits which consumers receive, with the capital cost of the expansion. If the former exceeds the latter then (subject to reservations on second-best grounds), the expansion should be undertaken. Note that this comparison is not a marginal one, in the sense of an infinitesimal change: it involves comparisons of finite, possibly large increments, of the kind that are usually associated with cost–benefit analysis. We can, however, draw some implications for planned prices: if the expansion is not made, and rationing by price is used, price will exceed marginal costs $v + \beta$ and profits will result. It is no longer sufficient for capacity expansion that there would be excess demand at a price equal to $v + \beta$. If the expansion is made, and marginal cost pricing principles are applied, then price will in general be below $v + \beta$, and possibly as low as v, so that losses will result. This follows because the expansion in capacity may be justified even when it will subsequently be under-utilized, and under-utilization of capacity implies a price equal to v. Note finally that it may be self-contradictory to expand capacity, and then set a high price to reduce the extent of the loss. For example, suppose that in figure 5.13, the expansion were undertaken on the basis that benefits exceed costs at output q_1^*, but then a price equal to $v + \beta$ is charged (which would reduce, but not eliminate, losses). It follows that the increment in consumers' surplus is approximately ceb, which is unlikely to have justified the capacity expansion in the first place. In other words, in taking the capacity expansion decision, the enterprise must base it on the pricing policy which will *actually* be adopted after the expansion takes place, if an inconsistency is not to result.

5.5 Conclusions

In this chapter we have considered three sets of problems which arise when the attempt is made to apply marginal cost pricing principles in practice. This treatment of these problems is by no means exhaustive. We have not tried to discuss the difficulties of estimating the cost and demand functions on which to base pricing policies, which are very large topics in themselves. Nor have we covered, even at the conceptual level, all the problems of defining cost, demands and outputs in practical situations. All these issues are best tackled in the context of some specific public enterprise. This is not the case however for two further problems, which have not been considered here, but which can fruitfully be discussed at the theoretical level. The first is concerned with the characteristics of an enterprise as an interdependent system over space and time.[28] For example, electricity is generated at a number of power stations, of differing ages, capacities, designs, and fuel sources, dispersed over the country. Likewise demands are spatially dispersed. At any point in time there exists a system planning problem of determining the production at each power station, and the sources of supply of each demand, in such a way as to minimize total system costs, given also the capacities and costs of the distribution network. Over time, capacity expansion must be planned not in terms of a single, homogeneous capacity variable K, but rather in terms of a mix of different kinds of capacity – coal-fired, oil-fired, nuclear, etc. – which mix must itself be optimized. Moreover, there is interdependence between capacity expansion at different points in time, since the cost characteristics of capacity installed in year $t + \zeta$ will affect the degree of utlization of capacity installed in year t, and hence the appraisal of the amount and kind of this capacity. All this is simply to say that the neat conceptual apparatus we have so far been using does not solve all real problems: more complex models have to be constructed, whose solutions are more likely to be achieved by simulation than by analysis.

The second problem is that of determining the optimal pricing and depletion policy of a non-renewable natural resource. Coal-mining, of course, has always been an extractive industry, and one in which this problem in principle occurs. However, this aspect of the industry's problems has always been ignored, perhaps because reserves are so large relative to consumption, which was in any case expected to decline, that they were regarded as virtually inexhaustible. However, recently gas supply has ceased to have a manufacturing technology and has become instead an extractive industry, while the public enterprise element in North Sea oil production also makes this a relevant problem. The UK energy sector is currently in the process of a transformation due to the increased importance of domestically-produced non-renewable resources. It would be of interest to examine the problems presented by this and in particular to examine the consequences for pricing policy of the ultimate exhaustibility of the resource.

Though both these problems are interesting and relevant, they would lead us beyond the limits of space and technique set on this book. We now turn, therefore, to an analysis of the conceptual problems which face the doctrine of marginal cost pricing.

chapter 6

some problems of the second best

Recall from chapter 3 that a second-best economy is one in which the market system is incapable of achieving unaided a Pareto-optimal resource allocation. One or more of the assumptions defining a first-best economy is not fulfilled, and we find in general that the market equilibrium resource allocation yields a lower level of welfare for everybody, than some resource allocations which are attainable with the resources and technological possibilities available to the economy. The analysis of second-best economies has had two sets of implications for public enterprise economics, one negative and the other positive and constructive. The former consists mainly of the undermining of the rationale for marginal cost pricing as a general optimality rule. The so-called[1] 'general theorem of the second best' can be interpreted as follows. In a second-best economy there are certain 'deviant sectors' (monopolies, oligopolies, generators of external effects) whose behaviour cannot be directly modified by a central planner. In trying to achieve a Pareto optimum in this second-best economy, the planner will find that the necessary conditions (pricing rules) which must be satisfied in the sectors he does control may differ in general from those which would obtain in a first-best economy. If these sectors are public enterprises, it immediately follows that marginal cost pricing (the first-best condition) may no longer be optimal. As a result of subsequent analysis,[2] rather more than this can be said. Where the equilibrium position of each deviant sector (for example, a monopolist's output) is unaffected by the choices made by a decision-taker in some other sector, then the first-best condition for the latter continues to apply. In other words, account need only be taken of changes which actually cause deviants to vary outputs, prices, etc. It is very doubtful if this qualification can rescue marginal cost pricing, however, since the important public enterprises, producing coal, gas, electricity, steel, rail, air, road transport, and postal and tele-communications services, are closely related economically to 'deviant' sectors, in one way or another. Thus, the general theorem of the second best makes the position of general advocacy of the marginal cost pricing rule untenable.

The constructuve aspect of the theory of the second best is that it suggests how we may set about developing pricing 'rules' which are more relevant to the real economy. Since the optimal conditions for any one sector will depend on the nature of its interdependence with the deviant sectors, actual pricing policies may have to be developed on a case-by-case basis. However, it is still possible to conduct analysis at the general level, to show what the broad outlines of such policies should be. This analysis is carried out with models which explicitly embody the main features of the second-best economy. In this chapter we shall adopt this positive approach and shall examine the nature of optimal pricing policies in a number of second-best situations.

Before following up this apparently quite reasonable approach, however, we ought to discuss a rather odd implication of it. In the course of the analysis, we find that we are implicitly making the assumption that public enterprise policies are the sole instruments of the economic policy by which the 'central planner' tries to achieve a Pareto-optimum in a second-best economy. This in spite of the fact that in many circumstances they do not appear to be the best instrument. In chapter 3 for example, we saw that direct price regulation of monopolies was a more effective instrument than indirect manipulation of their outputs through the price of their public enterprise competitor. Faced with monopolistic price–output policies of the private operators of cross-channel ferries, consumer welfare would appear to be better served by price regulation than by having British Rail join the cartel.[3] The point which then occurs to logical minds is: why does the planner not adopt policies which influence deviants directly, rather than confining himself to public enterprise policies as the sole policy instruments?[4] From this it is a short step to the belief that the economy can be treated as if more rational policies could indeed be implemented, which ultimately brings us back to marginal cost pricing policies for public enterprises. But then we have turned a full circle and again confront the proposition: implementation of marginal cost pricing rules cannot be justified because the appropriate policies are not in fact adopted.

A way out of the impasse is provided by the distinction between what is and what ought to be. To meet the case of what is, we should develop the theory on the assumption that the policy-maker constrains himself to use as instruments only public enterprise policies. This is rather like writing tunes for a pianist to play only with the left hand, when we know that if he also used the right hand we could write much better tunes. However, there are good reasons for developing the theory in this way. First, it allows us to evaluate the policies which are actually being carried out in the second-best world, or those which are proposed for implementation in it. It also helps us to understand why policies derived from first-best models tend to become incoherent when modified in the light of realities (that set out in the 'White Paper on Financial and Economic Obligations of the Nationalized Industries' (1967) is a good example). Secondly, many might argue that since more general policies aimed directly at achieving allocative efficiency stand no strong chance of being adopted, whereas (the presumption is) optimal public enterprise policies would be, the 'piecemeal' second-best approach is actually most relevant. This argument must rest on some view of the policy-making machine as fragmented, imperfectly co-ordinated, and internally inconsistent.[5] In terms of our earlier metaphor, the right hand does not know, does not care, or is too busy to notice what the left hand is doing, and is playing some other kind of tune altogether.

To take care of what ought to be requires an expansion in scope of the entire analysis. We would have to consider the entire set of aims of economic policy, and the entire set of instruments which can be designed to achieve them. This would involve analysis of the properties of taxes, subsidies, price regulation, and any other kind of policy instrument, as well as public enterprise pricing. In designing an optimal set of policies, comparisons would have to be made of the differential impacts of the instruments on the objectives, and the costs associated with each type of instrument. Any constraints which exist on the set of available instruments would have to be taken into account.[6] Thus, acceptance of the logic of the arguments against 'piecemeal' second-best policy leads to a complete analysis of optimal economic policy in the course of which optimal public enterprise policies would be determined, rather than to a reversion to first-best assumptions.

To embark on the second stage of this programme would lead us well beyond the scope of this book. In this chapter and the next two, we shall be mainly concerned with some aspects of the first stage. In accepting the limitations of the piecemeal approach, we can console ourselves with the thought that at worst it is realistic, and at best it is provisional.

6.1   Public enterprise pricing and monopoly[7]
We take the following situation first of all: in an otherwise competitive economy there is a single public enterprise, producing a good which is a close substitute to that produced by a single monopoly. We assume that the behaviour of the monopolist cannot be controlled directly, and that the only policy open to the 'central planner' is the choice of price for the public enterprise.[8] He wishes to maximize social welfare, which we take to mean that he seeks a Pareto optimum. The key element in the problem is the relationship between the output chosen by the monopolist, and the price chosen for the public enterprise. Assume that this relation can be exactly specified (this assumption is further discussed later), and can be written quite simply as

$$q_1 = \beta_1(p_2), \tag{6.1}$$

where q_1 is the monopolist's *chosen* output, p_2 is public enterprise price, and β_1 is some function with suitable properties of differentiability. Then, we can show[9] that the optimal public enterprise price p_2^* must satisfy the condition

$$p_2^* - MC_2 = -[p_1^* - MC_1]\,(dq_1/dp_2)\,(dp_2/dq_2), \tag{6.2}$$

where MC_1 and MC_2 are the respective marginal costs, dq_1/dp_2 is the derivative of the function $\beta_1(p_2)$, evaluated at the optimal point, and dp_2/dq_2 is the *total derivative* of price with respect to output, again evaluated at the optimal point. To interpret this condition: since q_1 is produced by a monopolist, $p_1^* > MC_1$, and so the term in square brackets is positive. If the two goods are substitutes, dq_1/dp_2 is likely to be positive, while $dp_2/dq_2 < 0$. Hence (because of the sign in front of the brackets) the term as a whole is positive. This tells us that in this case the public enterprise price should optimally exceed marginal cost, by an amount which is greater, other things being equal, the greater is the price-marginal cost divergence in the monopoly sector. If the two goods had been complements, then this result would have been reversed since then $dq_1/dp_2 < 0$. We see also that $dq_1/dp_2 = 0$ implies that price equals marginal cost in the public sector. The result can also readily be generalized beyond monopoly. If $p_1^* \neq MC_1$ for any reason, then equation (6.2) implies $p_2^* \neq MC_2$ (as long as $dq_1/dp_2 \neq 0$ of course). If a tax is imposed on good 1, for example, we have $p_1^* > MC_1$ and (6.2) applies;[10] alternatively, if a subsidy is paid, then $p_1^* < MC_1$, and a similar divergence is implied for good 2 (assuming the goods are substitutes). Thus (6.2) gives the basic qualitative result for the case of a public enterprise interdependent with a single, uncorrected 'deviant sector'.

To interpret further the condition in (6.2) first recall that the marginal net social benefit of output of a good is measured by price *minus* marginal cost. However, in the present case we have that the marginal net social benefit of the public enterprise good q_2 depends not only on its own price and marginal cost, but also *on the changes it induces* in the output of the monopoly. Thus, rewriting (6.2) as

$$[p_2^* - MC_2] + [p_1^* - MC_1]\, dq_1/dq_2 = 0 \tag{6.3}$$

we can interpret the first term as the *partial* marginal net social benefit of q_2 in market 2, and the second as the *partial* marginal net social benefit of q_2 in market 1, so that the sum of these could be called the *total* marginal net social benefit[11] of q_2. This condition then says that welfare is maximized when this total derivative is zero; a small variation in q_2 cannot increase total welfare. The second partial marginal net social benefit is the product of two terms. The first is the marginal net social benefit of output q_1, and the second is the derivative of q_1 with respect to q_2. The interpretation just placed on this product then follows from the 'function of a function' rule of differentiation.

A further explanation of the condition can be given with the help of figure 6.1. On the horizontal axis, we measure output q_2 *leftward*, beginning at the value $\bar{q}_2$, which is defined to be the output at which $p_2 = MC_2$. It is therefore the public enterprise output which would obtain if the first-best rule were implemented. Curve A shows the value of the difference $p_2 - MC_2$ as q_2 is reduced (and its price raised) from that initial point.[12] Thus, it shows the relation between the first *partial* marginal net social

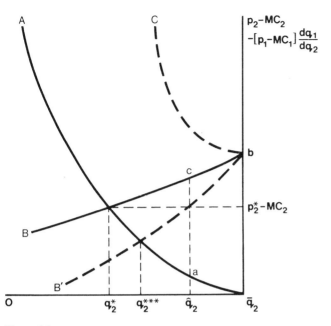

Figure 6.1

benefit and q_2. Given the usual assumptions about slopes of demand and marginal cost curves, it is reasonable to expect the difference $p_2 - MC_2$ to increase as q_2 is reduced. Curve B shows how the second partial marginal net social benefit varies with q_2. Thus, it shows $-[p_1 - MC_1] \, dq_1/dq_2$ as a function of q_2. We *assume* that the curve falls with reduced q_2, which may be due to one or both of the following: as q_2 falls (and p_2 rises) each successive reduction leads to a smaller increase in monopoly output q_1; and as q_1 increases, the difference $p_1 - MC_1$, which is the marginal net social benefit with respect to q_1, becomes smaller. This assumption, which is made essentially as a stability or second-order condition, will be discussed later. Taking it as given, we see that optimal output is at q_2^*, where A and B intersect. This is the point at which the two *partial* marginal net social benefits of q_2 are equal, thus satisfying equation (6.2). We can rationalize this as follows: at output $\bar{q}_2$, the loss of welfare in market 2 arising from a small reduction in q_2, is measured approximately by $p_2 - MC_2$ and is therefore zero. The gain in welfare in market 1, on the other hand, is measured at $\bar{q}_2$ approximately by $-[p_1 - MC_1]dq_1/dq_2$, represented by point b in the figure. Hence the gain in welfare in market 1 from a reduction in q_2 exceeds the loss in market 2, and there is scope for Pareto improvement. Consumers in market 1 can bribe those in market 2 to accept the reduction in output and diversion of resources, and still be better off. This holds true at any value of q_2 between $\bar{q}_2$ and q_2^*.

For example, at $\hat{q}_2$, the welfare loss to q_2 consumers of a further small reduction is shown by point a, while the welfare gain in market 1 is shown by point c, and so again there is a possibility of making everyone better off. Only at output q_2^* is there no such possibility, and so this is the Pareto-optimal point.

This illustration helps to make clear the nature of the second-best argument: in the initial situation, because of the monopoly in good 1, consumers in that market value their consumption at the margin sufficiently to be able to pay consumers of good 2 to reduce their consumption and release resources into production of good 1. The market fails to organize this mutually beneficial exchange. By adopting an appropriate pricing policy, the planner is able to bring about the required resource reallocation and, given the continued existence of the monopoly, to exhaust all possibilities for such exchange.[13]

The illustration also forces us to consider an important point which could easily be overlooked. We have to assume that the relationships are such that an intersection does take place.[14] For example, if curve B in figure 6.1 were replaced by C, then no optimal second-best policy for the public enterprise exists. Alternatively, we might have a curve which intersected A at several points, implying several local optima, among which we would have to find in some way the global optimum. There is, therefore, scope for further analysis of the more fundamental restrictions which have to be placed on cost and demand functions to ensure a 'well-behaved' result, although this will not be carried out here.

We can now generalize the condition in (6.2) by extending it first to the case of a single public enterprise with two monopolies, and then to that of a single monopoly and two public enterprises. These cases will serve as paradigms for the n-good case, for which the reader can construct his own combinations.

Let q_0 and q_1 be the monopoly outputs, and q_2 the public enterprise output. Again, the crucial elements in the analysis are the functions[15] relating the monopoly output choices to public enterprise price, $\beta_i(p_2)$, $i = 0, 1$. Given these, we can write the necessary condition[16] for optimal public enterprise price and output as

$$p_2^* - MC_2 = -\left\{ [p_0^* - MC_0] \frac{dq_0}{dp_2} + [p_1^* - MC_1] \frac{dq_1}{dp_2} \right\} \frac{dp_2}{dq_2}, \tag{6.4}$$

or alternatively as

$$p_2^* - MC_2 + [p_0^* - MC_0] \frac{dq_0}{dq_2} + [p_1^* - MC_1] \frac{dq_1}{dq_2} = 0. \tag{6.5}$$

Here, we have three *partial* marginal net social benefits of q_2, and condition (6.5) simply states that the sum of these must equal zero, this sum being the *total* marginal net social benefit of q_2. The chief point to note is that condition (6.4) implies a price-marginal cost divergence for the public enterprise which is a weighted *sum* of those in the monopolized markets, rather than an average, as is sometimes suggested. An intuitive explanation of this is as follows: the marginal welfare gains, net of the cost of the increased resources, accruing to consumers of q_0 and q_1 are $p_0 - MC_0$ and $p_1 - MC_1$, respectively, so that the *total* net welfare gain from a diversion of resources away from q_2 is the sum of these, weighted by the increases in their outputs which actually result. As long as this sum exceeds the welfare loss sustained by consumers of good 2, the possibility of a mutually beneficial exchange exists, and so a Pareto optimum has not been achieved. Only when the amount consumers of good 2 would require to compensate them for a marginal reduction in consumption is just equal to the total net welfare gain to the consumers of good 0 *and* 1, is a Pareto optimum achieved.

We can again work variations on the interpretation of condition (6.4). Thus, if goods 1 and 2 are substitutes, and 0 and 2 complements, the two terms on the right-hand side of (6.4) would be offsetting: consumers of good 1 would be prepared to bribe consumers of good 2 to reduce their consumption, while consumers of good 0 would be prepared to bribe them not to. Indeed, we could interpret the condition as implying in this case that consumers of goods 0 and 2 all have to be compensated for a reduction in q_2 by consumers of good 1. Whether p_2 ends up above or below MC_2 depends entirely on the price-marginal cost divergences in the two monopolized markets, and the relative values of dq_0/dp_2 and dq_1/dp_2, which measure the effects of the public enterprise price on the respective monopolized outputs. We have no reason for assuming, of course, that in general these all cancel out.

Similarly, if a tax existed in market 0, and a subsidy in market 1, while both 0 and 1 are substitutes for 2 (or both complements) then the terms would again be offsetting, and the price-marginal cost divergence for the public enterprise depends on their relative magnitudes.

Turning now to the case of a single monopoly and two public enterprises, let q_2 and q_3 be the outputs of the latter. The monopolist's chosen output q_1 is now a function of both public enterprise prices p_2 and p_3, so that we have the relation

$$q_1 = \beta_1(p_2, p_3). \tag{6.6}$$

The necessary conditions[17] for a Pareto optimum now are

$$p_2^* - MC_2 = -[p_1^* - MC_1] \frac{\partial q_1}{\partial p_2} \frac{dp_2}{dq_2} \tag{6.7}$$

and

$$p_3^* - MC_3 = -[p_1^* - MC_1] \frac{\partial q_1}{\partial p_3} \frac{dp_3}{dq_3}, \tag{6.8}$$

the interpretation of each of which follows directly from that given for condition (6.2). We then see that the *relative* price-marginal cost divergences in the two public enterprise markets are given by

$$\frac{p_2^* - MC_2}{p_3^* - MC_3} = \frac{\partial q_1}{\partial q_2} \bigg/ \frac{\partial q_1}{\partial q_3} \tag{6.9}$$

so that the public enterprise with the greater relative divergence is that with the greater impact on the monopolist's choice of output, at the optimum.

6.2   Some problems of strategic interdependence

The analysis of the previous section can be used to illustrate both negative and positive aspects of the theory of second best. The conditions in (6.2), (6.4), (6.7) and (6.8) show quite clearly that marginal cost pricing is not a necessary condition for a Pareto optimum in the second-best economy. They also give us quite useful insights into the general qualitative nature of the appropriate second-best policies. However, we now have to consider the difficulties of actually implementing such policies. It will in general be necessary to know the relevant demand and cost functions, and, most importantly, the functions which relate monopolists' output choices to public enterprise prices. In the latter case, there is a conceptual problem which goes beyond the usual difficulties of econometric estimation. It is usually assumed that the monopolist maximizes profit with respect to the cost and demand functions which he perceives to exist. He takes the public enterprise price as a parameter in the perceived demand function, and adapts to a change in it by recomputing his profit-maximizing output with respect to the new demand function. The β function then traces out the path of such output choices as the public enterprise price varies continuously.

However, this account misses an important point. The situation we have been analysing is essentially one of oligopoly,[18] and the basic term in condition (6.3), dq_1/dq_2, is what has been called in the literature of oligopoly theory a 'conjectural variation'. It is not simply derivable from a measured cross elasticity of demand, but rather must represent the planner's conjecture of the way in which the monopolist will vary his output when the public enterprise varies its own price and output. In the previous analysis, we assumed in effect that the monopolist acted as envisaged in the Cournot duopoly model, where a firm maximizes its profit, taking the other's output as given. This assumption may or may not hold in particular areas of the economy to which the above analysis may be relevant, but in any case it is important to be aware of its existence. This also suggests that there may be a class of cases in which second-best policies should be derived by examining explicitly the oligopolistic nature of the situation, i.e. by regarding it as one in which all participants recognize their strategic interdependence. We now consider two examples of such cases.

Suppose first that we have two enterprises, one private, one public, producing undifferentiated outputs, and supplying an entire market. This is a simplification of the kind of situation which, for example, faces British Rail in its cross-channel ferry and hotel operations, and the British Gas Corporation in the sale of gas to the industrial bulk fuel market (where all that matters is heat content per £, and so gas is effectively homogeneous with oil when both are measured in thermal units). The situation is shown in figure 6.2, where D is the market demand curve, and MC_1 and

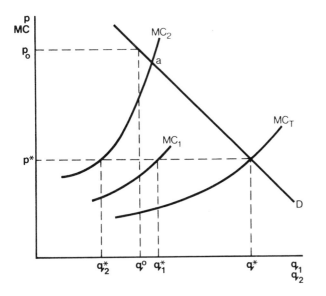

Figure 6.2

MC_2 are the marginal cost curves of the private and public enterprises respectively. The curve MC_T is the horizontal sum of MC_1 and MC_2, and so shows 'industry' marginal costs on the assumption that total output, q, is divided between private and public enterprise outputs, q_1 and q_2, respectively, in such a way as to equalize marginal costs. The 'competitive' or first-best solution in the market is at price p^*, with total output q^*, and individual enterprise outputs q_1^* and q_2^*. In this solution, price equals marginal cost and outputs are allocated in a cost-minimizing way (the rest of the economy is assumed perfectly competitive). Suppose now that the private enterprise, in a desire to increase profit, announces that it intends to set the price at p_0. The public enterprise may fall in with this, perhaps on the basis of the following argument: because outputs are homogeneous, only one price can prevail in the market. If the public enterprise maintains price at p^*, it captures the entire market, putting the private firm (which will no doubt claim unfair competition from a heavily subsidized public enterprise) out of business. If the public enterprise continues to set price at p^*, it will itself produce q^* at a marginal (and possibly average) cost well in excess of this price. If it raises price to equal marginal cost at a in the figure, then we have a price–output situation almost the same as that proposed by its private sector competitor.[19] Hence, the best policy is to accept the suggested price increase.[20] The private enterprise may gamble on its competitor's acceptance of this reasoning. On the other hand (assuming output q_1^* yielded at least normal profit for the private enterprise), if the public enterprise threatened to maintain price at p^* and if need be let the private enterprise go out of business, this would act as an effective constraint on the latter, and could forestall the price rise. Thus, given the nature of the situation, the optimal strategy for the public enterprise is to threaten, or, if the need arises, actually to adopt, maintenance of the price[21] at p^*.

The second case of strategic interdependence which we shall consider is that of bilateral monopoly, with the public enterprise as the sole buyer of a good, and the private enterprise as the sole seller. Again we assume that the rest of the economy is competitive. This is a simplification of the kind of situation in which the British Gas Council buys North Sea gas, the electricity industry buys generating equipment, and the Post Office buys telephone exchange equipment. In figure 6.3, D is the demand curve of the public enterprise, for the good to be exchanged, MC is the marginal cost curve of the private enterprise producing the good, and MR is the marginal revenue curve corresponding to D. We take it that D shows, at each level of output q, the

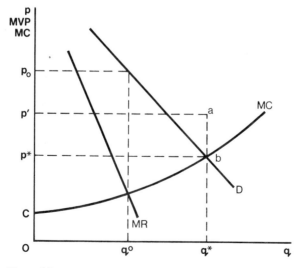

Figure 6.3

marginal value product of the good,[22] which in an otherwise first-best economy measures its marginal social value. The optimal quantity of the good which should be produced by the monopolist and bought by the public enterprise is q^*; at any other quantity, its marginal cost differs from its marginal value product, and so welfare could be improved by an output change. If the public enterprise can negotiate this quantity, therefore, it will actually be achieving the first-best solution for this second-best economy. There are two bargaining strategies it may adopt to achieve this solution, the first of which would require it effectively to have complete control of the situation, while the second takes a more realistic view of the bargaining process.

First, suppose that the public enterprise announced that it would accept any quantity, but would pay at most the price p^* in the figure. In effect, p^* *becomes the marginal revenue of the monopolist* – he can sell as much as he likes at that price. It follows that his profit-maximizing quantity is q^*, so this is the amount he will offer. Thus, if the public enterprise determines price, while the private enterprise determines quantity, the first-best solution can be achieved by this strategy.

However, that solution may yield the monopolist a smaller profit than he thinks he should get, and, given the realities of the bargaining situation, may not be possible. Suppose that instead, therefore, the public enterprise announces that it will buy an amount q^*, and is prepared to negotiate over the price. It is then possible to ensure that the monopolist can have his profit goals at least to some extent satisfied by deciding on a price greater than p^*, say p' in the figure. In that case, the monopolists' total revenue is $Op'aq^*$, his total costs are given by the area $OCbq^*$ under his MC curve, and so total profit is the area $Cp'ab$. It is obviously possible to find some price greater than p^* at which the monopolist's profit is as great as if he were able to exercise his monopoly power in full.

In order for this second strategy actually to lead to a first-best optimum, it is necessary that the public enterprise use, in its determination of input mix, output level and final price, the 'shadow price' p^*, rather than the actual price p'. This is because p^* measures the marginal cost of the good. The significance of p' is that it determines the monetary deficit or surplus of the enterprise, and so the result of paying a price p' instead of p^* can be viewed as essentially a transfer payment from the exchequer to the monopolist. Hence (given that there are no welfare effects associated with the deficit or surplus) the value of p' determines the distribution of income in the economy, rather than the allocation of resources.

In case this second strategy should appear fanciful, note that it is essentially the procedure which has been advocated for price and output policies in the coal industry, although in somewhat different terminology.[23] The monopoly in question is the National Union of Mineworkers which controls the sale of miners' labour services to the National Coal Board. In promoting the interests of its members, it uses its bargaining power to secure wage rates which exceed those which could be earned by coal-miners in alternative employment. We take the latter to be the 'marginal social cost' of mining labour services, since they represent the opportunity cost to the economy of having the miners producing coal rather than something else. Hence, the price of labour services exceeds their marginal cost, where the latter may even be regarded as zero if the miners would be otherwise unemployed.[24] However, it has been argued that in determining coal output, and evaluating, say, coal-fired power stations against alternative designs, mining labour should be costed at its opportunity cost, and not the wage rate. Hence, we have an exact illustration of the second strategy just analysed. Coal output and prices would be determined by a 'shadow price' calculation, while the wage rate affects the coal industry's surplus or deficit, and so determines the implied transfer from the exchequer to coal-miners. An interesting implication of this argument is that an increase in coal-miners' wage rates, with their true opportunity costs unchanged, would have no effect on price and output of coal, at least on resource allocation grounds. It would increase the size of transfer from the exchequer to coal-miners, and so require an increase in taxation, in government borrowing, or a reduction in other forms of public expenditure. The question of whether coal prices should then rise must therefore be discussed in terms of tax-expenditure policy, viewing the increase in coal prices essentially as a form of indirect taxation. Similarly, the question of how large the rise in wage rates should be relates primarily to considerations of income distribution and tax-expenditure policy, which explains why it is inevitable that a government would become involved in the bargaining process.[25]

To summarize the analysis of this section and the last: we have been considering second-best situations in which a public enterprise is economically interdependent with a private monopoly. We derived and interpreted some results for optimal pricing rules in such cases, suggesting in a qualitative way the kinds of departures from marginal cost pricing which would be required. In applying this approach, a major problem would be the estimation of the 'conjectural variation', defining the change in the monopolist's choice of output in response to a change in public enterprise price. This suggested that it may often be important to examine explicitly the oligopolistic nature of the markets concerned, taking into account the types of strategic interdependence perceived by the private and public sector participants. Some examples were analysed, where this analysis was intended to be suggestive rather than exhaustive. In the rest of this chapter, we shall look at a somewhat different second-best situation.

6.3   Uncorrected externalities
The existence of external effects implies that the market mechanism will not achieve, unaided, a Pareto optimum, and so also implies existence of a second-best economy.

It is in principle possible to design a set of policies which would 'correct for' all externalities, and bring about a first-best Pareto optimum, but it seems impossible to argue that the policies towards externalities which actually exist have this effect, and there are certainly many examples of uncorrected externalities.

Where a public enterprise generates external effects, we can envisage that appropriate corrections would be made, so that it makes choices on the basis of social rather than private costs. Here, we shall not be concerned with the problem of determining the corrections,[26] since nothing there is specific to public enterprise. Rather, we shall take the case of a public enterprise which does not itself generate externalities, but which is interdependent with a sector in which uncorrected externalities exist. The analysis will be conducted in terms of an example: there are two towns, Alpha and Omega, which are connected by a road and a railway line. The only form of road transport is the motor car (this could be generalized with no real gain in insight). Private motorists are assumed to reckon as the cost of a journey from Alpha to Omega, the cost of petrol, vehicle wear and tear and the value of their time (assumed always positive). Given the details of road conditions and of the characteristics of the cars driven by the motorists, we assume that it is possible to estimate the aggregate cost incurred by a given number of motorists q_m wishing to make the trip from Alpha to Omega within a specified time period. The relationship between this total cost C_m and q_m is graphed as the curve OC_m in figure 6.4(a). Its shape reflects the assumption that as traffic builds up average speed declines, thus (after some point) increasing the petrol consumption, wear and tear on the car and

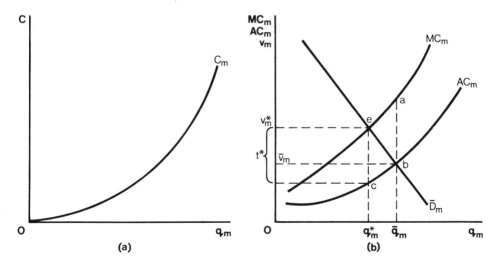

Figure 6.4

journey time of each motorist. Hence, after some point, total costs rise more than proportionately with the number of motorists, as shown by the curvature of OC_m. In figure 6.4(b), MC_m and AC_m are the marginal and average cost curves derived from OC_m in the usual way. From the curvature of OC_m, we know that MC_m lies above AC_m and has a steeper slope at every point. The important point to note for the subsequent analysis is that each motorist will take, as the cost to himself of the road trip, the *average* cost AC_m, at any given total number of road trips q_m. That is, assuming he knows the total number of motorists who will be on the road at that time, he will determine what it will cost him to be one of them; then, assuming that each motorist is identical in terms of time value and car characteristics, this cost is the same for each motorist and corresponds to the average cost AC_m. The nature of the situation, as one involving external effects, results from the fact that the *marginal* cost of a road journey is above the *average* cost. For example, at $\bar{q}_m$ in the figure, each motorist reckons the cost of the trip as the average cost at point b on AC_m, but the decision of the marginal motorist to take the trip has a cost given by point a on MC_m, since this represents the *increase in total costs* to all users, arising from his taking the trip. The distance ab then measures the divergence between the social cost and the private cost of the marginal road trip. To generalize this, we can write the relation between marginal and average cost as[27]

$$MC_m = AC_m + q_m \frac{\mathrm{d}AC_m}{\mathrm{d}q_m}, \tag{6.10}$$

where $\mathrm{d}AC_m/\mathrm{d}q_m$ is the derivative of average cost with respect to the number of motorists. Thus, the increment in total cost resulting from the marginal trip exceeds the average cost, on which the motorist bases his decision, by the amount $q_m(\mathrm{d}AC_m/\mathrm{d}q_m)$, which can be interpreted as the increase in cost to all motorists following from the marginal trip undertaken.

Denote the price of a rail trip from Alpha to Omega by p_r, and assume that it is fixed throughout the following analysis at the value $\bar{p}_r$. Now suppose that a price v_m were to be set for road trips from Alpha to Omega, which would be *inclusive of costs* incurred by each motorist. Effectively, therefore, v_m consists of the average cost of a road trip AC_m plus some *toll* t which the motorist pays. Given $\bar{p}_r$, by varying v_m we would trace out a demand curve for road trips, which is drawn as $\bar{D}_m$ in figure 6.4(b). We take the situation to be that in which no toll is actually levied on road trips, so that the 'price' of a road trip v_m is equal to the average cost, AC_m. It follows that the equilibrium number of road trips is given by $\bar{q}_m$ in the figure, since that is the number of motorists who will want to make the trip at the price $\bar{v}_m = AC_m$. We can give this position our usual welfare interpretation: the market price measures the value of the marginal unit of consumption. In this case, the value of the marginal trip is just equal to the private cost of undertaking it, AC_m, whereas the social cost of that marginal trip is the value of MC_m at point a in the figure, and so we have an 'uncorrected external diseconomy' in the amount $MC_m - AC_m$ at $\bar{q}_m$.

A first-best solution[28] would be to levy a toll such that the value of the marginal trip is just equal to its social cost. In the figure, we see that the optimal toll is given by t^*: with this toll, the 'price' of a road trip is v_m^*, resulting in the total number of trips q_m^*, and a market equilibrium[29] at e, where $v_m^* = MC_m$.

The second-best situation is created by the impossibility, for some reason, of imposing the optimal, or indeed any, toll on road users. The problem becomes that of determining the optimal price of rail trips, given the dependence on it of the demand for road trips. Thus, the rail price p_r becomes the only instrument with which to optimize the 'modal split', to use the jargon of transport economists, in the market for trips from Alpha to Omega.

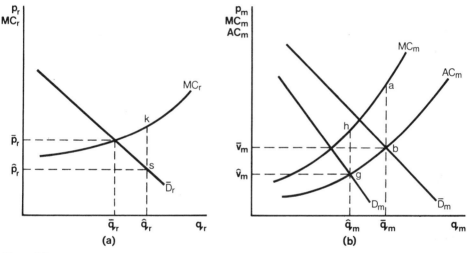

Figure 6.5

In figure 6.5(a) we show the marginal cost and demand curves for rail trips MC_r and $\bar{D}_r$, respectively. The position of the rail demand curve will in general depend on the 'price' of a road trip, AC_m, and so we assume that $\bar{D}_r$ corresponds to the value of AC_m at the number of road trips $\bar{q}_m$. Figure 6.5 therefore represents initial, mutually consistent equilibrium positions in the two markets, with $\bar{D}_m$ corresponding to a marginal cost price for rail, $\bar{p}_r$, and $\bar{D}_r$ corresponding to the average cost of a road trip at $\bar{q}_m$.

In this initial situation, there is a divergence between the marginal value of a road trip, and its marginal cost, of the amount $MC_m - AC_m$ at $\bar{q}_m$. Hence, a small reduction in the number of road trips would generate a welfare gain of approximately this amount. In the rail market, the marginal value of a rail trip p_r is equal to its marginal cost MC_r and so the welfare loss from a small increment in rail trips is approximately zero. By reducing the rail price from $\bar{p}_r$, we achieve the reduction in road trips and increase in rail trips, and hence generate a net welfare gain. In the figure, we illustrate this by reducing the rail price to $\hat{p}_r$, which expands rail trips to $\hat{q}_r$, causes the road demand to shift to D_m, and hence causes an initial fall in road trips to $\hat{q}_m$, thus reducing the marginal welfare loss $MC_m - AC_m$ to that at $\hat{q}_m$ (shown by the distance hg). However, the figure does not show the end of the story, since the fall in AC_m will cause a downward shift in $\bar{D}_r$, so that if $\hat{p}_r$ is held, there will be a smaller increase in rail trips than $\hat{q}_r - \bar{q}_r$. Because of the demand interactions, the figure is not well suited to find the final solution, but it indicates the general nature of the argument. The necessary condition which must be satisfied by the optimal rail price is[30]

$$p_r^* - MC_r = [MC_m - AC_m] \frac{\partial q_m}{\partial p_r} \frac{\partial p_r}{\partial q_r}, \tag{6.11}$$

which is clearly similar to the sorts of conditions we derived in the earlier sections of this chapter. Its interpretation and illustration are also essentially the same, and so we leave the reader to supply these. We note only that the term in square brackets is effectively the marginal welfare loss of road trips, since, in the absence of a toll, the value of the marginal road trip is always equal to AC_m. Moreover, this term is always positive, while the product of the two partial derivatives is negative, and so a rail price below marginal cost is called for. Finally, we emphasize that this 'correction' to the marginal cost price of the public enterprise good is made, not because it itself generates externalities, but because it is closely related in demand to a sector in which uncorrected externalities exist. If this demand relation did not exist (i.e. $\partial q_m/\partial p_r = 0$), marginal cost pricing would be optimal.

6.4 Conclusions

In this chapter we have considered second-best situations in which a public enterprise is interdependent with a 'deviant sector', which may be a monopoly, or a market in which non-optimal taxes or uncorrected externalities exist. The initial assumption is that the public enterprise price is the sole instrument of second-best policy, even though better ones can clearly be designed. To pursue the full implications of this assumption would require a more general analysis of the cost, effectiveness and feasibility of a wide set of policy instruments, which would be an important though large undertaking. We have here adopted the assumption provisionally, as being the most useful way to begin the analysis of what appear to be the real problems. We find that in general marginal cost pricing is not justified on the Paretian grounds from which it usually derives its support. If the public enterprise price is set equal to marginal cost, there is in general a way of reallocating resources so as to make everyone better off, and using the public enterprise price as a means of exhausting such possibilities will imply in the end a non-marginal cost pricing condition. There is a strong similarity among the forms of such conditions for the various cases analysed, and they can usually be rationalized in an intuitively appealing way. To implement pricing policies based on such conditions will in general require more information than that needed by any pricing rule which does not take into account interactions between sectors. Moreover, a particular problem arises in the class of cases in which the public enterprise is closely related to a 'monopoly', since here in effect we have a situation of oligopoly. In such a case, it may be difficult to measure the 'conjectural variation', which is a crucial element of the second-best pricing condition, and it has been suggested that the appropriate approach may be to set up a model of the situation which explicitly incorporates the types of strategic interdependence which exist. The overall conclusion of the analysis, which cannot possibly be exhaustive, is that actual pricing policies must be developed on a case-by-case basis, since the particular nature of the second-best situation may differ from enterprise to enterprise. However, the kind of analysis carried out here is useful in indicating the general forms such policies would take.

Finally, note that it is not valid to use the conceptual and informational difficulties of second-best solutions as a justification of marginal cost-pricing policies. There is no presumption that a marginal cost price is a better approximation to the optimal second-best pricing condition than any other rule, when no information on the parameters of the condition exist. Indeed, we would argue that often the pricing policies currently in existence may be closer approximations to the second-best optimal rules than the marginal cost-pricing rules which seek to supplant them. But this will have to be argued elsewhere.

chapter 7

profitability, taxation and income distribution

In the previous four chapters, we have been concerned with the characterization of pricing and investment policies which achieve allocative efficiency. The purpose was always to find necessary conditions under which the public enterprise resource allocation was Pareto optimal, and then to use these conditions to determine the appropriate policy. Implicit in this, therefore, is the assumption either that our 'policy-maker' is indifferent to the distribution of welfare, or that he is able to achieve any desired distribution by making lump-sum transfers which leave the marginal conditions unaffected (recall the discussion of chapter 3). Also implicit was the assumption that the profit or loss of the enterprise was a matter of indifference, presumably for a similar reason: that any deficit could be financed in a lump-sum way, and any surplus distributed in a similar fashion. Finally, although economic efficiency is a matter of both allocative efficiency and technological efficiency, the latter received no explicit attention: it was implicitly assumed that public enterprise managers would choose the technologically most efficient set of input combinations for each output, and then the cost-minimizing combinations within this set, so that the cost of producing each given level of output was at a minimum.

As we saw in chapters 1 and 2, however, a great deal of attention is paid by policy-makers to precisely these issues – profitability, income distribution and technological efficiency – to the extent that allocative efficiency may well be sacrificed in pursuit of them. Therefore, any attempt to formulate decentralized pricing and investment policies is incomplete unless it extends to these. It is worth while to recapitulate the reasons for the explicit attention which must be paid to these goals. Of prime importance is the impossibility of devising lump-sum taxes which would achieve distributional objectives, and provide finance for public enterprise deficits and other forms of public expenditures whose revenues do not cover costs. Thus, taxes are imposed on incomes and outputs.[1] These taxes are not only a means of raising revenue, but are also instruments of income redistribution. Public enterprise prices relate directly to the government's fiscal concerns, since gross trading surpluses are an important source of government revenue, and public enterprise investment constitutes a heavy claim on public expenditure. Thus, the surpluses of public enterprises can be looked upon as a form of indirect taxation.

In addition, the nature of most public enterprise outputs, as 'public utilities', raises important distributional issues, as does the fact that inputs, especially labour services, may be supplied by households whose real income it is desired to increase, for one reason or another. Clearly, therefore, public enterprise prices are likely to be seen as useful instruments in taxation and income redistribution policies.

Profitability has a further significance: the self-interest which is at the root of profit maximization leads an entrepreneur to seek to minimize costs at each level of output, and hence to pursue technological efficiency. Once the connection between efficiency and self-interest is removed, managers may pursue the 'quiet life', and adopt 'satisficing' goals, which may well imply technological and managerial inefficiency.[2] The problem as policy-makers see it is to find a way of stimulating managers to technological efficiency, by reintroducing profit as a goal but not as a maximand. The problem is compounded when income distributional goals exist, the pursuit of which appears in turn to imply technological inefficiency. This is a fine example of the policy conflict discussed in chapter 1.

In the rest of this chapter, we shall try to answer the question: how may pricing policies be defined, which meet profit and income distributional objectives with the minimum loss of economic efficiency? We shall conclude the chapter with a discussion of the way in which such policies might be operationalized in conjunction with the other second-best 'rules' derived in earlier chapters.

7.1   Profit targets
The way in which both profitability and efficiency goals have been brought to bear upon public enterprises is through the device of a 'financial target', described in chapter 3. For present purposes, we take this to be a specified value[3] of the gross trading surplus, or excess of revenue over direct operating costs. Thus, the surplus includes provision for those costs which can be taken as fixed with capacity. The value of the surplus reflects the contribution to the exchequer which it is desired that the enterprise should make. The precise way in which technological and managerial efficiency is supposed to be stimulated by the profit target is somewhat unclear, as is the relation between the strength of this stimulus and size of the target. We shall discuss this question later in this section. For the moment, we concern ourselves only with the question: how should prices and outputs be chosen, in a way which meets the profit target with a minimum loss of allocative efficiency?[4]

First, note that if the public enterprise produces only a single product then the problem is relatively trivial. Figure 7.1 illustrates. In the figure, p^* is the allocatively optimal price (assuming there are no other second-best problems) but at the corresponding output q^*, average total cost AC exceeds price, and so the enterprise makes a loss. Suppose it is required to 'break even', i.e. to cover total costs including fixed costs (in which case the required surplus is effectively equal to fixed cost): then

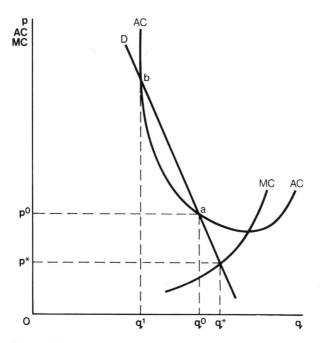

Figure 7.1

this requires price to equal average total cost, AC. There are two outputs at which this occurs in the figure, namely q^0 and q^1, corresponding to the points a and b at which AC intersects the demand curve D. Clearly there is a smaller welfare loss at a, and this is the optimal output. Thus, in the case of a single output, the set of output levels which satisfy the profit target will typically contain at most two values (or one if the target is for *maximum* profit) and so the problem of choice is very straightforward.[5]

In general, however, public enterprises produce more than one output, and so we have the important problem of the *allocation* of the profit target among different outputs. We shall, as is our usual practice, begin with the simplest possible case, in which the public enterprise produces two outputs, which in addition are unrelated in demand and cost: the cross-elasticities of demand are zero, and variations in production of one output do not affect costs of the other. We then have the problem of determining the optimal prices.

The argument underlying derivation of these can be described as follows: suppose that the two outputs, q_1 and q_2, are initially at the level at which their respective prices are equal to marginal cost. A small reduction in q_1 will reduce consumer welfare by its price p_1, since this is the marginal value of output to consumers; it will, however, release resources which can be used elsewhere, the value of this being measured by marginal cost, MC_1. Hence, the marginal net welfare loss corresponding to a reduction in q_1 is measured by $p_1 - MC_1$. Likewise, $p_2 - MC_2$ measures that of good 2. The effect of the change in output of good 1 on the profit it generates is given by the difference between marginal revenue, MR_1, and marginal cost. That is, the *marginal profit* of output 1 is $MR_1 - MC_1$, and that of good 2 is $MR_2 - MC_2$ (note that if outputs are *greater* than their profit-maximizing levels, which we take to be the case, these marginal profits are negative: a reduction in output increases profit, because $MC > MR$).

It can be shown[6] that the optimal outputs of the two goods must satisfy the condition:

$$\frac{p_1 - MC_1}{MR_1 - MC_1} = \frac{p_2 - MC_2}{MR_2 - MC_2} = \lambda < 0, \tag{7.1}$$

where λ is some negative number,[7] whose value is determined by S, the profit constraint. This condition is interpreted as follows: if the two ratios in (7.1) were unequal, we could always find a way of reallocating outputs, which would leave profit unchanged ($= S$), but lead to a greater welfare gain in one market than the loss in the other. Hence, everybody can be made better off by the reallocation, assuming appropriate compensation is paid, and so the initial allocation cannot be Pareto optimal. A necessary condition for such possibilities not to exist is that the ratios are equal.

To illustrate this, consider a numerical example. Suppose that the ratio[8] of marginal welfare loss to marginal profit in the first market is 3/1, and that in the second is 2/1. Then, by choosing to increase output in the first market so that the loss of profit is 1, we can increase welfare by 3 units; by choosing to reduce output in the second market so that profit increases by 1, thus restoring profit to the required level, we lose two units of welfare. Thus, consumers in the first market can more than compensate those in the second for the change, and so this situation cannot be Pareto optimal.

To obtain some further insight into the conditions, recall that marginal revenue of each good can always be written as

$$MR_i = p_i(1 - 1/e_i), \qquad i = 1, 2, \tag{7.2}$$

where e_i is the price elasticity of demand for good i, given by

$$e_i = -\frac{p_i}{q_i}\frac{dq_i}{dp_i}, \qquad i = 1, 2. \tag{7.3}$$

Now, from equation (7.1), we have that

$$p_1 - MC_1 = \lambda[MR_1 - MC_1] > 0 \tag{7.4}$$

and so, by using equation (7.2) and rearranging, we obtain

$$p_1(1 - 1/\hat{e}_1) = MC_1, \tag{7.5}$$

where

$$\hat{e}_1 = -\frac{(1 - \lambda)e_1}{\lambda} \tag{7.6}$$

and similarly we can show for good 2 that

$$p_2(1 - 1/\hat{e}_2) = MC_2, \tag{7.7}$$

where

$$\hat{e}_2 = -\frac{(1 - \lambda)e_2}{\lambda}. \tag{7.8}$$

The term $-[(1 - \lambda)/\lambda]$ must be greater than 1, since λ is negative.[9] The conditions in (7.5) and (7.7) then have the interesting interpretation: the public enterprise is, in effect, constrained to act like a 'quasi-monopolist', who must maximize profit, but with respect to a demand curve whose elasticity is increased by the factor $-[(1 - \lambda)]/\lambda$, the value of which depends on the profit constraint S. As S tends to maximum profit, so this term tends to unity,[10] as we would expect. Since the 'correction factor' to the two demand elasticities is the same, we have the result that the relative deviations of price from marginal cost of the two goods are entirely determined by their elasticities. Each deviation varies inversely with the elasticity of demand of the good: goods with less elastic demands have higher divergences of price from marginal cost.

An illustration of these results is given in figure 7.2. For simplicity, it is assumed that marginal costs are constant and equal for the two goods. The optimal outputs are q_1^* and q_2^*, respectively, it having been asumed that the value of S is such as to imply a value of λ of -1. Thus, condition (7.1) is clearly satisfied in the figure, since the relevant divergences are given by ab, bc, ef and fg, and we have that $ab/bc = ef/fg = -1$. The price-marginal cost divergence is clearly greater in market 2, which has the less elastic demand, and that market also makes the greater profit contribution, shown by the area p_2^* abk, as compared to that in the first market, area p_1^* efh. The lines $\widehat{MR}_1$ and $\widehat{MR}_2$ are the *adjusted* marginal revenue curves, corresponding respectively to the elasticities $\hat{e}_1$ and $\hat{e}_2$ rather than the true elasticities. Thus, the profit constraints induce the public enterprise to act as a 'modified' profit maximizer, restricting output, raising price, and 'charging what the market will bear' to an overall degree determined by the profit constraint.

Before going on to generalize these results, we can note a feature of them which is interesting from the viewpoint of empirical application. In practice, public enterprise

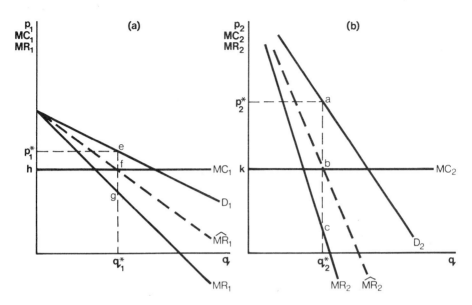

Figure 7.2

prices are often set on the basis of 'what the market will bear'. Profit margins are higher in 'captive markets', or, in the terminology of economics, markets with low demand elasticity, than in competitive markets. The pricing rule just derived would therefore make a lot of sense to those who currently set pricing policy. Moreover, this suggests that the existing pattern of outputs may lie closer to the optimum than would the one which follows from making all prices bear the same proportionate relationship to marginal costs.[11]

We can now generalize our earlier result by assuming that the two goods are interdependent in demand. It is then possible to show[12] that the optimal prices and quantities must now satisfy the relationship

$$\frac{p_1 - MC_1}{MR_{11} + MR_{12} - MC_1} = \frac{p_2 - MC_2}{MR_{22} + MR_{21} - MC_2} = \lambda, \tag{7.9}$$

where $MR_{ij}, i, j, = 1, 2$, is the effect of the ith output on the revenue of the jth. We can regard the sum $MR_{11} + MR_{12}$ as the *total* effect on the revenue of the enterprise, of a change in output 1, via the effects on both its own demand, and that of good 2. And likewise for the sum $MR_{22} + MR_{21}$. For example, if the two goods are substitutes, so that an increase in q_1, accompanied by a fall in its price, decreases demand and revenue of good 2, then MR_{12} will be negative. The basic rationalization of this condition is essentially as before: the only difference is that now the *total* effect of each output on the overall revenue of the enterprise must be taken into account. It follows that the price-marginal cost divergences will now depend not only on own-price elasticities of demand, but cross-price elasticities also. This of course increases the informational requirements for implementation of these conditions.

Similar conclusions follow when we consider the case of several public enterprises, each producing several outputs, many of which are interdependent in demand. This is the case in the energy and transport sectors, for example, where electricity and gas are close substitutes in the domestic space-heating market, coal and gas compete in the industrial bulk energy market, rail and air compete in long-distance interurban travel, and so on. Given that each enterprise is subject to a different profit constraint, the optimality condition for goods 1 and 2 now becomes[13]

$$\frac{p_1 - MC_1 - \sum_{i=2}^{n} \lambda_i MR_1}{MR_{11} + MR_{12} - MC_1} = \frac{p_2 - MC_2 - \sum_{i=2}^{n} \lambda_i MR_{2i}}{MR_{21} + MR_{22} - MC_2} = \lambda_1, \qquad (7.10)$$

where λ_1 is determined by the profit constraint imposed on the first public enterprise. The condition clearly differs only by the subtraction from each numerator of the term $\sum_{i=2}^{n} \lambda_i MR_{ji}$, $j = 1, 2$, which is the sum of the effects of a change in q_j, on the revenues of all other profit-constrained public enterprises, weighted by *their* values of λ, the λ_i, $i = 2, 3, \ldots, n$. The significance of λ lies in its interpretation as the marginal welfare cost of the profit constraint;[14] i.e. its value measures the reduction in consumer welfare which would result from a small increase in the required profit. Thus, the term $\lambda_i MR_1$ is the indirect effect on consumer welfare of a change in q_1, via its effect on the revenues (and therefore profits) of the other enterprise. It is essentially the product of derivatives $\partial B/\partial S_i$, $\partial S_i/\partial q_1$, which, from the 'function of a function' rule, translates into the indirect effect of q_1 on net social benefit B, given its effect on the profit requirement S_i. Now since λ_i is negative, if MR_1 is negative (the goods are substitutes) this term is positive, and therefore, in (7.10), plays the part of a 'social cost': by reducing the profits of the other enterprise, an increase in q_1 causes them to make up for this by raising their prices and thus reducing welfare in their own markets. Such effects have to be taken into account in determining the output level of every good produced in the public enterprise sector. To do so is simply to recognize the common sense argument that it is pointless to make one enterprise achieve its profit target, while ignoring the fact that this makes it harder for another to do so, and in the end leads to a greater welfare loss over all. The condition in (7.10) essentially imposes the requirement for a *co-ordinated* public enterprise policy.

This suggests two further points of interest. First, how should we determine the *relative* profit targets of different public enterprises? And second, what should be the approach towards sales of intermediate goods *within* the public sector? We consider each of these in turn.

To examine the first question, let us return to the simple case of two goods and no demand interdependence, but assume that they are produced by different public enterprises (which produce other outputs as well). The optimum conditions relating to each good will now be

$$\frac{p_1 - MC_1}{MR_1 - MC_1} = \lambda_1 \quad \text{and} \quad \frac{p_2 - MC_2}{MR_2 - MC_2} = \lambda_2, \tag{7.11}$$

where λ_1 and λ_2 are determined by the target surpluses in the two industries. Recall that they are interpreted as the marginal welfare loss arising from the profit constraint on each enterprise. Now presumably, the subject of concern to the policy-maker is the *total* surplus generated by all enterprises, since this is the effective inflow into the exchequer. It follows that the allocation of this surplus among enterprises is inefficient if $\lambda_1 \neq \lambda_2$, because in that case it would be possible to reallocate resources and vary outputs between the two enterprises in such a way as to make everyone better off, while leaving the total *sector* surplus unchanged. The argument proceeds exactly as before, since in terms of welfare and the total profit contribution of the public enterprise sector, it makes no difference that the two outputs are produced by different public enterprises. An efficient allocation of *profit targets* among public enterprises then requires that the marginal welfare loss of each target in each enterprise be the same, which implies $\lambda_1 = \lambda_2$ and the condition in equation (7.1) must hold throughout the public sector. Thus, other things being equal, we would find that a public enterprise whose outputs tended to be elastic in demand would have a low target, while one which had inelastic demands would be constrained to be highly profitable. The separate profit targets should, however, be *implied* by the optimality conditions set out here, *given* the desired surplus required from the public enterprise sector as a whole.

Consider now the case in which public enterprises buy from and sell to each other. In terms of the overall public sector surplus, the profits or losses made on these sales are simply transfers from one enterprise to another, which in the aggregate cancel out: what matters is the total revenue earned from sales outside the sector and the total costs of inputs brought in. The relevant analogy here is to a large, divisionalized, vertically integrated firm, and the problem is essentially to determine the correct set of *transfer prices*, i.e. the prices which co-ordinate and optimize transfers of intermediate goods between divisions in a decentralized way.[15]

Given a set of profit targets which are separately imposed on public enterprises, each enterprise will be constrained to make some profit on its sales to other public enterprises, even though this leads to distortions and welfare losses. This is more clearly seen, if we take the case of a single public enterprise, E, which produces two outputs, one of which it sells to public enterprise A, the other to public enterprise B. E is the sole producer of these outputs. The rest of the economy is assumed perfectly competitive. Given the profit constraint which is imposed upon it, E will have to set its prices above marginal cost, and the relative profit contribution from sales to A and B will depend on the elasticities of their demands for E's output, as we have already seen.[16] These elasticities depend partly on the technological possibilities of input substitution in A and B, and partly on the price elasticities of demand for their final outputs. Given that A and B must meet *their* profit targets, they will substitute other inputs for the public enterprise input, thus buying in from outside the public sector, and will also raise their own prices. But since E's profit simply represents higher costs to A and B, the *total* surplus of the three enterprises must be derived from the revenues of A and B in their sales to final consumers. Suppose instead that this total surplus were allocated only to A and B, and that the third enterprise is instructed to sell to them at marginal cost i.e. no financial target is imposed upon it. There is an efficiency gain, because the input combinations chosen by A and B would then be based on a minimization of social costs. Given that the prices of inputs supplied by the private sector equal their marginal costs (i.e. we are in an otherwise first-best economy) a price of the public enterprise input above *its* marginal cost would distort the relative input prices which A and B face, and lead them to choose input combinations which do not minimize social cost.[17] Thus, the conclusion is that transfers within the public enterprise sector should be made at marginal cost, given that such transfers do not involve interdependence with 'deviant' markets in the private sector. The overall surplus required by the public sector should be generated by profits on sales to non-public enterprise buyers. Thus for example if it were not for the fact that oil is supplied under conditions of oligopoly coal would be sold to the electricity and steel industries at a price equal to marginal cost, while coal sold to outside buyers would make a positive contribution (over and above that which is anyway implied by pricing at marginal cost in an increasing cost industry) to profit.[18]

The argument so far has led to the conclusion that given the total required surplus from the public enterprise sector, which is determined by the government on revenue-raising grounds, the objective of minimizing the loss of allocative efficiency determines the way in which it can be allocated among all public enterprise outputs. The total surplus generated by any one enterprise is then a *derived* value: it will be the sum of the individual surpluses on the outputs the enterprise produces. By examining the converse case, in which targets are separately allocated to enterprises and then the effects on price-marginal cost divergences of specific outputs determined, we were able to show that the former is a better second best. This means that a public enterprise which sells most of its output to other public enterprises, and which in outside markets faces elastic demands, would be relatively 'unprofitable' (recalling that the 'surplus' includes interest and depreciation).

This conclusion cannot be left to stand, however, without a discussion of the second reason for the existence of 'financial targets', as stimuli to managerial and technological efficiency, and a yardstick of performance.[19] Clearly, there is no direct connection between profit targets and efficiency, since they can be achieved by price increases. There must exist some system by which price increases are monitored, so that the profit target is made to exert pressure on costs. Since this must be done by the 'sponsoring Departments' and the Treasury,[20] we immediately lose many of the advantages which a decentralized system would bring. If the monitoring is to be effective, it would require exploration of the reasons for cost increases, analysis of productivity levels, and so on – price control alone cannot suffice. More often in the past decade or so, price increases have been refused or scaled down in the (presumed) interests of counter-inflationary policy, with no monitoring of cost levels. Thus, public enterprises have been able to point to this as a reason for non-fulfilment of profit targets, and it has been *impossible to determine* whether or not this is true, whatever dark suspicions may be held.

This suggests, to the writer at least, that the pursuit of technological and managerial efficiency should be divorced from the question of profitability, and should be undertaken directly, rather than indirectly through pricing policy. The appropriate instrument would be the 'efficiency audit' suggested by Professor Robson[21], which in fact bears a resemblance to the kind of work done by the Prices and Incomes Board[22] when it existed. An 'efficiency audit commission' would be exclusively concerned with producing analyses of the efficiency of all parts of the public enterprise sector, choosing its own areas of investigation, and having full rights to information. The gains in decentralization would come about because this commission would not be involved in the process of formulating decisions, but rather in appraising and monitoring the outcomes of decisions and operational and decision-taking procedures. In this way, the attempt to stimulate managerial and technological efficiency could be made consistent with greater decentralization of pricing and investment decisions.

To conclude this discussion of public enterprise profitability, we can note one further generalization. Recall the demonstration that to allocate surpluses to public enterprises, which must then be allocated to each group of outputs, leads to a worse second-best outcome than to allocate the total desired surplus optimally across all public enterprise outputs, so that the 'profit target' of each enterprise becomes derived rather than predetermined. This argument can be extended to the whole economy: given the overall tax revenue required by the government, this could be allocated optimally across all goods in the economy, and thus the total surplus to be generated by the public enterprise sector is derived from the tax revenue accruing from public enterprise outputs rather than being pre-determined.

The determination of 'optimal taxation' has a long history of study in economics, and given the nature of the problem, it is not surprising to find that the conditions for the optimal tax on goods in general are precisely those given earlier in equations 7.1,

7.5 or 7.9,[23] λ would now be determined by the total tax revenue requirement, and is interpreted as the marginal welfare loss, through the entire economy, of a change in the government's 'budget constraint', i.e. the relation between revenue and expenditure. Thus, if we define the specific tax on the ith good t_i as the difference between price and marginal cost of the ith good,

$$t_i \equiv p_i - MC_i, \tag{7.12}$$

then it can be shown that the optimal *rate* of tax, t_i/p_i, is given (in the demand independence case) by

$$t_i/p_i = 1/\hat{e}_i, \tag{7.13}$$

where, as before, $\hat{e}_i = -[(1-\lambda)/\lambda]e_i$, and e_i is own-price elasticity of demand for good i. It can be shown[24] that this is exactly equivalent to condition (7.1), assuming that the values of λ are in each case the same, which in turn requires that the 'target surplus' which is allocated to the public enterprise producing good i, is precisely that implied by the set of optimal taxes on all the outputs it produces. Thus, if an optimal taxation policy is applied throughout the economy, public enterprise prices are determined as part of this, and there is no separate public enterprise pricing problem.[25]

In reality, optimal taxation policies do not seem to be generally pursued. Again, we are led to the implication of the present analysis: we are searching for optimal policies in one part of the public sector, presuming they would be implemented, while assuming that policies in other parts of the public sector are non-optimal. In that case, the aggregate surplus required from public enterprises is not determined on a globally optimal basis, and public enterprise pricing policy (now in a world of 'deviant sectors' if taxes in the rest of the economy are non-optimal) becomes a separate problem.

There is one important result of this generalization, however, which will be taken up at the end of this chapter: we can express optimal public enterprise prices in terms of a tax-rate applied to marginal cost,[26] which may be useful from the point of view of decentralization.

7.2 Two-part tariffs

In the previous section, we considered the case in which the only revenue-raising instrument was public enterprise price. It is often the case, however, that a public enterprise adopts a pricing structure consisting of a fixed charge, which might be called a licence fee, rental or connection charge, and then a price per unit of consumption. We shall see that in the second-best situation created by the existence of profit targets, a smaller welfare loss may result from such a *two-part tariff*, than from a single unit price. Essentially, the device of making the consumer pay for the *right* to buy any desired amount at the given unit price scoops out some consumer surplus, and so leads to a smaller distortion in resource allocation than if the entire profit target were met by increases in the unit price. On the other hand, the fixed charge does affect total demand for the public enterprise good, and hence resource allocation, first, because of the income effect on demand, and secondly, because some consumers will choose to go without the good altogether, than pay the charge, which is in effect larger than their 'consumer surplus'. If we were to assume that the latter effect does not hold, we would be getting rid of the entire problem: by use of the fixed charge, we could meet the required surplus, and indeed *all* taxation requirements, and prices could be set equal to marginal cost. In effect, we would have assumed the existence of the very lump-sum taxes, the impossibility of which causes the problem in the first place.[27] The problem is, therefore, to determine jointly the values of fixed charge and price, which generate a required surplus with the minimum loss of allocative efficiency.[28] We assume throughout that the fixed charge is uniform across all consumers, and so cannot be varied to match the degree of willingness to pay of individual consumers. In other words, we rule out 'perfect price discrimination'.

First, we analyse the consumer's choice problem. We assume that he has a given income, y_0, and consumes two goods, q_1 and q_2, which he buys at given prices, p_1 and p_2. The consumer's budget constraint, in the absence of any fixed charge, is drawn as the line y_0 in figure 7.3. Given the nature of his preferences, which are represented in the relevant range by indifference curve u_0, he buys q_1^0 of good 1. Now suppose that a

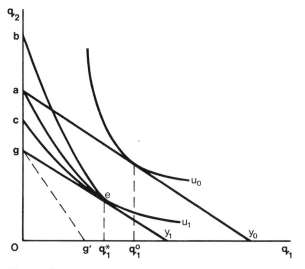

Figure 7.3

fixed charge F is imposed on good 1, while its price remains the same: in order to buy any desired amount of q_1 at price p_1 the consumer must first pay F. If he chooses to pay F, then his income is reduced to $y_1 = y_0 - F$, which defines the new budget constraint shown as y_1 in the figure. On the other hand, if he does not pay F, then his budget constraint remains at y_0, but he is *constrained to consume nothing* of q_1; that is, he must spend all of y_1 on q_2, implying that he must be at point a in the figure. The question then is: under what conditions will he choose to pay F and so buy q_1^*. The answer is given in the figure: there are three possible cases, each corresponding to a possible indifference curve. Consider first the indifference curve beu_1. If the consumer chooses to pay the fixed charge, he will then buy q_1^* of q_1, since e is the point of tangency between the indifference curve and the budget constraint in that case. Now the intercept b of this indifference curve,[29] on the q_2 axis, is higher than point a. This implies that the consumer is better off *at all points* along beu_1, including point e than at a. Hence, the consumer will choose to pay F, and will then buy q_1^* of good 1 at price p_1. Note that $q_1^* < q_1^0$, which is due to the income effect of the imposition of F.

Consider next the indifference curve ceu_1, having its intercept at c on the q_2 axis. Again, *if* he pays the fixed charge, the consumer would buy q_1^*. But now, c is below point a, implying that the consumer is worse off at all points on ceu_1 than at a, including e. Hence, he will be better off by buying none of q_1, not paying F, and spending all his income on q_2.

Finally, consider indifference curve aeu_1, whose intercept is at point a. If the fixed charge is paid, q_1^* will again be bought. In this case, however, all points along aeu_1 are indifferent to a, and so the consumer is indifferent between paying and not paying the fixed charge. We call such a consumer *a marginal consumer*.

This analysis formalizes the common sense notion that the consumer simply asks himself: suppose I pay the fixed charge and then choose the quantities of goods I would like to consume with my remaining income; would I be better off, or worse off, than if I simply consumed nothing of the good for which I have to pay the fixed charge? Then, figure 7.3 characterizes the conditions under which the consumer will be better off, worse off, or indifferent between the two alternatives. By the use of this figure we can see clearly that a change in F (downward shift in the budget line) will reduce consumption of the good first because of an income effect on those who continue to consume it (assuming it is not an inferior good), and secondly because marginal consumers will cease to consume it at all. Because of this second effect, the *number* of consumers falls. Note also that changes in the price p_1 will change *both* consumption (through the usual income and substitution effects) and the number of consumers; for example, an increase in p_1 will cause marginal consumers of good 1 to cease paying the fixed charge and consume nothing of it, as can be seen by considering the budget line gg' in figure 7.3. If the consumer is marginal at the initial price, then the intercept of the indifference curve which is tangential to gg' *must* be below point a, given that indifference curves do not intersect. Thus, consumption and the number of consumers each depend on *both* price and the fixed charge F.

We now consider the optimization problem of the public enterprise, which is assumed to produce good 1 only.[30]

Let q_1 be the *total* market demand for good 1, with n the number of buyers, so that $p_1 q_1$ is revenue from sales, and $F n$ is revenue from payment of fixed charges. Then, the requirement that profit must equal some value S leads to the profit constraint

$$p_1 q_1 + F n - C(q_1) = S, \tag{7.14}$$

where $C(q_1)$ is the cost function,[31] and S is the required surplus.

We have that

$$q_1 = f_1(p_1, F) \qquad \frac{\partial q_1}{\partial p_1}, \frac{\partial q_1}{\partial F} < 0 \tag{7.15}$$

and

$$n = f_2(p_1, F) \qquad \frac{\partial n}{\partial p_1}, \frac{\partial n}{\partial F} < 0, \tag{7.16}$$

where each function is differentiable. This involves the assumption that the relation between total demand q_1 and the fixed charge F is appropriately smooth and continuous. Thus, the derivative $\partial q_1/\partial F$ measures two effects: the fall in consumption of non-marginal consumers, due to an income effect, and the switching of marginal consumers out of the market. We are then assuming that the latter does not cause sharp drops in demand but represents, rather, a smooth continuous relationship. This is equivalent to assuming that consumers are smoothly and densely distributed along the whole spectrum, from low willingness to pay a fixed charge, to high willingness.[32] A similar assumption is involved in respect of the second function. Strictly speaking, n is an integer, and so cannot be differentiated. However, if we assume that, over the relevant range of values of p_1 and F, n is large, then we can regard it as approximately a real number.[33]

It can be shown[34] that the optimal price and fixed charge, which in turn, through (7.15) and (7.16), determine total demand and the number of consumers, must satisfy the conditions

$$\frac{p_1 - MC_1}{MR_1 - MC_1 + \phi_1} = \frac{(p_1 - MC_1)\dfrac{\partial q_1}{\partial F}}{MR_F + [p_1 - MC_1]\dfrac{\partial q_1}{\partial F}} = \lambda, \tag{7.17}$$

where

$$\phi_1 = F \frac{\partial n}{\partial p_1} \frac{\partial p_1}{\partial q_1} > 0. \tag{7.18}$$

The meaning of these conditions is as follows: the first term is the ratio of the marginal welfare loss of output to the marginal profit of output, adjusted for the effect of changes in output on the revenue from the fixed charge. The proposition that $p_1 - MC_1$ measures the marginal welfare loss from a reduction in output is by now familiar, and so is the proposition that $MR_1 - MC_1$ measures the marginal profit gain resulting from a reduction in output (when S is below maximum profit). The term ϕ_1 captures the effect on revenue from the fixed charge, of a change in output, which requires a change in price and hence a change in the number of consumers who pay the fixed charge. This term is positive because a reduction in output is accompanied by a rise in price, and a corresponding fall in the number of consumers and in the total revenue from the fixed charge. Thus, the *total* marginal revenue with respect to changes in output is $MR_1 + \phi_1$, and its overall marginal profitability is the difference between this and marginal cost.

The second term is the ratio of the marginal welfare loss with respect to the fixed charge, to the marginal profitability of the fixed charge. Thus, to interpret the numerator we apply the 'function of a function' rule, i.e. we have the marginal welfare loss due to a fall in output, $p_1 - MC_1$, multiplied by the fall in output due to an increase in the fixed charge, and so the overall term gives the marginal welfare loss due to the fixed charge. The denominator consists of two terms. The first is the change in total fixed charge revenue, resulting from the change in the fixed charge itself, which is denoted by MR_F and can be written as

$$\frac{d[Fn]}{dF} = n + F\frac{\partial n}{\partial F} = n(1+v), \tag{7.19}$$

where v is the elasticity of the number of consumers with respect to the fixed charge. This is clearly quite analogous to the marginal revenue of output.[35] The second term, which will partly offset the first, is the effect of changes in the fixed charge on the profitability of output. Thus, holding price constant, an increase in F will cause: a fall in demand, and hence a fall in revenue, equal to price times the fall in output; and a fall in costs given by marginal cost times the fall in output. Then, the difference between these is the change in profit. At the optimum, we expect that $p_1 > MC_1$, and so, since $\partial q_1/\partial F < 0$, this term will be negative. In the absence of a 'marginal cost per consumer', due to our earlier assumption of no consumer-related costs (or at most a fixed *overhead* consumer cost), this term, expressing the loss of profit due to increases in F, is the effective marginal cost.

Thus, we find that these conditions yield an interpretation similar to that of the conditions derived earlier for the case of two outputs, despite the fact that the precise terms they contain are somewhat different. We could again rationalize the conditions by showing that if the ratios were unequal, it would always be possible to find variations in the price and fixed charge which increase welfare (assuming appropriate compensation is paid) while leaving total profit unchanged. Similarly, we could re-express the optimal price and fixed charge in terms of appropriately chosen elasticities. Since all this would reproduce fairly closely the material set out earlier, it is left to the reader.

7.3   Pricing policy and income distribution

The foregoing analysis has been concerned with pricing policies which meet profit targets with minimal losses in allocative efficiency, and so continued to assume that income distribution was a matter of indifference. We now assume that the 'policy-maker' has explicit objectives toward income distribution, which cannot be pursued through lump-sum taxation: he must achieve them through taxing goods and services. In particular, income distributional considerations will be brought to bear on public enterprise prices.

In actual practice, income distributional aims are pursued by direct *ad hoc* intervention: proposed price increases may be rejected, loss-making services perpetuated, and manpower policies, whose purpose is to eliminate over-manning, may be refused implementation (examples were discussed in chapter 1). Our purpose here is to examine whether income distributional aims can be incorporated into pricing policies in a systematic way, so that they become consistent with decentralized control, and do not require *ad hoc* intervention.

We take the case of a public enterprise producing two goods, x_1 and x_2, subject to a profit constraint of the kind considered earlier. We shall be interested in formulating pricing policies which take into account the policy-maker's income distributional preferences, as well as generating the required surplus. To simplify the analysis, we again assume that outputs are independent in demand; in addition, we assume there are only two consumers in the economy. This latter assumption generalizes easily;[36] the reader may like to think of them as in fact two *groups*, say 'poor' and 'rich'. Although there are other goods in the economy, we suppose that the policy-maker operates only on the prices of the public enterprise, so that, effectively, we can suppress all other goods, and write the consumers' utility functions as:

$$u^i = u^i(x_{i1}, x_{i2}) \qquad i = 1, 2, \tag{7.20}$$

where x_{ij} is the ith consumer's consumption of good $j = 1, 2$. Each is constrained by the budget equation:

$$p_1 x_{i1} + p_2 x_{i2} = y_i, \qquad i = 1, 2. \tag{7.21}$$

where the p_j are prices, and y_i consumer's income. Given tastes, incomes and prices, there will be a pair of demand functions for each consumer

$$x_{i1} = f_{i1}(p_1, p_2, y_i) \qquad i = 1, 2, \tag{7.22}$$

and

$$x_{i2} = f_{i2}(p_1, p_2, y_i) \qquad i = 1, 2, \tag{7.23}$$

which show how his consumption choices vary with prices and income. It follows that we can substitute from these into the utility function, to obtain the consumer's utility as a function of prices and income. That is:

$$u^i = u^i \left[f_{i1}(p_1, p_2, y_i), f_{i2}(p_1, p_2, y_i) \right] \tag{7.24}$$
$$= v^i(p_1, p_2, y_i) \qquad i = 1, 2, \tag{7.25}$$

where v^i is called the consumer's *indirect utility function*. Its derivatives show the effect of changes in prices and income, on the utility of the consumer, *via* their effect on his consumption choices. Now consider the 'policy-maker', whose role is to determine the allocation of resources. We assume that he is not indifferent to the distribution of utility, but rather has specific preferences concerning the utility level which each consumer enjoys. We can put this formally by saying that there exists a *social welfare function*

$$W = W(u^1, u^2) \qquad \frac{\partial W_i}{\partial u} > 0, \qquad i = 1, 2, \tag{7.26}$$

which gives us a representation of the policy-maker's preference ordering over pairs of utilities for the two consumers. The condition on the sign of the partial derivatives of this function was discussed earlier, in chapter 3. It says that, other things being equal, the policy-maker would prefer to see a consumer better off than worse off; this does not, of course, preclude his wanting to make one consumer better off *at the expense* of the other.

Before analysing the optimal pricing conditions, let us examine the partial derivatives of W with respect to prices p_1 and p_2. We have that:

$$\frac{\partial W}{\partial p_1} = \frac{\partial W}{\partial v^1} \frac{\partial v^1}{\partial p_1} + \frac{\partial W}{\partial v^2} \frac{\partial v^2}{\partial p_1} \tag{7.27}$$

and

$$\frac{\partial W}{\partial p_2} = \frac{\partial W}{\partial v^1} \frac{\partial v^1}{\partial p_2} + \frac{\partial W}{\partial v^2} \frac{\partial v^2}{\partial p_2}, \tag{7.28}$$

where we have expressed W as a function of the indirect utility functions v^i. Now, it can be shown[37] that:

$$\frac{\partial v^i}{\partial p_1} = -\lambda_i x_{i1} \quad \text{and} \quad \frac{\partial v^i}{\partial p_2} = -\lambda_i x_{i2} \tag{7.29}$$

In words, the marginal *indirect* utility of a change in price p_1 to the ith consumer is equal simply to the negative of that consumer's marginal utility of income, λ_i, multiplied by the quantity of good 1 he consumes, and likewise for good 2. Thus, we can rewrite (7.27) using $a_i = \dfrac{\partial W}{\partial v^i}$, as

$$\frac{\partial W}{\partial p_1} = -[a_1\lambda_1 x_{11} + a_2\lambda_2 x_{21}] \tag{7.30}$$

and similarly for (7.28). Now, in our two person world, we must have:

$$x_{11} + x_{21} = x_1 \tag{7.31}$$

and so

$$x_{11} = \theta_{11}x_1, \; x_{21} = \theta_{21}x_1 \tag{7.32}$$

where

$$\theta_{11} = \frac{x_{11}}{x_1}\theta_{21} = \frac{x_{21}}{x_1}\theta_{11} + \theta_{21} = 1. \tag{7.33}$$

and similarly for good 2. Thus, $\theta_{ij}, i, j = 1, 2$, is the proportion of the total output of good j consumed by consumer i. It follows therefore that we can write (7.30) as:

$$\frac{\partial W}{\partial p_1} = -[a_1\lambda_1\theta_{11} + a_2\lambda_2\theta_{21}]x_1 = -D_1 x_1 \tag{7.34}$$

where D_1 is defined to be the term in brackets, and can be called the *distributional characteristic* of good 1.[38]

Likewise, we can write:

$$\frac{\partial W}{\partial p_2} = -[a_1\lambda_1\theta_{12} + a_2\lambda_2\theta_{22}]x_2 = -D_2 x_2 \tag{7.35}$$

where D_2 is the distributional characteristic of good 2, and will differ from D_1 if and only if the fractions of total output x_2 consumed by consumers 1 and 2, θ_{12} and θ_{22} respectively, differ from θ_{11} and θ_{21}. This is so because the *marginal social utility of income* to consumer 1, $a_1\lambda_1$, is the same for both D_1 and D_2, as is that for consumer 2.

To see the significance of the distributional characteristic of a good, let us suppose that the marginal social utility of income to consumer 1, given by $a_1\lambda_1$, is greater than that of consumer 2, at the given income levels (for example, consumer 1 is poor and considered relatively deserving, consumer 2 rich and relatively undeserving). Suppose also that consumer 1 consumes a large proportion of good 1 and a small proportion of good 2, so that $\theta_{11} > \theta_{12}$, and, correspondingly, $\theta_{21} < \theta_{22}$. It follows[39] that $D_1 > D_2$: the distributional characteristic of good 1 exceeds that of good 2, because relatively more of it is consumed by the 'more deserving' consumer.

To complete the specification of the model, we assume that production is carried out with use of an input z, which is bought by the public enterprise on a competitive market at price w. Then, production of good j is subject to the relations:

$$x_j = f_j(z_j) \qquad j = 1, 2, \tag{7.36}$$

where z_j is the quantity of z used in producing x_j. The budget constraint can be written

$$\sum_{j=1}^{2} p_j x_j - w \sum_{j=1}^{2} z_j = S, \tag{7.37}$$

which simply constrains the difference between revenue and costs to a certain value, S.

The policy-maker then wishes to choose prices p_j and inputs z_j in such a way as to maximize W, subject to production and budget constraints, and given the demand functions for the two goods. It can be shown[40] that the necessary conditions which determine optimal prices are

$$p_j\left(1 - \frac{k_j}{e_j}\right) = MC \qquad j = 1, 2, \tag{7.38}$$

where

$$k_j = 1 + \frac{D_j}{\beta} \tag{7.39}$$

and β is the Lagrangean multiplier associated with the profit constraint, or, in other words, the marginal welfare loss arising from the profit constraint. Recalling our earlier analysis of optimal pricing under a profit constraint, we again see that the public enterprise acts as a quasi-monopolist, equating marginal cost of each good to a 'corrected' marginal revenue. In the present case, however, we have that the 'correction' depends not only on the profit constraint's marginal welfare loss, but also on the distributional characteristic, D_j. It is of interest to see how this affects the results. To isolate its effects, let us assume that the two goods have identical demand elasticities, so that from our earlier analysis we know that, in the absence of distributional considerations, the ratios of their prices to their marginal costs would be the same. Let us suppose, however, that in the present case we have:

$$p_1/MC_1 > p_2/MC_2 \tag{7.40}$$

That is, the optimum conditions imply a greater relative divergence for good 1 than for good 2. From (7.38), this must in turn imply

$$1 - \frac{k_1}{e_1} < 1 - \frac{k_2}{e_2} \tag{7.41}$$

so that, from the equal elasticity condition, we must have:

$$k_1 > k_2 \tag{7.42}$$

But from (7.39), this implies that

$$\frac{D_1}{\beta} > \frac{D_2}{\beta}. \tag{7.43}$$

Recalling that $\beta < 0$ (an increase in the profit target causes a reduction in welfare), we have

$$D_1 < D_2. \tag{7.44}$$

Thus, we conclude that the good with the greater relative divergence of price from marginal cost is, other things being equal, the good with the lower distributional characteristic. When the profit target is allocated over goods, relatively smaller welfare losses are imposed on those goods, large proportions of which are bought by consumers with high marginal social utilities of income.

More generally, the distributional characteristic may offset or reinforce the effects of different demand elasticities among goods. A good with both a high demand elasticity and high distributional characteristic will have a relatively lower price/marginal cost ratio than one with opposite characteristics. Thus, the overall allocation of the profit target among outputs will depend in part upon the relative losses in allocative efficiency, as represented by demand elasticities, and in part upon relative losses in distributional equity, as measured by the distributional characteristics.

This analysis has shown that it is in principle possible to define pricing policies which incorporate considerations of distributional preference.[41] The main requirement for their operationalization is a specification of the distributional 'weights' or marginal social utilities, $a_i \lambda_i$. The distributional characteristic of a good, by its definition in (7.35), depends partly on the way in which consumption is distributed over particular households or groups (the θ_{ij}), and partly on the marginal social utility attached to each of these. The former can be estimated from expenditure survey data, assuming the classifications of households into groups in these surveys reflects the classification which is relevant for the policy-maker's distributional preferences. The latter, however, requires explicit information on these preferences, and this may be very hard to obtain. We are led back to the issues raised in chapters 1 and 2: a necessary condition for a greater degree of decentralization in the public enterprise control system, is an explicit statement of preferences over the conflicting aims of policy. Without this, there will tend to be a great deal of *ad hoc* intervention in specific decisions, with consequent increases in the cost of control.

7.4   Second best pricing policies

We can now bring together the various strands in the analyses of the last two chapters, where we have analysed a number of second-best situations in isolation from each other. In practice, some or all of those situations occur together, and so the actual optimal prices will be the resultants of the interaction of profit targets, distributional concerns, and relationships between each public enterprise and the 'deviant sectors'. Nothing would be gained here by setting out the 'general conditions'.[42] This is best done at the operational level, where specific models would have to be constructed for particular sectors, and numerical estimates made of at least the most important terms in the optimal pricing conditions. At that stage, information availability and the tractability of the models will determine approximations, simplifications, and all the compromises with generality which have to be made at the practical level. The aim here has been to give as much insight as possible into the general principles which must underlie the practical models.

We have seen that it is possible to determine, in principle, pricing policies which can reconcile the various objectives which public enterprises have been urged to pursue. Thus, decentralization by the use of such pricing policies is in principle possible. The control system envisaged here could be described as follows. Ignoring for the moment profitability, pricing policies could be devised for public enterprise outputs, which would pursue allocative efficiency and distributional aims along the lines examined in this chapter and the last. The aggregate surplus over all public enterprises implied by these policies could then be computed. If it is smaller than desired then, through a system of fixed charges and price increases for only those goods which are sold outside the public sector, the desired revenue could be generated in a way which does least damage to allocative efficiency and income distributional objectives. These policies will then *imply* a surplus for each enterprise, rather than the converse. Once optimal pricing structures have been determined, under which the appropriate prices may be expressed in terms of 'tax rates' or 'mark-ups' on marginal cost, public enterprises can be left to take their own pricing and investment decisions (given the cost of capital, the determination of which will be discussed in the next chapter). The problem of improving managerial and technological efficiency would be approached through the 'Efficiency Audit Commission', which would not participate in the decision-taking process, but would instead examine the *outcomes* of decisions which have been taken, and the *procedures* by which plans are formed and implemented. Improvements suggested by this Commission would then be enforced on public enterprises by 'directions of a general nature'.

The analysis of the last two chapters has been very much concerned with what could be called the '*dual second-best problem*'. The problem is to find prices, or, more generally, pricing policies, which guide decentralized decision-takers to an optimum. The reason for framing the problem in terms of choice of pricing policies, rather than direct choice of outputs, is the concern with the possibilities of decentralization. The major obstacle to implementation of the policies is not so much the technical one of formulating and quantifying the relevant models, although that is difficult enough; it is rather that of obtaining the stable, consistent set of relative valuations of different objectives, which we discussed at some length in chapter 1. Without some kind of explicit preference ordering, or, as it has been represented in this chapter, a 'social welfare function',[43] it is not possible to devise decentralized rules which make the correct trade-offs between the various policy objectives. This remains therefore the central problem of public enterprise policy.

chapter 8

the public enterprise cost of capital

The analyses of optimal pricing policies in the previous five chapters have all presupposed the existence of an interest rate, r, which determines the cost of capital to a public enterprise. It is possible to discuss, quite adequately, pricing problems involving fixed capacity, without concern for this cost of capital, but once we treat capacity as variable it becomes an important parameter of the analysis. In this chapter we shall discuss theories of the determination of the public enterprise cost of capital.

Recall that the cost of capital enters into the analysis in two ways. First, in choosing the cost-minimizing way to produce any given output level, it will, in relation to the prices of all other inputs, determine the least-cost input combination or production process. Secondly, since it thereby partly determines the relation between total costs and output, it is an important component of marginal cost, and so will influence the planned price and output, and the current investment programme. This second role of the cost of capital can be described somewhat differently, using the results of chapter 4. The cost of capital is the rate used in discounting net social benefits of future consumption, so as to determine that level of investment which maximizes their net present value. Sophisticated pricing rules are unlikely to achieve economic efficiency, therefore, if the value of the cost of capital is non-optimally chosen, given its pervasive influence on the solution.

The question of the optimal public sector cost of capital has a wider relevance than to public enterprises only. Much of the investment made by the State will provide future outputs of 'non-marketed goods' – education, health services, defence, police services, roads – and appraisal of these investments will also require a cost of capital. The analysis we shall set out is quite capable of application to these (and indeed much of it originated in this way), but for present purposes we shall proceed as if public sector investment took place entirely in public enterprises. It should also be noted that the literature on this topic is large and growing, and at some points quite controversial. No attempt can be made here to survey this. Instead, we shall provide an introductory exposition of what seems to be the most fruitful line of recent research.[1] As we shall see, the problem of determining the optimal public sector cost of capital is essentially one in the second best, and so falls logically in sequence with the last two chapters. To begin with, however, we examine the problem in the context of the first-best economy.

8.1   The cost of capital in a first-best economy

The first-best economy to be defined here is a little different to that considered earlier, in that we assume there exists only a single good. This is a very useful simplifying assumption, the relaxation of which would make no essential difference to the results as long as we assume complete certainty, which we do. A simplifying, but not so innocuous,[2] assumption which we shall also make is that there are only two periods, year 0 and year 1, to be considered. The economy works as follows: each consumer in year 0 owns a given endowment of the good which he may divide between consumption and saving. Alternatively, he can augment his consumption in year 0 by borrowing against the amount of the good he will have in year 1. Saving is effected by buying bonds; borrowing by selling them. There are two firms in the economy, one public the other private. The public firm acquires, by selling bonds, some quantity of the good in year 0, which it invests to produce a corresponding output of the good in year 1. This output will then be distributed to consumers. The private firm invests some amount of the good in year 0, made available to it by its shareholders, who then receive its output in year 1 in proportion to their shareholdings. Thus, the total amount of the good which will be available for consumption in year 1 will be the sum of public and private sector outputs. The only market which exists in this economy is the bond market, on which individuals borrow and lend and the public firm borrows, all at the same interest rate r.

Each consumer chooses his consumption and borrowing or lending in such a way as to maximize a utility function

$$u_i = u_i(x_0^i, x_1^i), \qquad i = 1, 2, \ldots, n, \tag{8.1}$$

where u_i is the ith consumer's utility, x_0^i his consumption in year 0, and x_1^i that in year 1. His budget constraints in year 0 and 1 are, respectively,

$$y_i + \hat{x}_0^i + b_i = \bar{x}_0^i \tag{8.2}$$

and

$$x_1^i = (1+r)b_i + g_i + s_i x_{\mathrm{p}}. \tag{8.3}$$

The first says simply that the sum of his contribution to private investment, y_i, consumption, x_0^i, and bond purchases or sales, b_i, must equal the initial endowment $\hat{x}_0^i$; where $b_i > 0$ if he buys bonds and $b_i < 0$ if he sells them. The second budget constraint says that his consumption in year 1 equals the sum of the interest plus repayment of principal on his bond holdings $(1+r)b_i$; plus the payment from the public firm, g_i; plus his share, s_i, in the output of the private firm, x_p. By solving for b_i in (8.3) and substituting into (8.2), we obtain the single *wealth constraint*

$$y_i + x_0^i + \frac{x_1^i}{1+r} = \hat{x}_0^i + \frac{g_i + s_i x_p}{1+r}. \tag{8.4}$$

If we take as predetermined for the moment the values of y_i, g_i, x_p and s_i, then we can solve[3] for the consumer's utility-maximizing choice of consumption time-stream ($\bar{x}_0^i$ $\bar{x}_1^i$) (implying a corresponding bond sale or purchase) which must satisfy the necessary condition

$$\frac{-\partial u_i}{\partial x_0^i} \Bigg/ \frac{\partial u_i}{\partial x_1^i} = (1+r), \tag{8.5}$$

where the left-hand side is the consumer's marginal rate of substitution, dx_1^i/dx_0^i, between consumptions in years 0 and 1. It is usual to express this marginal rate of substitution in a way which gives additional insight into the solution. We define ρ_i as the *i*th consumer's *rate of time preference*, which is a kind of subjective interest rate with the following interpretation: given the consumer's levels of consumption x_0^i and x_1^i, ρ_i is the rate at which he would have to be compensated for giving up some x_0^i in exchange for some x_1^i, in such a way as to remain just as well off. Then, we can show[4] that the marginal rate of substitution can be written as

$$-\frac{\partial u_i}{\partial x_0^i} \Bigg/ \frac{\partial u_i}{\partial x_1^i} = \frac{dx_1^i}{dx_0^i} = (1+\rho_i). \tag{8.6}$$

Hence, putting (8.5) and (8.6) together gives, as the consumer's optimality condition,

$$1+\rho_i = 1+r, \quad \text{or simply } \rho_i = r. \tag{8.7}$$

A simple interpretation of this condition is that each consumer who lends, does so up to the point at which the rate at which he requires to be compensated for a marginal reduction in current consumption is just equal to the rate at which he actually is compensated (given by the market interest rate); while each consumer who borrows, does so up to the point at which the rate at which he values the marginal bit of current consumption (which rate is measured by ρ_i) is just equal to the price of that current consumption, r. Individual consumers may in equilibrium be either borrowers or lenders, depending on their tastes, initial endowments and the interest rate, but, in the aggregate, the borrowing and lending of individuals must cancel each other out, so that we have

$$\sum_i b_i = b_g, \tag{8.8}$$

where b_g is the value of the public firm's bond issue, and also the amount it invests.

Note finally the important point, that since all consumers face the same interest rate, r, and since the condition in (8.7) is satisfied for each of them, then in equilibrium all consumers' time preference rates are equal, their common value being measured by the market interest rate.

Given the market interest rate, each consumer's choice of consumption is determined, and, from the budget constraint in (8.2), this in turn determines his choice of a bond-holding[5] b_i, positive if lending and negative if borrowing. Thus, we can write each individual's demand (or, equivalently, supply) function for bonds as

$$b_i = f_i(r), \tag{8.9}$$

where, in the normal case,[6] we will have

$$db_i/dr > 0, \tag{8.10}$$

i.e. the higher the interest rate, the smaller the borrowing or greater the lending.

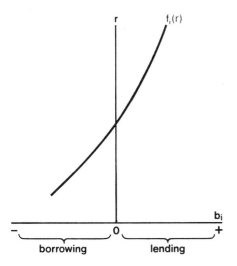

Figure 8.1

Figure 8.1 illustrates the relation for a typical consumer; aggregating over all consumers would give a curve of the same shape. Note that the analysis from which this curve is assumed to be derived took as given the amount devoted to private investment, y_i, and the amounts to be received as income from private and public firms next period, g_i and $s_i x_p$, respectively. Hence, changes in any of these from their pre-assigned values would *shift* the curve in figure 8.1. It will become important to explore this further in the next section.

Now let us turn to the production side of the economy. The public and private enterprises each take some amount of the good in year 0 and invest it, to produce some amount of the good in year 1. Let y_g and y_p be the amounts invested by public and private firms, respectively, and x_g and x_p their outputs in year 1. Then we have the 'investment production functions'

$$x_g = g(y_g) \qquad \frac{\mathrm{d}x_g}{\mathrm{d}y_g} > 0; \qquad \frac{\mathrm{d}^2x_g}{\mathrm{d}y_g^2} < 0 \tag{8.11}$$

and

$$x_p = p(y_p) \qquad \frac{\mathrm{d}x_p}{\mathrm{d}y_p} > 0; \qquad \frac{\mathrm{d}^2x_p}{\mathrm{d}y_p^2} < 0. \tag{8.12}$$

The first derivatives of these functions can be called the 'marginal productivity of investment' in the two sectors, and are always positive, while the negativity of the second derivatives expresses the diminishing marginal productivity of investment.

Consider now the behaviour of the private enterprise. It can be shown[7] that if it acts in the best interests of its shareholders, it will choose its investment, y_p, in such a way as to maximize the net present value of its profit stream, which can be written as

$$v_p = \frac{x_p}{1+r} - y_p, \tag{8.13}$$

where v_p is the net present value, and r is as before the market interest rate on bonds. The value of y_p which maximizes v_p must satisfy the condition

$$\frac{\mathrm{d}v_p}{\mathrm{d}y_p} = \frac{\mathrm{d}x_p}{\mathrm{d}y_p}\frac{1}{1+r} - 1 = 0, \tag{8.14}$$

which therefore gives the condition

$$\mathrm{d}x_p/\mathrm{d}y_p = 1+r. \tag{8.15}$$

Again, we obtain more insight into this condition by noting that we can always find[8] some number m_p which, at a given level of y_p, satisfies

$$\mathrm{d}x_p/\mathrm{d}y_p = 1+m_p. \tag{8.16}$$

We can interpret m_p as an interest rate or *rate of return on investment*, and in fact we shall call it the marginal rate of return on investment. Then, the condition in (8.15) becomes

$$1+m_p = 1+r, \quad \text{or simply } m_p = r. \tag{8.17}$$

This has a straightforward interpretation: the private enterprise invests up to the point at which the marginal rate of return on investment is just equal to the market rate of interest. This is because the latter measures its shareholders' opportunity costs of consumption. Note also that from condition (8.7) we have that $\rho_i = m_p$ for every i, since each consumer is in equilibrium with $\rho_i = r$. Thus, the private enterprise does not need to find directly the preferences of its shareholders: it can take the market interest rate as measuring their rates of time preference, and so optimizes for them by using this in its investment appraisal.

Now we turn to the principal question of this section: what is the optimal allocation of resources between consumption and investment for the economy as a whole? We put ourselves once again in the place of a central planner who wishes to find a Pareto optimum. Ignoring the details of bond markets, ownership of the private firm, etc. we have that the economy is constrained by the equations

$$\sum_i x_0^i + y_g + y_p = \sum_i \hat{x}_0^i \tag{8.18}$$

and

$$\sum_i x_1^i = g(y_g) + p(y_p). \tag{8.19}$$

The first says that the total consumption plus total investment in year 0 must equal the total endowment of the good available to the economy,[9] and the second that total consumption in year 1 must equal output. This implies that consumption in year 1 can only be increased by reducing consumption in year 0, and investing in the two firms. The resource allocation problem can then be divided into three subproblems:

(a) how should the reductions in year 0 consumption, and increases in year 1 consumption, be allocated among consumers?

(b) how should the total investment be allocated between public and private enterprises?

(c) how should the total investment be determined?

We shall give the solutions to these subproblems in that order. First, if a Pareto optimum is sought, then the allocation of consumptions among consumers must satisfy the condition that the time preference rates of all consumers be equal. To see this, suppose that any two, say ρ_1 and ρ_2, were not, and in particular that $\rho_1 > \rho_2$. Then consumer 1 could take one unit of consumption in year 0 from consumer 2, and would be prepared to give him more year 1 consumption in return, than 2 requires in order to be left just as well off. Hence, both can gain from the exchange, and this cannot be a Pareto-optimal situation.[10] If no such possibilities exist, we must have $\rho_1 = \rho_2$.

To solve the second problem, suppose that there is some given total amount of investment in the economy, $\bar{y}$, which must be divided between private and public enterprises. Given this total, we would expect that it is optimally allocated when the resulting total output in year 1 is maximized, which in turn implies the necessary condition[11]

$$\frac{\mathrm{d}x_g}{\mathrm{d}y_g} = \frac{\mathrm{d}x_p}{\mathrm{d}y_p}. \tag{8.20}$$

Given that, analogously with m_p, we can define the public enterprise marginal rate of return an investment, m_g, this condition becomes

$$m_p = m_g, \tag{8.21}$$

which has the straightforward interpretation that investment is allocated between the two sectors in such a way as to equate marginal rates of return. If this were not so, investment could be diverted from the low rate of return enterprise to that with the higher rate, and so we could increase year 1 output (which, given non-satiation, makes everyone better off).

The solution to the third problem then follows immediately. The optimal total investment will be found when

$$\rho_i = m_p = m_g, \qquad i = 1, 2, \dots, n, \tag{8.22}$$

i.e. when the time preference rate of each consumer is equal to the marginal rate of return on investment in each sector. Again, the reasoning is straightforward: if $m_p = m_g > \rho_i$, for all i, then by reducing consumption in year 0 (in a way which keeps the ρ_i all equal) and investing it (in a way which maintains $m_p = m_g$), consumers can be more than compensated for this sacrifice. If $\rho_i > m_p = m_g$, on the other hand, the increase in year 0 consumption following from a reduction in investment would more than compensate consumers for the loss of year 1 consumption. If such improvements are not possible, we must have the equality in (8.22). Thus, we have three sets of conditions which characterize a Pareto-optimal resource allocation in this two-period economy.

In fact, of course, there is no central planner in control of the entire economy. Consumers in our model take their own consumption and bondholding decisions, the private enterprise invests on behalf of its shareholders, and the planner has only to determine the optimal investment policy for the public enterprise. Putting together all the steps in the analysis so far enables us to see what this policy requires. Since all consumers confront the same interest rate, we know that the ρ_i will all be equal in an equilibrium. In addition, since the private enterprise acts in the best interests of its shareholders, we then have that $m_p = r = \rho_i$. Thus, to satisfy the necessary conditions for a Pareto optimum, the investment of the public enterprise must satisfy the condition

$$m_g = r = m_p = \rho_i. \tag{8.23}$$

An obvious way in which this would be achieved is by the adoption of an investment appraisal rule similar to that used by the private enterprise: the public enterprise should maximize the net present value of its investment,

$$v_g = \frac{x_g}{1+r} - y_g, \tag{8.24}$$

using the market interest rate in discounting.

The equilibrium of the economy, at which the conditions in (8.23) are all satisfied, is shown in figure 8.2. In (a) we have the equilibrium of an individual consumer. The 'budget line' $\bar{w}_i$ is derived from the wealth constraint in equation (8.4) by writing

$$\bar{w}_i = \hat{x}_0^i - y_i + \frac{g_i + s_i x_p}{1+r}, \tag{8.25}$$

where $\bar{w}_i$ will be, *in equilibrium*, a given constant to each individual. The wealth constraint can then be written as

$$x_1^i = \bar{w}_i - (1+r)x_0^i, \tag{8.26}$$

which gives the straight line $\bar{w}_i$ in figure 8.2(a), with slope equal to $-(1+r)$. The equilibrium choice $(\bar{x}_0^i \bar{x}_1^i)$ by the consumer occurs at the point of tangency between this line and an indifference curve $\bar{u}_i$. Recalling that $dx_1^i/dx_0^i = (1+\rho_i)$ is the (absolute value of the) slope of an indifference curve at a point, the tangency solution implies that $r = \rho_i$, which is the necessary condition we derived earlier.

In figure 8.2(b) we have the equilibrium position of the public enterprise. Its

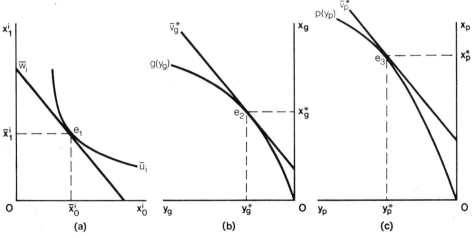

Figure 8.2

investment, y_g, is measured leftward from the origin, and the curve $g(y_g)$ shows how output in year 1 varies with y_g. It clearly embodies the assumption of positive but diminishing marginal productivity of investment, and its slope at any point is given by $1 + m_g$. The line $\bar{v}_g^*$ is one of a whole family of such lines, which are derived as follows. Given the expression for the net present value of investment, v_g, in equation (8.24), we can set v_g equal to some fixed value, say v_g^0, and rearrange to get

$$x_g = (1+r)v_g^0 + (1+r)y_g. \tag{8.27}$$

Then, by defining $\bar{v}_g = (1+r)v_g^0$, we have the relation

$$x_g = \bar{v}_g + (1+r)y_g. \tag{8.28}$$

By varying the fixed value of v_g, we generate a family of parallel straight lines, with slopes equal to $1 + r$; the higher the fixed value of v_g, the higher will be the corresponding line when graphed in the figure. The problem of *maximizing* v_g can then be expressed as the problem of choosing values of y_g and x_g which are on the highest possible such line, given the set of technological possibilities defined by $g(y_g)$. The solution is of course a point of tangency, and is shown in figure 8.2 (b). The line $\bar{v}_g^*$ is the highest which can be attained with a feasible pair (y_g, x_g), and the values which generate it are (y_g^*, x_g^*). At the point of tangency, the slope of the line, $1 + r$, equals the slope of the curve, $1 + m_g$, and so we have the necessary condition given earlier, $r = m_g$.

In figure 8.2(c) is shown the equilibrium position of the private enterprise. The discussion of it exactly matches that just given for the public enterprise, and so the reader is left to supply it for himself.

This completes the analysis of the equilibrium position for the first-best economy. Its conclusion is that the public enterprise should choose its investment by maximizing net present value, using the market interest rate in discounting. However, the real economy is not first best, and so it is important to examine the validity of this result in a model which captures at least some features of the second-best reality.

8.2   The cost of capital in a second-best economy

A crucial assumption underlying the first-best model is that the capital market is perfect: there is a single interest rate, which is the same for all buyers and sellers of bonds, and whose value measures two things, from the point of view of the public-sector planner. First, it measures the time preference rate of every consumer, and hence provides information on the value of current versus future consumption; and secondly, it measures the marginal rate of return on investment in the private sector, and so provides information on the opportunity cost of resources devoted to public rather than private investment. The essential feature of most second-best models is that, because of market imperfections, the market rate of interest no longer measures *both* these values and, at best, is equal only to one of them. The problem then is to determine the appropriate public-sector cost of capital, taking explicit account of the failure of the market interest rate to provide all the necessary information.

There are several reasons for suspecting that real capital markets are imperfect. The existence of uncertainty leads to devices such as credit rationing, which place a limit on an individual's ability to borrow or 'issue bonds', and to different interest rates for different borrowers. Transactions in capital markets are effected through financial intermediaries, and there is the possibility that non-competitive conditions lead the spread between borrowing and lending interest rates to exceed the marginal costs of organizing these transactions. Taxation of various kinds exists, which, as we shall see, drives a wedge between time preference rates and the marginal rate of return on investment. There are, therefore, several ways in which we could characterize a second-best economy. Here, we adopt the following assumption:[12] the second-best economy differs from that of the previous section *only* in the existence of a tax, t, which is levied on the profits of the private enterprise. This tax is not optimally chosen: it is a parameter of the problem, rather than a variable of optimization. The proceeds of the tax are distributed, along with the profit of the public enterprise, among consumers in year 1.

This assumption raises the same questions about the consistency and rationality of the 'central planner' as we discussed in chapter 6. It is possible to show that if he chose the tax optimally, a first-best resource allocation could be attained, while, because he does not, an inferior solution is the result. We accept this on the same grounds as before: actual taxation practice does not conform to optimality rules, so that the realistic formulation of the second-best problem must embody this inconsistency.

Thus, we wish to determine the optimal investment plan for the public enterprise, given that a tax is levied on private enterprise profit. First we examine the effects of the profits tax. For the purpose of the tax, profit is defined as $x_p - y_p$: the value of output in year 1 *minus* the investment required to generate it.[13] Hence, the after-tax income available for distribution to shareholders in year 1 will be $x_p - t(x_p - y_p)$. If it is acting in the best interests of its shareholders, the firm will maximize net present value *after tax*, and so it will wish to maximize:

$$v_p^1 = \frac{x_p - t(x_p - y_p)}{1 + r} - y_p, \tag{8.29}$$

which yields the necessary condition

$$\frac{dv_p^1}{dy_p} = \left[\frac{dx_p}{dy_p} - t\left(\frac{dx_p}{dy_p} - 1 \right) \right] \frac{1}{1+r} - 1 = 0. \tag{8.30}$$

On rearranging, this gives the necessary condition as

$$\frac{dx_p}{dy_p} = 1 + m_p = 1 + \frac{r}{1-t} = 1 + r',$$ (8.31)

where we again define m_p as the marginal rate of return on investment in the private enterprise (given $x_p = p(y_p)$). This condition implies that the private enterprise invests up to the point at which the marginal rate of return is just equal to the *tax-adjusted* interest rate, r', which must exceed the actual interest rate, r, since t is defined on the interval $0 < t < 1$. Effectively, the private enterprise responds to taxation by acting as if it faced a higher market interest rate. An equivalent and intuitively more obvious way of expressing this is as follows: from (8.31) we see that the condition requires that

$$m_p = r' = \frac{r}{1-t},$$ (8.32)

thus implying that

$$m_p(1-t) = r,$$ (8.33)

where the term on the left-hand side is the after-tax marginal rate of return on investment. The enterprise then equates this to the actual market interest rate.

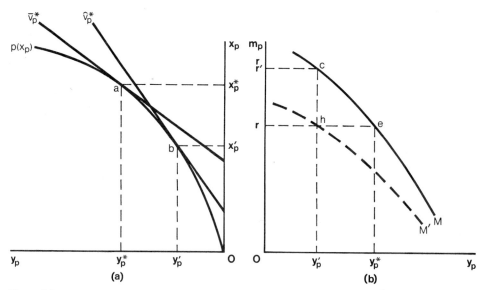

Figure 8.3

The effect on the investment of the private enterprise is shown in figure 8.3, where panel (a) reproduces (c) of figure 8.2, with the addition of the line $\hat{v}_p^*$. This line is derived from equation (8.29) in the same way as $\bar{v}_p^*$ was derived earlier, and so relates to *after-tax* net present value. Its slope is equal to $1 + r'$, which is why it is steeper than $\bar{v}_p^*$. The solution to the investment decision is now at y_p' and not y_p^*, so we conclude that the imposition of the profits tax reduces investment in the private enterprise. Figure 8.3(b) shows this result in somewhat different form. Given the function $x_p = p(y_p)$, we can take the derivative dx_p/dy_p and then graph the marginal rate of return $m_p = dx_p/dy_p - 1$ against the amount of investment y_p. This is shown as the curve M. Its negative slope follows from the curvature of $p(x_p)$. In an economy without tax, the private enterprise is in equilibrium when $m_p = r$, and this is shown at point e in the figure. We can represent the after-tax equilibrium in either of two ways: the tax can be viewed as increasing the interest rate to r', giving the equilibrium at c; or as reducing the marginal rate of return as shown by the curve M', thus giving the equilibrium at h. In each case, of course, the investment level is at y_p'.

The tax, since it is levied on private enterprise profits, does not directly affect the rate of interest at which consumers borrow and lend. Hence, as in the previous section, the ith consumer will be in equilibrium where $\rho_i = r$, which immediately gives us the result that $m_p > \rho_i$. Thus, the result of the profits tax is that investment is too low in the private enterprise: at the margin, a little more investment would yield more than enough output in year 1 to compensate shareholders for their current sacrifice, but because of the tax the shareholders would not in fact be compensated, and so the investment is not made. The non-optimality of private enterprise investment is the central feature of the second-best solution.

The second-best optimization problem can now be described as follows: the central planner must choose a Pareto-optimal allocation of resources in the economy, taking the behaviour of the 'deviant' private sector as given. The relevant aspect of this behaviour is contained in the responses which are made to variations in the market interest rate, r. From our earlier analysis, we expect that increases in the interest rate will increase consumers' purchases of bonds, and hence reduce their consumption in year 0, and reduce the investment of the private enterprise (refer back to figure 8.3).

We now give the solution [14] to this second-best problem, again putting ourselves in the position of a central planner. We can in this case break the overall problem into two subproblems:

(a) that of allocating consumptions in the two periods among consumers, and

(b) that of determining the total amount of investment in the economy, where the only instrument available for doing this is the investment in the public enterprise. (Thus, once again, the second-best situation can be thought of as arising out of some limitation on the set of economic agents which can be directly controlled by the planner, and on the set of instruments he has available.) This problem is therefore, equivalently, the problem of choosing optimal public enterprise investment.

The solution to the first problem can quickly be given, and follows that for the first-best economy: the allocation of consumptions must be such that all time-preference rates are equal. If not, reallocations could be found (leaving *total* consumption and investment undisturbed) which would make everybody better off. The argument here replicates that given earlier. Thus, in the optimal allocation, the ρ_i are all equal.

In determining public enterprise investment, the planner must reason as follows: an increase in investment y_g will require an increased bond issue and hence a rise in the market interest rate, r. This will cause reductions in consumption and private enterprise investment to an extent determined by their sensitivity to the interest rate. (There are some complications here, arising out of the *income effects* of changed year 1 outputs, which we ignore for simplicity.) The increase in public enterprise investment will cause a corresponding increase in its output in year 1, which must be weighed against the loss of year 1 output from the private enterprise, and the loss of year 0 consumption. Let dx_1/dy_g represent the *total* derivative of year 1 consumption[15] with respect to public enterprise investment; that is, it shows the *total* effect on year 1 output, x_1, of a change in y_g, taking account of the repercussions throughout the entire economy (we shall shortly identify these more formally). Similarly, let dx_0/dy_g represent the total derivative of year 0 consumption[16] with respect to public enterprise investment. We could then define the *total marginal product* of public investment as

$$MP_g = -\frac{dx_1}{dy_g} \Big/ \frac{dx_0}{dy_g} = \frac{dx_1}{dx_0}\Big|_{y_g}. \qquad (8.34)$$

The minus sign in this definition is included because we wish MP_g always to be positive, and, at least in equilibrium, we expect the numerator dx_1/dy_g to be positive, and the denominator dx_0/dy_g to be negative. (The notation $dx_1/dx_0\big|_{y_g}$ is adopted to emphasize that the variations in x_0 and x_1 are brought about by changes in y_g.) This definition simply expresses the idea that a given increment in y_g will change current consumption and give rise to changed future consumption, where these changes are the total effects of the increment in y_g. The necessary condition for the optimal amount of public enterprise investment is then[17]

$$MP_g = \frac{dx_1}{dx_0}\Big|_{y_g} = 1 + \rho_i, \quad \text{for all } i. \qquad (8.35)$$

We can rationalize this condition in the following way: ρ_i is the rate at which, in equilibrium, each consumer requires to be compensated for a reduction in current consumption. MP_g is the rate at which reductions in current consumption generate future consumption (via changes in the value of y_g). If these were not equal, it would be possible to make at least one consumer better off by changing total current consumption[18] (and y_g). The absence of such a possibility implies the equality in (8.35).

By itself, of course, this condition tells us very little – it is almost a platitude. The interest stems from expressing in greater detail this 'total marginal product' MP_g. To do this, first recall the constraints on consumption in the economy, given earlier in equations (8.18) and (8.19). These can now be written as

$$x_0 + y_g + y_p = \bar{x}_0 \tag{8.36}$$

and

$$x_1 = p(y_p) + g(y_g), \tag{8.37}$$

where $\bar{x}_0$ is the total initial endowment in year 0. By solving for y_g in (8.36), and substituting into (8.37), we obtain the single constraint

$$x_1 = p(y_p) + g[\bar{x}_0 - x_0 - y_p]. \tag{8.38}$$

Differentiating totally, we therefore have

$$dx_1 = \frac{dx_p}{dy_p} dy_p + \frac{dx_g}{dy_g} [-dx_0 - dy_p]. \tag{8.39}$$

But we know that both y_p and x_0 depend on y_g, since variations in y_g change the interest rate. In fact we have

$$dy_p = \frac{\partial y_p}{\partial r} \frac{dr}{dy_g} dy_g \quad \text{and} \quad dx_0 = \frac{\partial x_0}{\partial r} \frac{dr}{dy_g} dy_g, \tag{8.40}$$

which express this dependence. The partials $\partial y_p/\partial r$ and $\partial x_0/\partial r$ give the effects on private investment and consumption of an interest rate change, and dr/dy_g gives the effect on the interest rate (via its bond issue) of a change in public investment.

Then, substituting from (8.40) into (8.39) and rearranging gives

$$\frac{dx_1}{dy_g} = \left[\frac{dx_p}{dy_p} \frac{\partial y_p}{\partial r} - \frac{dx_g}{dy_g} \left\{ \frac{\partial x_0}{\partial r} + \frac{\partial y_p}{\partial r} \right\} \right] \frac{dr}{dy_g}. \tag{8.41}$$

Thus, we have an expression for the numerator of the ratio in (8.34). Also, note that from (8.40) we have

$$\frac{dx_0}{dy_g} = \frac{\partial x_0}{\partial r} \frac{dr}{dy_g} \tag{8.42}$$

and this gives us the denominator. Thus, we can now restate the condition in (8.35) as

$$
\left.\frac{dx_1}{dx_0}\right|_{y_g} = \frac{-\left[\dfrac{dx_p}{dy_p}\dfrac{\partial y_p}{\partial r} - \dfrac{dx_g}{dy_g}\left\{\dfrac{\partial x_0}{\partial r} + \dfrac{\partial y_p}{\partial r}\right\}\right]\dfrac{dr}{dy_g}}{\dfrac{\partial x_0}{\partial r}\dfrac{dr}{dy}} . = 1+\rho_i \tag{8.43}
$$

The final step is made by rearranging (8.43) to obtain

$$
\frac{dx_g}{dy_g} = \frac{(1+\rho_i)\dfrac{\partial x_0}{\partial r} + \dfrac{dx_p}{dy_p}\dfrac{\partial y_p}{\partial r}}{\dfrac{\partial x_0}{\partial r} + \dfrac{\partial y_p}{\partial y}} , \tag{8.44}
$$

which gives more insight if written as

$$
1+m_g = \theta_1(1+r) + \theta^2\left(1+\frac{r}{1-t}\right), \tag{8.45}
$$

where $0 < \theta_1, \theta_2 < 1$, and $\theta_1 + \theta_2 = 1$. In going from (8.44) to (8.45) we have simply used some earlier definitions and results, and in particular that $dx_g/dy_g = 1 + m_g$, $\rho_i = r$, for all i, and $dx_p/dy_p = 1 + [r/(1-t)]$.

The equation in (8.45) is a useful way of expressing the condition for the optimal level of public enterprise investment. It says that the equilibrium marginal rate of return on this investment must be a simple weighted average of the market interest rate (= consumers' time preference rate) on the one hand, and the marginal rate of return to private sector investment on the other, where the latter can be found by a simple correction to the market interest rate. The weights are

$$
\theta_1 = \frac{\partial x_0}{\partial r}\left/\frac{\partial x_0}{\partial r} + \frac{\partial y_p}{\partial r}\right. \quad \text{and} \quad \theta_2 = \frac{\partial y_p}{\partial r}\left/\frac{\partial x_0}{\partial r} + \frac{\partial y_p}{\partial r}\right., \tag{8.46}
$$

which are positive (because numerators and denominators all have negative signs) and sum to 1. Thus, the weight which the market interest rate receives depends entirely on the strength of the interest effect on current consumption (strictly speaking, corrected for income effects – see Sandmo and Drèze (1971)) relative to that on investment. The reason is that these determine the extent to which the public enterprise investment displaces, at the margin, consumption or private investment. The opportunity cost of displaced consumption is measured by r, and that of displaced investment by $r/(1-t)$, and so condition (8.45) expresses the equality between the marginal rate of return on public enterprise investment and its opportunity cost, measured according to the precise displacement of consumption and private investment it makes at the margin.

Finally, note a further aspect of this result. Let us define

$$r^* = \theta_1 r + \theta_2 \frac{r}{1-t} \tag{8.47}$$

as the optimal public enterprise cost of capital. Then, the public enterprise can satisfy the necessary condition for optimal investment if it maximizes net present value[19]

$$v_g = \frac{x_g}{1+r^*} - y_g \tag{8.48}$$

using r^* in discounting. Thus, we have a complete solution to the public enterprise investment decision problem.

8.3   Conclusions

The analysis and results of the previous section throw a great deal of light on the appropriate basis for the public sector cost of capital, and lead to some interesting conclusions for public sector investment appraisal generally.

The first of these relates to the cost of capital currently in use, the so-called 'test discount rate', or TDR. Both in concept and measurement, it is based on estimates of the marginal rate of return on private investment, on the grounds that public sector investments should not be undertaken if they yield a lower return, at the margin, than private investment. From the preceding analysis, we see that this implicitly assumes that $\partial x_0/\partial r = 0$, i.e. that variations in the interest rate do not affect consumption, so that public sector investment displaces only private investment. No empirical evidence for this seems to have been adduced, and it certainly conflicts with theoretical reasoning.

The intuition underlying it seems at first sight to be reasonable, but, as we have just seen, is misleading, at least in the general case, because there we must have

$$r < r^* < \frac{r}{1-t}, \tag{8.49}$$

so that the marginal rate of return in the public sector is optimally less than that in the private sector. The reason, of course, is that private investment is itself 'too low': consumers would be prepared to undertake more investment, but the market fails to organize this and so the public enterprise partially compensates for this. On the other hand, the public enterprise should not in general invest until its marginal rate of return is *equal* to the market interest rate, because the resulting sacrifices in private sector investment would actually make the *total* return to the public investment too low.

We can note a further interesting aspect of the way public enterprise investment decisions are taken in practice.[20] The procedure is to use the TDR to find the least-cost input combinations to produce a given level of output (e.g. in evaluating nuclear against coal-fired power stations), but to use the actual interest rate paid on their borrowing (which is very close to the interest rate on government bonds) to determine *scale* of output.[21] Given the relative significance of choice of scale and choice of technique in determining their total investment, therefore, we find that the bulk of the investment programme is basically determined by r (= the interest rate used for choice of scale) while marginal adjustments in it will be influenced by $r/(1 - t)$ (= the TDR). We therefore have the interesting conclusion: although not really using a weighted average cost of capital, this hybrid procedure, which is quite inconsistent with the rationale of the TDR, may actually be nearer the correct solution than would be achieved by consistent application of the TDR. This is more likely the greater the displacement, at the margin, of consumption relative to private investment.

A second point concerns the possibility of finding the optimal level of public enterprise investment by a discounting procedure. This issue is an important one, and is part of the general question of the possibility of achieving second-best optima by decentralized procedures. Consider the first-best case. It is possible to regard the optimum as being achieved in one of two ways. There could be a centralized solution, in which the 'planner' specifies to the public enterprise the amount of investment it should undertake. For this, the planner would have to find the solution to the entire resource allocation problem, where that solution was set out in figure 8.2. Alternatively, he could simply instruct the public enterprise 'manager' to maximize net present value, taking as cost of capital the market interest rate. Given certain assumptions to ensure the stability of the process,[22] an optimum could then be achieved without the need for a complete central solution. The manager would compute a net present value at the prevailing interest rate, and try to issue the implied number of bonds. If this caused the interest rate to change, he would recompute a net present value at the new interest rate, and restate his bond requirement. This procedure would be reiterated until an equilibrium is achieved, at which point the necessary conditions for a first-best optimum would be satisfied.

In the second-best case, we could again envisage two solution procedures. The central planner could again solve the entire problem, and determine an amount of investment which the public enterprise should undertake. To do this, of course, he would require knowledge of the relevant lending and investment functions. The decentralized procedure would again be to specify a net present value maximization rule, as in equation (8.48) above, but the problem arises: what is the appropriate way in which to specify the cost of capital r^*? Now, in the special case in which the weights θ_1 and θ_2 are constant with respect to public enterprise investment y_g, the problem would be solved if the planner gives the manager the 'formula' for computing r^*, in conjunction with the market interest rate r, and the private sector rate of return $r/(1-t)$. In that case, again assuming the stability conditions to be satisfied, a decentralized procedure will converge on the second-best optimum. The problem arises if θ_1 and θ_2 vary with y_g, since in that case, the 'formula' has to be recomputed at every step. This problem may perhaps be better perceived if we think in terms of a group of public enterprises, whose total investment is financed by bonds issued by the central planner. Then, each individual manager is not in a position to recompute the appropriate weights, and therefore cannot compute the necessary r^* value; this must be done by the central planner. But in that case, the benefits of decentralization are lost (at least those associated with information and computation costs) and the planner might just as well specify physical investment programmes. This point applies *a fortiori* to the case in which the planner might specify to managers the value of r^* which actually obtains at the equilibrium point. As the condition in (8.45) makes clear, to find this value he actually has to solve the problem for the optimal investment level, and so the value of r^* cannot be used to *find* this solution in a decentralized way.[23] This argument suggests, therefore, that except under fairly special circumstances, in which the weights θ_1 and θ_2 are unresponsive to public investment, the possibilities for decentralization of public sector investment decision-taking take a particular form: given centralized determination of total public enterprise investment expenditure, public enterprises could make their own detailed allocations of these by the use of a discounting procedure, using the value of r^* *implied by* the centralized choice of total investment. Thus, the relevance of the discount rate is to the decentralized allocation of given total investment budgets, rather than to the determination of these budgets themselves.[24]

This raises a further issue, which can be dealt with only briefly here. Recently, a controversy has developed[25] concerning the precise way in which the investment appraisal procedure should be formulated to take account of the second-best considerations analysed in the previous section. There, a natural formulation was that of equation (8.48) in which we maximize net present value, using r^* as a discount rate. However, Feldstein has argued that such a procedure will lead to non-optimal investment choices, and suggests instead a procedure whereby discounting is carried out only at 'the' time preference rate, which we take to be r, and a correction made to the value of investment, y_g, to take account of its true opportunity cost, in terms of the consumption and private investment it displaces. In a two-period world, this opportunity cost would be calculated as follows: first, suppose a fraction ϕ_1 of the increment in public sector investment dy_g represents displaced current consumption, while a fraction ϕ_2 ($=1-\phi_1$) represents displaced private investment. Thus, we have $dx_0 = -\phi_1 dy_g$, and $dy_p = -\phi_2 dy_g$, where dx_0 and dy_p are the reductions in consumption and private investment. The private investment which is displaced would have yielded output next period of the amount $(1+m_p)\,dy_p$, since m_p is the marginal private sector rate of return. The present value of this, discounting at 'the' time preference rate, is $[(1+m_p)/(1+r)]\,dy_p$. Thus, the marginal social opportunity cost of one unit of public investment is defined as

$$k = \left[\phi_1 + \frac{(1+m_p)}{(1+r)}\,\phi_2\right], \tag{8.50}$$

since this gives the present value of the reduction in consumption caused by an increment dy_g in public investment. Feldstein's procedure suggests that we then maximize

$$\tilde{v}_g = \frac{x_g}{1+r} - ky_g. \tag{8.51}$$

This maximization leads to the solution

$$\frac{dx_g}{dy_g}\frac{1}{1+r} - \left[\phi_1 + \frac{(1+m_p)}{(1+r)}\,\phi_2\right] = 0. \tag{8.52}$$

But rearranging this equation gives

$$1+m_g = \phi_1(1+r) + \phi_2(1+m_p), \tag{8.53}$$

and so, provided that $\theta_1 = \phi_1$, and $\theta_2 = \phi_2$, we have precisely the solution in (8.49). Since the θs and ϕs measure the same thing, namely the proportions of public investment which are provided by displaced consumption and private investment, respectively, the Feldstein procedure is equivalent to that derived earlier.

Although this equivalence is easy to demonstrate for the two-period case, moving to n periods makes the problem much more difficult. The analysis in Vanags (1975), however, suggests that, under a wide range of circumstances, the two procedures are approximately equivalent in the n period case.

To conclude: in this chapter we have considered some elements of a theoretical approach to determination of the public enterprise cost of capital. The second-best model ignored many aspects of reality, and could be extended in various ways. In this writer's opinion, however, it gives considerable insight into the nature of optimal second-best investment planning, and the general nature of its results are likely to be very robust to changes in the model's specifications.

chapter 9
pricing and investment under uncertainty

Consider the following planning problem:[1] the planners in the electricity supply industry must choose, in year t, an investment programme which will make new capacity available for production in year $t + 6$. The aim will be to provide capacity to meet the peak demand expected in that year. Two problems would confront the planners in applying the approach, say, of chapter 5: the first is that the peak demand curve cannot be known with certainty; and the second is that cost curves cannot be known with certainty, not only in respect of the level of costs, but also in respect of the capacity output which is attainable from any given amount of *installed* capacity. The uncertainty concerning demand arises from its dependence on variables such as income, prices of complements and substitutes, weather conditions, consumer durable technology and ownership, and so on, whose future values cannot be known in year t. The uncertainty about costs and output availability arises because future input prices, productivities, and incidence of plant failures cannot be known in year t. How then should the planners approach the problem of choosing prices, outputs and investment programmes? This chapter is concerned with a general theoretical approach to that question.

First, let us generalize from this example, to obtain a model of the decision problem under uncertainty, which will have a wider applicability than to just one public enterprise. The planner has to choose one *alternative* from some given set of alternatives, where in the above example this consists of the set of all possible investment programmes. Resulting from this choice will be an *outcome*, consisting of a value of some variable in which we are ultimately interested. In the case of electricity investment, this outcome could be the net social benefit of a particular investment programme, or its profitability.[2] Uncertainty exists when any alternative has more than one possible outcome, and it is not known which will occur. The plurality of possible outcomes arises because the underlying determinants of the outcome can take a number of possible values. Those which in fact occur can be thought of as being 'chosen' by some chance mechanism, outside the planner's control. We assume, however, that the planner is able to set out each of the possible outcomes which may follow his choice of any one alternative, and that he can do this for all possible alternatives. In terms of the electricity investment problem, this would mean that for any one investment programme, the planner can set out all the possible levels of net social benefit which may result. He would calculate any one of these by, on the one hand, assuming a particular set of values for future incomes, prices of complements and substitutes, weather conditions, etc. to define a specific demand curve; and, on the other hand, by assuming a particular set of values for future input prices, productivities and incidence of plant failure, to define a cost curve. Given an appropriate pricing rule, a net social benefit outcome can be found for that set of assumptions. By varying the assumptions, the entire set of outcomes can be generated.

This is not what happens in the planning of electricity investment, however. Part of this procedure is completed, but not all. We can learn a great deal from an examination of why this is so, and that will be the subject of the next section. For the moment, we shall continue to develop the theoretical model.

We said earlier that the outcome which results from a given choice of alternative can be thought of as being 'chosen' by some chance mechanism outside the planner's control. We assume that he can assign a probability to the event that any one outcome will be 'chosen', and so associated with each alternative will actually be a *probability distribution* of outcomes. We can, therefore, describe the problem of choice under uncertainty as that of evaluating alternative probability distributions of outcomes, and finding the alternative which yields the most preferred distribution. Applying this to the theory of public enterprise pricing and investment, we can define a two-stage 'programme': the first stage is to consider how probability distributions of outcomes can be ranked on a scale of social preference, such a scale being necessary if we are to be able to discuss *optimal* decision-taking; and the second stage is to apply this to specific types of pricing and investment problems. Although the programme would logically be carried out in that order, a rather more interesting approach is to reverse it, and to consider how a method of ranking may arise out of an analysis of specific problems. This is the approach we adopt here.

9.1 The capacity margin problem

We consider here how the planners in the electricity supply industry solve their decision problem under uncertainty.[3] Their first step is to construct a probability distribution of peak demands for year $t + 6$. This is done by combining two other probability distributions. A forecast of the most probable demand, given '*average cold spell*' weather conditions, is made for year $t + 6$. This forecast is obtained by putting best estimates for future incomes, prices, etc. into an equation which relates these to demand, and solving for future demand.[4] Then, taking a probability distribution of forecasting errors[5] and applying this to the forecast demand, the first probability distribution of future demands is obtained. From past evidence on the relationship between deviations in demand from the 'average weather condition' level, and deviations in weather conditions from this standard, together with a probability distribution of weather conditions, the second probability distribution of demands can be generated. Combining these two distributions using standard probability laws then gives an overall probability distribution of demands in year t + 6. Figure 9.1 illustrates this distribution, $f(q)$, on the assumption that it is normal. Demand in year $t + 6$ is denoted by q, and the most probable demand is $\bar{q}$.

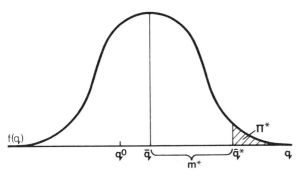

Figure 9.1

The planners now see themselves faced with the following problem: let K_0 be the level of installed capacity which will be available in year $t + 6$, as a result of past investment decisions. The investment plan to be chosen in year t will bring installed capacity up to some value K^* in year $t + 6$. Now, the question is should K^* be just sufficient to enable the system to meet the most probable demand, $\bar{q}$, or should it be greater? In other words, should there be a *margin of capacity* over and above that required to meet the most probable demand, and, if so, how great should that be? Thus the problem of investment planning resolves itself into that of determining the appropriate size of the *capacity margin*.[6]

The capacity margin is chosen as follows: referring to figure 9.1, suppose that the investment plan adopted in year t was just enough to increase capacity output from q_0 to $\bar{q}$. In that case, since half the distribution lies above $\bar{q}$, there is a 50 per cent chance that peak demand will actually exceed $\bar{q}$. The consequence of excess demand would be 'load-shedding' – some consumers have to be completely deprived of supply for the duration of the excess demand (which may be only a few hours of the year – but also the coldest hours) so that output is restrained to capacity.[7] If planned capacity output were to exceed $\bar{q}$, however, the risk of excess demand is less, since the area of the distribution above it will be smaller. Given the precise parameters of the probability distribution $f(q)$, we can find, for each possible level of capacity output, $\hat{q}$, the probability that demand will exceed it. The planners then choose a critical 'risk level' or probability that demand will exceed capacity, shown by the area π^* in figure 9.1, and find the capacity output corresponding to this, which we call $\hat{q}^*$. This is then the output level for which capacity will be installed. The procedure is illustrated in figure 9.2. The curve $F(\hat{q})$ shows the relation between capacity output, $\hat{q}$, and the probability that demand will exceed it, π, derived from the probability distribution $f(q)$.[8] As we expect from figure 9.1, the value of π (= the area under $f(q)$ to the right of $\hat{q}$) falls rapidly at first as $\hat{q}$ increases, but then approaches zero asymptotically. Then, in the figure, the chosen risk level π^* determines the capacity output $\hat{q}^*$, and hence the margin of capacity output over most likely output, $m^* = \hat{q}^* - \bar{q}$. Consequently, there is a margin of installed capacity over the capacity most likely to be required, $K^* - \bar{K}$. At the present time, this capacity margin is roughly 24 per cent of the value of $\bar{K}$, the capacity required to meet $\bar{q}$.

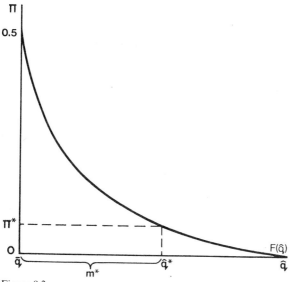

Figure 9.2

The interesting question is: on what basis is the choice of π^*, the risk level, made? To quote Mr Berrie, the planners 'must, in practice, choose a risk standard which enables the good image of electricity with consumers at large to be maintained, but without committing those consumers to too heavy a capital burden'. Thus, there is a trade-off between cost and risk: the greater the capacity margin, the greater must be total capacity costs, and so given the financial target the higher must be electricity prices; while a greater margin implies lower risk that consumers will lose supply, with consequent benefits. It is this latter part of the trade-off, however, which is put rather vaguely in the quotation. To explore this further, let us retrace our steps, and approach the problem from a different, and more general point of view.

The capacity margin problem is essentially an inventory problem. In general, a firm would confront the problem of uncertain demand by determining a capacity level and a level of inventory of finished goods, where the latter would absorb the uncertainties. In determining its inventory level, the firm would weigh up on the one hand the costs of carrying inventory, and on the other the loss of profit from failing to meet demand. The latter has two aspects: there is the direct result, that the firm will lose the profit it might have got from making a sale, if output had been available; and the more conjectural, long-term result, that the firm may have permanently lost a customer because of its failure to meet the order. Given the firm's estimate of the probability distribution of future demand, it will weigh up the cost of an addition to inventory, with the expected loss it would incur if it did not make that addition to inventory. We expect it to end up roughly[9] at a point at which the cost of the marginal addition to inventory is just about equal to the expected loss of not making that marginal addition. We now consider how this relates to electricity supply.

The first difference is that, because of its technology, electricity can only be 'stored' in the form of the capital equipment required to generate it, so that the inventory must consist of capacity, and not output. In general, this is a more expensive way of holding inventory than is the type of storage facility required for most goods.[10] Nevertheless, in terms of finding a solution, it is quite possible to quantify these costs, and so this aspect of the calculation is essentially unchanged.

The important difference arises in *valuing* an increment in the capacity margin. In the case of electricity supply, the direct loss of profit from failure to meet demand is negligible.[11] In any case, of course, profit is not the objective of a public enterprise. If the objective of the investment is to maximize net social benefit, then we can suggest the general form of the solution: capacity should be increased up to the point at which the marginal social benefit of the reduced risk of supply interruption just equals the marginal cost of adding to capacity. This formula does not get us very far, but at least it forces us to state the problem: how can we determine the marginal social benefit of additions to capacity?

The answer which appears to be accepted by planners in the electricity supply industry is that no solution to this problem exists. It is thought to be impossible to measure (and perhaps even to define) this marginal social benefit, and so the capacity margin decision must be made to maintain 'the good image of electricity'. This seems to mean in effect that the capacity margin is determined by the planners' preferences. There are two kinds of effects of power cuts which may concern planners. The immediate effects are public irritation, criticism and political pressure. The longer-run effect may be a decline in the growth of electricity demand, as consumers switch to substitutes for electricity whose supply seems to be more reliable. We would expect planners to prefer investment programmes involving less public irritation and criticism, and faster growth, to those with more irritation and criticism, and slower growth. This must be weighed up, of course, against the costs of providing a margin of (probably) spare capacity. The unpopularity of power cuts and their damage to long-run demand growth must be balanced against the unpopularity of price increases and *their* damage to demand growth, and the 'security level' π^* chosen accordingly. However, it should be noted that the costs of providing the capacity margin are typically spread over consumption by all the consumers at all times, and are not imposed only on peak demand, the uncertainty of which is essentially the source of the need for a capacity margin. Thus, the relevant group of consumers is not made to bear the cost of their being provided with the degree of supply reliability they enjoy, and we would expect as a result that it is over-demanded – in part because they are not induced to substitute cheaper ways of providing their peak energy demands.

Let us now compare the planners' practical solution of the capacity margin problem with our theoretical model. The latter saw the problem as that of choosing between alternative probability distributions of net social benefits, each distribution corresponding to an investment programme. The planners' procedure effectively collapses this distribution into two parameters: the probability, π, associated with each investment programme, that the capacity it provides will be exceeded by demand; and the capital cost of the investment programme. The value of π becomes a proxy for the complex of factors which determine the benefit of reduced risk. In the absence of any conceptual framework within which to analyse the social benefits of risk reduction, we have no real grounds for criticizing this procedure or rejecting its results.[12] Some elements of such a framework will be examined in the following sections. Before going on to these, we first consider the relevance of the capacity margin problem to the general issues of public enterprise pricing and investment under uncertainty.

The 'capacity margin problem' is a way of defining what is in fact the *general* problem of choosing capacity and price for a non-storable good.[13] As such, it is directly applicable to other public enterprises, the nature of whose technology is such that inventories must be held in the form of capacity rather than output. This is true of virtually all transport and communications services, but not of steel, coal and gas, whose outputs can be stored. For example, telephone connections at 4.30 pm on 15 April cannot be produced at 4 am on the previous 10 August and stored. Similarly trips from Alpha to Omega by rail, sea and air cannot be produced at one point of time and consumed at another. Inventories can only exist when production and consumption are separable in time, and are the means by which stable production can be reconciled with fluctuating and uncertain demand.

There is an important set of differences among public sector outputs concerning the way in which excess demands can be coped with (assuming for the moment that price adjustments are not used to eliminate them). In the case of outputs such as coal and steel, available output could be rationed among consumers in a way which implies *marginal* reductions for all consumers. Excess demand for transport and communications services, on the other hand, is generally coped with by queuing: the time-profile of demand accommodates itself to the time-profile of capacity as consumers adjust to the delays with which their demands will be met, and the costs of the excess demand are borne by consumers as time costs. Electricity, and to a lesser extent gas, differ in yet another respect: excess demand results in complete withdrawal of supply from some consumers, and maintenance of full consumption by others. The total welfare loss is likely to be greater in this case than in any other, because of the difference in *marginal* and *total* utilities. Thus, suppose a cut in electricity consumption of x kWh were spread evenly over all consumers. Then, since each consumer is able to make a marginal reduction in consumption, and since the value of the marginal unit to each consumer is approximately equal to its price p, per kWh, then the welfare loss in this case is measured approximately by the loss of revenue, px, which we already know to be negligible in practice. On the other hand, if the cut is imposed on a group of consumers who suffer a total loss of consumption, then the welfare loss is equal to the total amount of their 'consumers' surplus' which, in the middle of winter, may be very high. The obstacle to choosing capacity in a way which maximizes net social benefits appears to consist largely in the problem of measuring these surpluses. There is an important problem here of quite a general kind: 'reliability' of supply is a public good, in that no consumer can be excluded from enjoying it, and one person's consumption of it does not reduce that of someone else. The choice of a particular capacity margin determines the risk of failure to meet demand, and hence of power cuts, and a reduction in this degree of risk benefits everyone. The attempt to find, by consulting consumers, the appropriate level of provision of this public good 'reliability', therefore, encounters the general public good problem: it pays individual consumers to conceal their *true* preferences, in a way which influences the final choice in the direction they desire. For example, if a man from the electricity board were to go around asking consumers how much they would be prepared to pay to avoid power cuts, and the consumers know: (a) that they will not actually have to pay whatever sum they state; (b) the risk of power cuts will be smaller, the greater this sum; (c) over a wide range, the cost to them of increased reliability is less than its benefit; then clearly each consumer will rationally over-state his willingness to pay for the reduced risk of power cuts. In this situation, we may be forced back upon the planners' judgements, and preferences, as the second best. This also provides one way of rationalizing the belief that current capacity margins are too high: it pays individuals to pressurize, express extreme irritation, and vote for higher capacity margins than those for which they would in fact be prepared to pay, if payment were related to benefit.

This discussion has formulated the problem to which we must now apply some economic analysis. The analysis will be essentially concerned with the evaluation of probability distributions of outcomes in terms of social welfare. It therefore has a general applicability to optimal decision-taking under uncertainty in all areas of the public sector. However, it will be useful to continue to relate the analysis to the capacity margin problem, not only for expositional purposes, but also as a test of the potential contribution to solution of real problems which the theory can make.

9.2   A model of price and capacity choice under uncertainty

In this section, we examine a model[14] which deals simultaneously with pricing and investment policy. It can be regarded as the extension of the fixed-capacity model of chapter 5, to situations in which demand is uncertain. We shall set out the analysis, and then consider its implications for the issues discussed in the previous section.

The situation is as follows: the enterprise, at the first instant of year 0, must choose an investment plan, which will determine capacity in year 1. Costs in year 1 are known with certainty, but demand is not. There are two possible states of the world[15]

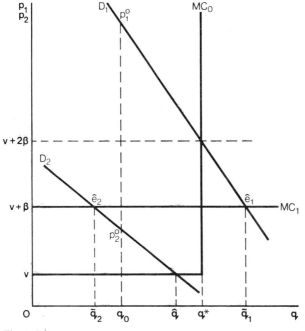

Figure 9.3

which may prevail in year 1, in each of which there will be a demand curve. Each state will occur with probability 1/2. The demand curves, D_1 and D_2, and cost curves relating to the optimal capacity, q^*, are drawn in figure 9.3. The cost curves take the form familiar from the analysis of the fixed capacity case in chapter 5. Note that for simplicity we have assumed that there is no peak-load problem: q measures the annual rate of output in year 1, with a uniform level of demand throughout the year. It is straightforward to relax this assumption to obtain the realistic case, and this is done once the basic results have been derived.

The following two assumptions are substantive rather than simplifying, and are basic to the model:

I. Price is set at the first instant of year 1, when demand will be known with certainty, and is always set in such a way as to restrain demand to capacity.

II. The value placed by a consumer, at the first instant of year 0, on the marginal unit of consumption in state s, $s = 1, 2$ is $\frac{1}{2}w_s$, where w_s is the value he will place on that unit when he knows that state s has occurred.

Each of these requires further discussion. The first is not entirely unrealistic. Prices do not normally have to be set at the time at which investment plans are being made, but rather can be announced relatively soon before peak demand.[16] For example, prices of electricity are not set six years in advance, but rather within, at most, twelve months of system peak. This seems generally true of other public enterprises. The degree of uncertainty confronting pricing decisions is therefore very much smaller than that for investment decisions,[17] and assumption I sets it equal to zero.

The second part of assumption I may be invalidated by constraints placed on the levels of prices, and on the extent of price adjustments, which may well exist in practice. By assuming the possibility of rationing by price initially, however, we are led to some interesting conclusions about the source and nature of the welfare losses due to supply interruptions.

Assumption II can be illustrated as follows: assume that the good concerned is electricity, and that state 1 corresponds to cold weather and high income for a consumer, while state 2 corresponds to mild weather and low income. Given some level of his consumption in state 1, say $\hat{q}_1$, suppose that the consumer is prepared to pay 50p for the marginal unit, when he knows that state 1 prevails. Likewise, he would pay 10p for the marginal unit of consumption when he knows state 2 prevails. Then, if the probability of each state occurring is 1/2, the assumption says that at the first instant of year 0 he would be prepared to pay 25p to assure himself of the marginal unit of consumption *if* state 1 occurs, and 5p to assure himself of the marginal unit if state 2 occurs. It also follows that he will pay a total of 30p to assure himself of the marginal units of consumption in both states. The assumption, therefore, implies that, in year 0, the consumer is willing to pay for an increment of consumption in each state, an amount equal to the *expected value* of what he would pay when he knows for certain which state exists. A justification for this assumption, based on an explicit analysis of consumer choice under uncertainty, is given in the next section.

In figure 9.3, we analyse the determination of the optimal price and capacity level, q^*. It can be shown that the general necessary condition for optimal capacity is

$$\tfrac{1}{2}(p_1^* - v) + \tfrac{1}{2}(p_2^* - v) = \beta, \qquad p_s^* \geq v, \qquad s = 1, 2, \tag{9.1}$$

where p_1^* is the optimal price which will be set in state 1, and p_2^* that which will be set in state 2. If, as in the present case, we have $p_2^* = v$, then equation (9.1) becomes

$$p_1^* = v + 2\beta \tag{9.2}$$

as in the figure.

The argument underlying this result is straightforward, and takes a form familiar from the earlier analysis of peak-load pricing. Thus, in figure 9.3, suppose that capacity is initially at q_0. Then, in state 1, the marginal value of output to consumers is shown by the price corresponding to point p_1^0 on demand curve D_1; while in state 2 the marginal value of output to consumers is shown by point p_2^0 on D_2. Now consider the differences between these prices, p_1^0 and p_2^0, and v. These differences, $p_1^0 - v$, and $p_2^0 - v$, can be thought of as the amount consumers would pay for an increment of output in each respective state, over and above the direct cost of producing the output. In other words, $p_1^0 - v$ measures, at capacity q^0, consumers' willingness to pay for an increment in capacity in state 1, while $p_2^0 - v$ measures the same thing for state 2. But from assumption II, we have that at the first instant of year 0, when the future state of the world is unknown, consumers' valuations of the increment of output in each state are $\tfrac{1}{2}p_1^0$ and $\tfrac{1}{2}p_2^0$, respectively. It follows from this assumption that their willingness to pay for the increment in capacity, at the first instant of year 0, is $\tfrac{1}{2}(p_1^0 - v) + \tfrac{1}{2}(p_2^0 - v)$. Note that here we again have a case of *joint products*: an increment of capacity will enable an increment of output to be produced in *each state*, and so its value, *before* the state of the world is known, is the *sum* of its values across states.

From this reasoning, it follows that an increment in capacity can make everyone better off, as long as

$$\tfrac{1}{2}(p_1^0 - v) + \tfrac{1}{2}(p_2^0 - v) > \beta. \tag{9.3}$$

By rewriting this condition as

$$p_1^0 + p_2^0 > 2(v + \beta), \tag{9.4}$$

we can see from figure 9.3 that the inequality is satisfied at capacity q^0, since $p_1^0 > v + 2\beta$, and $p_2^0 > v$. Hence, everyone can be made better off by increasing capacity. The inequality in (9.4) is clearly satisfied, right up to output $\hat{q}$. Since at this point $p_2 = v$, we know that output in state 2 should not exceed $\hat{q}$. If output in state 2 *were* to exceed $\hat{q}$, that would imply that resources at the margin are worth more in other uses than they are to consumers of this good in state 2. However, it is still the case that at capacity $\hat{q}$, $p_1 > v + 2\beta$, or alternatively, $\frac{1}{2}(p_1 - v) > \beta$, implying that consumers still value an increment of capacity at an amount greater than its cost, because of the *expected value of its benefit to them in the 'cold weather, high income' state* 1. Hence, even though no benefit will be derived from it if in fact state 2 occurs, everyone can be made better off by an expansion in capacity before the state of the world is known, because of its benefits if state 1 occurs. This clearly continues to hold up to capacity q^*, at which point $p_1^* = v + 2\beta$, or $\frac{1}{2}(p_1^* - v) = \beta$, and the expected value of benefit from a capacity increment is just equal to its cost.

Associated with this solution for optimal capacity choice is a pricing policy which is conditional on the state of the world. If state 1 occurs, then price will be set at $p_1^* = v + 2\beta$, since, following assumption I, this rations demand to capacity. If state 2 occurs, then price will be set at $p_2^* = v$, implying output $\hat{q} < q^*$, and this of course corresponds to the usual optimal pricing rule for given capacity. If state 1 occurs, the enterprise will make a profit, of the amount

$$P_1 = p_1^* q^* - (v + \beta)q^*, \tag{9.5}$$
$$= (v + 2\beta)q^* - (v + \beta)q^* = \beta q^*, \tag{9.6}$$

whereas if state 2 occurs, the enterprise makes a loss of

$$P_2 = p_2^* \hat{q} - v\hat{q} - \beta q^*, \tag{9.7}$$
$$= -\beta q^*. \tag{9.8}$$

It follows that the *expected value* of profit,
$$\bar{P} = \tfrac{1}{2}P_1 + \tfrac{1}{2}P_2, \tag{9.9}$$

is exactly zero, implying that in the long run (taking one year with another) the enterprise will break even.

Given the two assumptions underlying this model, therefore, we have a complete solution for the pricing and capacity choice problem, which is formally identical to the peak-load pricing solution, and can be generalized and operationalized in a similar way. Indeed, it is possible to consider a further case, analogous to the 'shifting peak' case, in which, if state 2 occurs, output will also equal capacity, and $p_2^* > v$. It is in this case that the general condition in equation (9.3) applies. The details of this extension are left for the reader to supply.

It is instructive to compare the solution just derived to the 'planners' solution' to the capacity margin problem given earlier. The essential difference lies in the role of price. In the planners' procedure which determined the capacity margin. a future price was assumed in generating the central estimate of future demand, and prices then vanished from the analysis. In the present case, because of assumption I, pricing policy and capacity choice are interdependent. The use of price to ration output means that in each state of the world, price measures the marginal value of consumption, and this, in conjunction with assumption II, provides us with the valuation of the benefits of increments in capacity which eluded the planners. Thus, we have the result that *if* pricing policy is used optimally, then we also have the basis of a solution to the investment planning problem.

We can relate the solution obtained here to our general formulation of the decision problem under uncertainty in the following way. The set of alternatives consists of the possible values of capacity output (which of course uniquely imply corresponding investment plans). Consequent on any capacity output choice will be a net social benefit of consumption in state $s = 1, 2$, which we could write as

$$N_s = B_s(q_s) - vq_s, \qquad q_s \leq \hat{q}, \qquad s = 1, 2, \tag{9.10}$$

where $\hat{q}$ is capacity. Thus, the 'probability distribution of net social benefits' consists of the two values N_s, for given choice of q_s (determined by the pricing policy), each with probability $1/2$. The only property of B_s which we need to specify is that

$$\frac{dB_s}{dq_s} = p_s(q_s), \qquad s = 1, 2, \tag{9.11}$$

where $p_s(q_s)$ is the market demand function in state s. In other words, marginal social benefit of output in state s is measured by price. Assumption II then allows us to act as if we could value the distribution of net social benefits corresponding to any one capacity choice, at the *expected value*,

$$\bar{N} = \tfrac{1}{2}N_1 + \tfrac{1}{2}N_2 = \bar{N}(q_1, q_2). \tag{9.12}$$

Hence, we have the solution to the crucial valuation problem: different capacity choices are compared on the basis of their values of $\bar{N}$, and we choose that capacity q, which is a solution to the problem

$$\text{maximize } \bar{N}(q_1, q_2) - \beta\hat{q} \tag{9.13}$$
$$\{q_s, \hat{q}\}$$

subject to $q_s \leq \hat{q}, \qquad s = 1, 2,$

which gives the solution in equation (9.3).

We can apply our solution to consider the conditions under which, *given our assumptions I and II*, the planners' solution to the capacity margin problem will be optimal. First, suppose that there are now three states of the world, which again will occur with equal probability. Extending the earlier reasoning, the optimality condition will now become

$$\tfrac{1}{3}(p_1^* - v) + \tfrac{1}{3}(p_2^* - v) + \tfrac{1}{3}(p_3^* - v) = \beta, \qquad p_s \geq v, \qquad s = 1, 2, 3. \qquad (9.14)$$

In figure 9.4 we show two possible solutions to the capacity choice problem. In both (a) and (b), the demand curves in the three states are shown as D_1, D_2 and D_3, and optimal capacity is q^*. In (a), we have that at the optimum, $p_2^* = p_3^* = v$, and so the necessary condition in (9.10) is satisfied with $p_1^* = v + 3\beta$. In (b), we have that $p_2^* = v$, and so $\tfrac{1}{3}(p_1^* - v) + \tfrac{1}{3}(p_2^* - v) = \beta$. We now need to characterize the capacity margin solution in these cases.

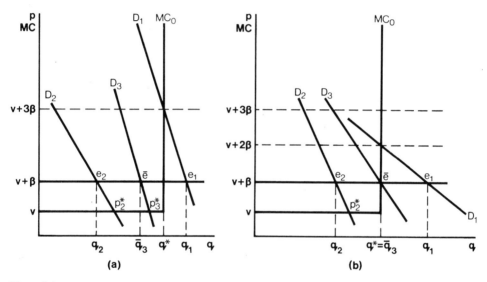

Figure 9.4

Suppose that the planners choose as their *given* price level the value $v + \beta$, so that in figure 9.4(a) they generate the 'demand forecasts' q_1, q_2 and $\bar{q}_3$, and in (b) the same. By construction, $\bar{q}_3$ is, in each case, the expected value of the forecast demands.[18] Hence, in each case, the capacity margin approach chooses some arbitrary risk level and installs capacity above $\bar{q}_3$. In case (a), we see that a capacity margin of the amount $q^* - \bar{q}_3$ is justified. At a capacity of $\bar{q}_3$, we have that the expected value of the benefits in states 1 and 3, of a capacity increment, exceeds the cost of the increment, and so everyone can be made better off by a positive 'capacity margin'. In (b), however, this is not the case: it happens that the optimal capacity level q^* is just equal to $\bar{q}_3$, and so no capacity margin is implied.

In terms of our figure, everything clearly depends on the height and slope of the demand curve D_1 relative to D_3: the higher and steeper this curve, the more likely it is that a positive capacity margin will be implied. To put this in economic rather than geometric terms, what matters is the value of marginal consumption in higher demand states of the world: where this is high relative to the 'mean' state of the world, a positive capacity margin is likely to be implied, whereas when this is low, no margin may be implied.

This statement could be a 'shattering glimpse of the obvious', were it not for the operational implications. The solution tells us that we can compute the optimal capacity margin by finding those prices which ration demand to capacity in each state of the world. Given these prices, we can also define a simple qualitative test to determine whether the existing capacity margin is too large. This test can usefully be stated in its most general form. Thus, let $p_s(q_s)$ be the (inverse) demand function in state s, where $s = 1, 2, \ldots, S$, and π_s the probability of occurrence of state s. Denote the capacity output under the 'planners' solution', by $\tilde{q}$. Finally, let S_1 be the set of states of the world, which have the property that

$$p_s(\tilde{q}) > v, \qquad s \in S_1. \tag{9.15}$$

In other words, at the chosen capacity level, the prices which equate demand to that level exceed marginal running cost for all states in $S_1 \subset S$. Then, capacity $\tilde{q}$ is too large if

$$\sum_{s \in S1} \pi_s[p_s(\tilde{q}) - v] < \beta, \tag{9.16}$$

which means that the expected value of willingness to pay for the marginal unit of capacity, over those states in which consumers benefit from it, is less than its cost.[19]

The discussion so far relates essentially to *peak* demand. If we explicitly incorporate peak-load considerations, then the conditions can be generalized in obvious ways. Given the probability distribution of off-peak demands, we can define the stochastic counterparts of the 'shifting peak' and 'non-shifting peak' cases. In the latter, off-peak demands in all states of the world are less than capacity chosen purely on peak-load considerations, in which case the off-peak demand distribution plays no part in capacity determination, and off-peak price will certainly be equal to v. If the distribution of off-peak demands overlaps with that of peak demands, then the expected value of willingness to pay for capacity in off-peak states of the world, weighted for duration of off-peak demands, will be added to (9.3) (in which the peak demands will correspondingly be weighted for duration). Off-peak prices will then be distributed over a range of values, required to equate demand to capacity in each state, and with a minimum value of v.

Returning now to the general discussion of the optimality of the capacity margin, a planner might argue that assumption I effectively assumes away the whole problem.[20] The use of price to restrain demand to capacity *once* the state of the world is known, means that power cuts are in effect eliminated, since excess demand is always priced away. Thus, the problem, as perceived by the planners, is made to disappear.[21] If assumption I is capable of being met in practice, however, then this analysis is in effect demonstrating how a solution to the problem can be derived, if pricing policy is used appropriately. Only if pricing policy cannot be used to ration demand to capacity, does the solution fail.

There are a number of reasons for the failure of assumption I to hold. It may not be possible technically to set a price when the state of the world is known: there may still be significant demand uncertainty confronting the pricing decision. Alternatively, there may be constraints on the level to which price may be raised, or on the size of any price adjustment. Referring back to figure 9.3, it is clear that quite wide price variations might be necessary from year to year, if price is used as a rationing device. Suppose, for example, that state 2 has occurred in year 0, so that price equals v. Then, if state 1 occurs in year 1, price will have to rise to $v + 2\beta$, while if state 2 occurs again in year 2, price will fall again to v. These price fluctuations might be regarded as too extreme, although whatever costs are associated with this 'extremeness' would have to be weighed against the costs of power cuts, and possibly excess capital expenditure, which occur when price rationing is not adopted.

There are clearly many cases which could be analysed. We might assume that price variation may take place between v and some upper limit below $v + 2\beta$; or that it may take place between bounds which lie within v and $v + 2\beta$; or that a uniform price must be set, which will prevail in all states of the world. Furthermore, we could assume that the constraints on pricing policy are arbitrarily given, or that we may choose them in some way which minimizes the welfare loss they generate. Limitations of space preclude analysis of all of these. We now consider what appears to be a representative case.

9.3 Uniform pricing of uncertain demands

Let us take the case in which a price is to be specified before the state of the world is known, with no adjustment possible once the state *is* known. This would correspond either to the situation in which there is unavoidable demand uncertainty at the time at which prices are set, or to that in which there are extreme constraints on pricing policy. To begin with, we assume that the 'uniform price' – uniform, that is, across states of the world, and not necessarily over periods of the day or year – is arbitrarily set equal to $v + \beta$. We shall in a moment consider the question of an optimal uniform price.

Referring back to figure 9.3, we see that if a price equal to $v + \beta$ is to be set before the state of the world is known, then, if state of the world 1 occurs, demand will be at

$\tilde{q}_1$, and if state 2 occurs, demand will be at $\tilde{q}_2$. Now suppose that capacity happened to be at q^*. Then, if state 1 occurs, there will be excess demand in the amount $\tilde{q}_1 - q^*$, which will have to be met by reducing consumption by some consumers to zero. The welfare losses are then the value of these total consumptions, and these will in general exceed the losses due to increasing price to $v + 2\beta$, for reasons already discussed. Essentially, those who lose their consumption would be able to compensate all other consumers for sharing their losses with them, and still be better off than when they suffer power cuts, but the enterprise fails to organize this mutually beneficial exchange through its pricing policy.

If state 2 occurs there will also be a welfare loss, arising from the fact that price in state 2 exceeds the marginal cost of state 2 consumption, given by v. Now, the lower the uniform price, the smaller is the welfare loss if state 2 occurs, and the larger is that in state 1. At a uniform price of v, the former is zero and the latter at a maximum; at a price of $v + 2\beta$ the converse is the case. Hence, the determination of the optimal uniform price follows from trading-off the expected values of the two kinds of welfare loss, which of course cannot be done unless we know the welfare cost of power cuts.[22]

Let us again assume an arbitrary uniform price at $v + \beta$, and consider the capacity choice decision, as one of optimizing subject to the fixed price constraint. We again make use of figure 9.3 to analyse this case. For any capacity greater than $\tilde{q}_2$, welfare in state 2 is unaffected by capacity choice (ignoring possible welfare effects arising from the way in which its costs are allocated). Thus, capacity choice appears to be determined *entirely* by an evaluation of the costs of capacity, on the one hand, against the welfare losses arising from non-price rationing of demand in state 1, on the other. Since the latter are the costs of power cuts, this describes precisely how planners view the problem. Until we have examined further the nature of these welfare losses, we cannot characterize in precise terms the nature of the solution. We can, however, establish the following qualitative result: in general, in the second-best situation created by the pricing constraint, the optimal capacity level will exceed q^*, the level which would be chosen when pricing policy is unconstrained. To see this, suppose that capacity is set at q^*. From our earlier analysis, we know that this corresponds to the point at which the cost of an increment of capacity, β, is equal to the expected willingness to pay for an increment, $\frac{1}{2}(p_1^* - v)$, where $p_1^* = v + 2\beta$ is the price at which demand in state 1 is q_1^*. However, price is actually equal to $v + \beta$, and excess demand is eliminated by totally depriving some consumers of supply. It follows that the value of an increment of capacity above q^* is not determined by its *marginal* value to all consumers, but rather by the *total* value of consumption to the marginal consumers, i.e. to those consumers who can *now* be supplied, and who would otherwise not have been. Therefore, on the grounds that the total value of consumption to these consumers is greater than the marginal value of consumption to all consumers, this increment in capacity will be justified. Thus, capacity will, in the second best optimum, be greater than q^*, but we cannot say by how much at this point.

This analysis has suggested the importance of the restriction on pricing policy, and has recast, in terms of the standard framework of economic analysis, the problem as seen by the planners. Its inconclusiveness at this point has the same cause as the arbitrariness of the planners' solution: the problem of determining the welfare losses due to total losses of consumption of some consumers. We now have to confront this problem.

9.4   The value of a risk reduction

The problem which faces the planners in trying to determine the level of future supply capacity in the face of uncertain demand is to obtain a valuation of the benefits to consumers of a reduction in the risk of a supply withdrawal. There are two steps necessary to solving this problem: first to construct a model which allows us to say what these benefits consist of in principle; and second to quantify these benefits by empirical measurements guided by the theoretical model. Consistent with the aims and scope of this book, we consider here only the first step. We cannot therefore claim to have solved the problem, but nevertheless will have made progress towards its solution.

We proceed by considering only the individual consumer and derive a money measure of the value to him of a reduction in risk of supply interruption (total benefit measures would follow from aggregation across consumers). The situation which confronts the consumer is as follows. In year 1, if the state of the world 1 occurs, he will have particular tastes, receive a particular income y_1, face a set of prices, and will choose to consume some set of quantities of goods and services. However, because of the unreliability of supply of one good, there are in fact two 'substates' in state 1. Either the consumer will be able to buy the desired amount of the good, or he will not be able to buy any of the good.[23] These two substates can differ only in that respect: in all others, especially in respect of the consumer's income, tastes and the prices he faces, the substates are identical. Denote by α the substate in which he cannot buy the good (e.g. he is subjected to a power cut) and by β that state in which he can. Given that state 1 has occurred, let π be the probability of substate α, and so $1 - \pi$ is that of substate β. We shall discuss the determinants of π in a moment.

If, in year 1, state 2 occurs, then the consumer will again have particular tastes, receive an income, y_2, and face a set of prices, and in the light of these will choose a set of consumption quantities. State 2 differs from state 1 in that he will certainly be able to buy all of these quantities.

We can effectively regard the consumer as being faced with three states of the world, therefore: state 1α, state 1β, and state 2. The probability of 1α is $\frac{1}{2}\pi$, since the probability of state 1 was 1/2; likewise, the probability of state 1β is $\frac{1}{2}(1-\pi)$; and state 2 will still occur with probability 1/2. The probability π that the consumer will not be able to buy any of the good in state 1 depends on three things: first, the total market demand for the good in state 1, which we take as given, since the good's price is predetermined; secondly, the capacity output available in state 1; and thirdly, the mechanism by which choice is made, of the particular consumers who will be refused supply (in the case of electricity, disconnected from the supply system). This last element is also taken as given: we specify nothing more about it than that it leaves every consumer with a value of π on the *open* interval $0 < \pi < 1$, given that there is excess demand. In other words, nobody is certain to be refused supply, or certain not to be, when total demand cannot be met. This therefore embodies a very mild notion of 'fairness'.

Hence, given market demand in state 1 on the one hand, and the mechanism of choice of supply withdrawals on the other, the value of π depends entirely on the level of capacity output, q. The greater is capacity, the smaller is π, and it becomes zero when capacity equals demand, $\tilde{q}$. Formally, we can write

$$\pi = f(q)\frac{\mathrm{d}\pi}{\mathrm{d}q} < 0 \lim_{q \to \tilde{q}} f(q) = f(\tilde{q}) = 0, \qquad f(q) < 1, \quad \text{for all } q > 0. \tag{9.17}$$

We are concerned with the problem of defining the value to the consumer, of a capacity increment which lowers the probability, π, that he will be refused supply. One measure which suggests itself naturally, as an extension of welfare analysis under certainty, would be the *expected value of consumer surplus*. This could be defined as follows: given his income, tastes and the set of prices prevailing in state 1, there is some amount the consumer would pay for the right to buy the desired quantity of the good, at its given market price, rather than go without it completely. For example, if, one minute before the power cut, the man from the electricity board were to ask a consumer how much he would pay to avoid it, then this is the sum he would name. This measure of consumer surplus would then provide a basis for valuing investments which reduce the probability that the consumer will be deprived of the good. It is clear that it is this kind of value measure which, however vaguely and impressionistically, is in the minds of the planners when they choose a critical risk level, and fix a capacity margin accordingly. We now have to develop an analytical framework which, among other things, will allow us to evaluate the appropriateness of this particular value measure.

The central assumption of the analysis is that a consumer's preference ordering over uncertain prospects conforms to the von Neuman-Morgenstern axioms,[24] so that he chooses as if he were maximizing the expected value of a cardinal utility function. Thus, let q_j^s, $s = 1, 2, j = 1, 2, \ldots, n$, be the quantities of the goods he will consume in state s. Then, we can write this utility function as

$$u^s = u^s(q_j^s), \qquad s = 1, 2, \qquad j = 1, 2, \ldots, n. \tag{9.18}$$

We use the superscript ^{s} to express the assumption that the utility function may differ between states of the world 1 and 2: for example, the consumer's taste for electricity will depend on how cold the weather is.

Although there are two 'primary' states of the world, the consumer in fact faces three: 1α, 1β and 2, in the first of which he must consume nothing of one good, which we designate the nth. It follows that although his income and tastes, and the prices he faces, are the same[25] in states 1α and 1β, we expect that in general his choice of consumption will differ, as he compensates in 1α for the zero value of q_n. Thus, denote by q_j^α the consumption of good j in state 1α, $j = 1, 2, \ldots, n$, and $q_n^\alpha = 0$; and by q_j^β that in state 1β. It follows that the consumer's *expected utility* is

$$\bar{u} = \tfrac{1}{2}\left[\pi u^1(q_j^\alpha) + (1 - \pi)u^1(q_j^\beta)\right] + \tfrac{1}{2}u^2(q_j^2), \qquad j = 1, 2, \ldots, n. \tag{9.19}$$

Let us now consider the consumer's choice problem. In each state he faces a budget constraint which can be written

$$\sum_j p_j^1 q_j^\alpha - y_1 = 0, \qquad \sum_j p_j^1 q_j^\beta - y_1 = 0, \qquad \sum_j p_j^2 q_j^2 - y_2 = 0. \tag{9.20}$$

In addition, in state 1α there is also the constraint

$$q_n^\alpha = 0. \tag{9.21}$$

Thus, in state 1α, the consumer maximizes his utility function $u^1(q_j^\alpha)$ subject to the budget constraint and constraint (9.21), and the optimal consumption choices must satisfy

$$\frac{\partial u^1}{\partial q_j^\alpha} - \lambda_\alpha p_j^1 = 0, \qquad j = 1, 2, \ldots, n-1 \tag{9.22}$$

and

$$\frac{\partial u^1}{\partial q_n^\alpha} - \lambda_\alpha p_n^1 - \lambda_n = 0, \qquad q_n^1 = 0, \qquad \lambda_n \geq 0, \tag{9.23}$$

together with the budget constraint, λ_α is the Lagrangian multiplier associated with the budget constraint, and so measures the marginal utility of income in state 1α; and λ_n is the multiplier associated with (9.21). Taking the interesting case in which $\lambda_n > 0$ (an increase in q_n^1 from zero increases utility) we have

$$\frac{\partial u^1}{\partial q_n^\alpha} > \lambda_\alpha p_n^1, \tag{9.24}$$

implying

$$\frac{\partial u^1}{\partial q_n^\alpha} \bigg/ \frac{\partial u^1}{\partial q_j^\alpha} > p_n^1/p_j^1, \qquad j = 1, 2, \ldots, n-1. \tag{9.25}$$

As we would expect, 'not enough' of good n is available to the consumer in state 1α. In states 1β and 2, however, the conditions take the 'normal' form

$$\frac{\partial u^1}{\partial q_j^\beta} - \lambda_{\beta} p_j^1 = 0, \qquad j = 1, 2, \ldots, n \tag{9.26}$$

for 1β, and, for state 2

$$\frac{\partial u^2}{\partial q_j^2} - \lambda_2 p_j^2 = 0, \qquad j = 1, 2, \ldots, n, \tag{9.27}$$

together with the relevant budget constraints in each case.

This analysis leads to several useful results. First, suppose that, as in the previous section, price in state 1 will always be used to restrain demand to capacity. In that case, state 1α cannot occur, and expected utility becomes:

$$\bar{u} = \tfrac{1}{2}u^1(q_j^1) + \tfrac{1}{2}u^2(q_j^2). \tag{9.28}$$

It follows that *marginal expected utility* of good j in state s is

$$\frac{\partial \bar{u}}{\partial q_j^s} = \tfrac{1}{2}\frac{\partial u^s}{\partial q_j^s}, \qquad s = 1, 2. \tag{9.29}$$

Now, using the conditions in (9.26) (with $\beta = 1$) and (9.27) we have

$$\frac{1}{\lambda_s}\frac{\partial u^s}{\partial q_j^s} = p_j^s, \qquad s = 1, 2. \tag{9.30}$$

In other words, since the left-hand side is a 'money measure' of the marginal utility of good j, in state s, the price of the good in that state also gives us that money measure. In *expected* utility terms, we have that

$$\frac{1}{\lambda_s}\frac{\partial \bar{u}}{\partial q_j^s} = \tfrac{1}{2}p_j^s, \qquad s = 1, 2, \qquad j = 1, 2, \ldots, n, \tag{9.31}$$

and so the expected value of price of good j in state s measures the monetary value of the marginal expected utility of good j in state s. This provides us with the justification for assumption II in the earlier section. Also, we see, by using condition (9.24), that when the consumer is not able to buy good n, the expected value of its price understates the money value of its marginal expected utility, as we would expect.

Next, from the conditions for consumer equilibrium in each state of the world 1α,

1β and 2 (again assuming non-optimal pricing policy), we can derive demand functions:

$$q_j^\alpha = \phi_j^\alpha(p_j^1, y_1), \qquad q_j^\beta = \phi_j^\beta(p_j^1, y_1), \qquad q_j^2 = \phi_j^2(p_j^2, y_2), \tag{9.32}$$

which relate the equilibrium quantity of each good, in each state, to prices and income in that state. By substituting these demand functions into the utility functions, we obtain the *indirect* utility functions

$$v^\alpha = v^\alpha(p_j^1, y_1), \qquad v^\beta = v^\beta(p_j^1, y_1), \qquad v^2 = v^2(p_j^2, y_2), \tag{9.33}$$

which show how utility in each state varies with prices and income, via the effects of changes in these on the consumer's equilibrium choices. Throughout the analysis, we shall assume that the set of prices prevailing in each state is given and constant, and so these indirect utility functions will be written as functions of incomes, y_s, alone. Hence, we can write the indirect expected utility function as

$$\bar{v} = \tfrac{1}{2}\left[\pi v^\alpha(y_1) + (1-\pi)v^\beta(y_1)\right] + \tfrac{1}{2}v^2(y_2), \tag{9.34}$$

in terms of which we shall carry out the remainder of the analysis.

We are now in a position to answer the question: what is the value in utility terms to the consumer, of a marginal change in the probability π, that he will be unable to buy any of good n? The answer is found directly from (9.34) as the derivative

$$\frac{\partial \bar{v}}{\partial \pi} = \tfrac{1}{2}\left[v^\alpha(y_1) - v^\beta(y_1)\right] < 0. \tag{9.35}$$

The term in square brackets is the difference between the utility the consumer obtains from his income in state 1 (*given* the prices in that state) when he cannot obtain good n, and the utility he derives when he can. Since we expect the latter to be greater, this difference is negative, and so a fall in π increases expected utility, as we would expect. Given y_1, the derivative is a constant. Thus, we have that the gain in expected utility from a reduction in the probability of supply withdrawal is given by the expected value of the difference in utility in state 1, with and without consumption of good n.

Since the expression in (9.35) is in terms of utility it is not quite the final answer to the problem. We need to have a money measure, since we want to aggregate over consumers and compare total benefits with capital expenditures. To derive such a money measure, first note that the investment which reduces π must be planned at time 0, before the future state of the world is known. That is the expenditure must be incurred *for certain*. It follows that the comparable measure of the benefit to the consumer is the amount he would pay *for certain*, to bring about a reduction in the probability that good n will be unavailable to him in one state of the world. We can interpret a certain payment as one which will be subtracted from the consumer's income in year 1, whichever state of the world occurs.[26] To identify this payment, which we denote by $\hat{P}$, suppose that the probability of withdrawal of supply from the consumer is reduced to $\hat{\pi}$ from π, which, other things equal, will increase his expected utility. Then define $\hat{P}$ as the maximum sum the consumer is prepared to pay for certain, to bring about this reduction in probability. Now from equation (9.34), we know that the consumer's expected utility in the 'initial position' is

$$\bar{v} = \tfrac{1}{2}[\pi v^{\alpha}(y_1) + (1-\pi)v^{\beta}(y_1)] + \tfrac{1}{2}v^2(y_2). \tag{9.36}$$

Then given the change in probability, together with the payment of $\hat{P}$, the consumer's expected utility is

$$\hat{v} = \tfrac{1}{2}[\hat{\pi}v^{\alpha}(y_1 - \hat{P}) + (1-\hat{\pi})v^{\beta}(y_1 - \hat{P})] + \tfrac{1}{2}v^2(y_2 - \hat{P}). \tag{9.37}$$

It follows that if $\hat{P}$ is the largest payment the consumer is prepared to make in exchange for the probability reduction, we must have:

$$\bar{v} = \hat{v} \tag{9.38}$$

since in that case he will be just indifferent between the initial situation on the one hand, and the reduced probability plus certain payment (= a subtraction from income in all states of the world) on the other.

In principle, from equation (9.38) we could calculate the relevant value of $\hat{P}$ for given π and $\hat{\pi}$ if we knew the consumer's utility functions. For our present theoretical purposes however, it will be more useful to use the equation to define an analytical expression which shows us the general determinants of the 'willingness to pay' for a small reduction in π from its initial value. Thus the term $\hat{P}/d\pi$ gives us in effect the price the consumer is prepared to pay for a small reduction in π, when $\hat{\pi} = \pi - d\pi$ and P^* satisfies (9.38), since it measures the amount of money given up per unit decrease in probability. It can be shown that[27]

$$\frac{\hat{P}^*}{d\pi} = \frac{-[v^{\alpha}(y_1) - v^{\beta}(y_1)]}{\pi\lambda_{\alpha} + (1-\pi)\lambda_{\beta} + \lambda_2} > 0, \tag{9.39}$$

or, in words, that the price a consumer will pay for a small reduction in the probability of supply withdrawal before the state of the world is known, depends positively on the utility difference with and without supply, and inversely on the marginal utilities of income in each state, *including* those of states in which no risk of supply withdrawal exists (in this case state 2). It also depends on the existing probability, π, of a supply withdrawal, but in a way which is determined by the relative values of marginal utilities of income in states 1α and 1β, λ_{α} and λ_{β} respectively.

One conclusion we can immediately draw from equation (9.39) is that concentration on the value of the good to consumers, *given* the existence of state 1, is likely to overstate their true willingness to pay for investments which reduce the likelihood of supply withdrawal before the state of the world is known. This is because such a procedure ignores the significance of the sacrifice of income in other states of the world, as represented by λ_2 in the equation. This conclusion may be strengthened if we revise the assumption that the 'primary' states 1 and 2 have equal probabilities. Suppose, more generally, that they will occur with probabilities γ and $1 - \gamma$ respectively. Then it can be shown that (9.39) becomes

$$\frac{\hat{P}*}{d\pi} = \frac{-[v^\alpha(y_1) - v^\beta(y_2)]}{\pi\lambda_\alpha + (1-\pi)\lambda_\beta + \left(\dfrac{1-\gamma}{\gamma}\right)\lambda_2}. \tag{9.40}$$

Thus if the probability of state 2 is significantly greater than that of state 1, relatively more weight should be given to the marginal utility of income in state 2, something which may be neglected if attention is paid only to the value of consumption in state 1.

This concludes the analysis of this section. As we began by saying, we cannot claim to have solved the practical problem. However, we have clarified the theoretical issues and derived some conclusions about the kinds of measurement which should and should not be made.

9.5 Conclusions

We began this chapter by stating the problem of choosing optimal capacity for a non-storable good under uncertainty. Although we took, as an example of the way in which it is solved in practice, the 'capacity margin' approach of planners in the electricity supply industry, the problem has wide application throughout the public sector. The purpose of the chapter has been to provide a conceptual framework for further analysis and empirical work. We saw that if pricing policy can be used to ration output, then the corresponding prices give us the required information for investment planning. This is no more than an extension of a standard result to the case of uncertainty. Given that pricing policy cannot be so used, we have to analyse the determinants of the consumer's valuation of changes in the probability that he will be refused supply, given prices and incomes in each state of the world. We were led to an expression for the willingness to pay for a probability change, which provides us, in principle at least, with the relevant measure. Although related to, it is not in general identical with, the expected value of consumer surplus, and the analysis allows us to suggest circumstances in which the latter might overestimate the 'true' value. It is clear that the planners' procedure for determining the capacity margin is distinctly *ad hoc*. On the other hand, we have not suggested in this chapter any operational procedure which would replace it. We have, however, taken the first important step towards this, which is to clarify the conceptual issues, and to establish the kinds of measurements which need to be made.

notes

chapter 1
1   This begs a number of questions concerning the exact nature of a 'subsidized price'.
2   Although it should be noted that the textbook illustration of this uses cost concepts which are *not* the counterparts of the real-world accounting costs. It is these latter which form the basis for calculation of actual public enterprise profits and losses. There is no simple relation between a profit or loss using an economist's definition of costs (i.e. opportunity costs) and that using an accountant's definition of costs (i.e. outlays).
3   The best accounts of these are to be found in the *Select Committee on Nationalized Industries' Report* (1968), Foster (1971) and Coombes (1971).

chapter 2
1   In the case of public enterprises, a general statement of preferences over alternative 'bundles' of the four aspects of policy concern – economic efficiency, profitability, income distributional effects and macroeconomic impact – would be provided *independently* of any specific decisions to be taken.
2   Set out primarily in the two White Papers on 'Financial and Economic Obligations of the Nationalized Industries', Cmnds 1337 and 3437.
3   In Robson (1960) p. 47.
4   This is very well discussed by Foster (1971).
5   Early 1975.
6   In chapter 7 we examine how a set of decentralized rules can be defined, which resolves this inconsistency. The point made here is not that consistency is impossible, but that it was not achieved in the policy which was suggested.
7   Although the contribution by Pryke (1971) suggests that productivity improvements have taken place over the twenty years or so since nationalization at a faster rate than in much of private enterprise. On the other hand, it is not possible to say whether this was due to the fact of ministerial control, or to the changes in structure, capacity, organization and management of the industries consequent upon nationalization.
8   Coombes (1971).
9   Robson (1960) p. 424.

chapter 3
1   See Mishan (1960). The definition given here varies slightly that due to Mishan.
2   After the economist Vilfredo Pareto (1848–1923), who is credited with having first proposed them.
3   Historically, impetus towards adoption of these 'mild' value judgements was given by the

criticism that paternalism and readiness to make interpersonal comparison are 'unscientific' (see Robbins, 1932). This argument does not appear to have a great deal of force today.

4 This is an important point, also discussed in Mishan (1960). It is not usually possible to 'test' normative propositions empirically, and so we could not adopt Friedman's position (Friedman, 1953) of ignoring the 'assumptions' of a model, even if we should want to. Rather, we base our faith in the propositions on the view we have about the 'realism' of the assumptions.

5 That is to say, each individual's preference ordering over all possible consumption bundles, current and future, is known to him, and is exogenous to the analysis. This does not imply, of course, that the individual's preferences between perambulators and sports cars will not be different in year 10 than in year 0, but rather that these preferences are *known* in year 0 and do not change.

6 The resource allocations and price systems are determined as the equilibria of the market system in each period. We assume here that the conditions sufficient for these equilibria to exist and to be attained are always satisfied. For discussions of these conditions, at increasing levels of difficulty, see Gravelle and Rees (1977), Arrow and Hahn (1971), and Debreu (1959).

7 The description of the economy given here refers to a 'sequence economy', where there is a succession of market systems through time. An alternative characterization is given by the 'Arrow–Debreu' economy, in which the markets are held *only* at $t = 0$, and contracts are made at that time for sales and purchases at all future dates. The rest of the time is spent simply honouring these contracts. Given the assumptions made here, these two characterizations of the economy are equivalent.

8 Note that there is no *mechanism* by which these plans are made consistent and 'true' expectations formed, so assumption 5 is pretty heroic. In the Arrow–Debreu economy, the fact that all exchanges *actually* take place at $t = 0$ implies that the market mechanism does ensure consistency of all future consumptions and productions, but this hardly constitutes a gain in realism.

9 For discussions and proofs of these propositions, see Rees and Gravelle (1977), Malinvaud (1972), Arrow and Hahn (1971), and Debreu (1959).

10 As always, we make the two-person assumption to permit two-dimensional representation. All statements we make in this context generalize to an *n*-person world.

11 These utility values are unique only up to a positive monotonic transformation, since they correspond to the usual *ordinal* utility functions of consumer theory. It follows that we cannot rely on specific sets of *u*-values for any of our propositions: they have to hold for all permissible transformations. This is true for all the propositions stated in this chapter.

12 These public enterprises may control industries with increasing returns, which would otherwise act monopolistically. Other reasons for the existence of public enterprises are hard to find in a first-best economy.

13 Briefly: that consumers' marginal rates of substitution between any two goods (including inputs they may supply) be equal to each other, and to the corresponding marginal rates of transformation of the two goods (including inputs) in production. It is assumed here that the reader is thoroughly familiar with these necessary conditions.

14 It can be shown that application of this rule in the case of capital goods *implies* a

procedure of maximizing net present value of investment discounting at the market rate of interest. This implication is shown to hold in chapter 4 below. Consequently, when in this chapter we wish to draw specific attention to investment, we shall speak of the first-best rule of maximizing net present value calculated by discounting at the market interest rate. That is, it should be stressed, simply one aspect of condition (b).

15 If returns to scale are constant, then marginal cost = average cost, and so average cost pricing (in the theoretical sense used here, rather than in the empirical accounting sense) would imply marginal cost pricing. Non-constant returns imply, in general, inequality between marginal and average costs, hence the statement in the text.

16 Note that here we are attaching significance to points on the curve F_1F_2 in a way that is not really valid. For example, by transforming the utility scales appropriately, we could make point A look very inegalitarian, representing a great deal of 'utility' for 1 and not much for 2. It must be supposed that the planner interested in wealth redistribution is able to see 'beyond' the ordinal utility scale, to the real levels of well-being of the individuals. Then, simple transformations of the utility indexes would not change his policy. Thus, although useful for purposes of illustration, too much weight should not be placed on the 'egalitarian' nature of a specific point on F_1F_2.

17 It seems to be the case that the analysis of uncertainty involves a more fundamental departure from the first-best economy than any other of the 'second-best' issues. Some aspects of this analysis are presented in chapter 9 below, where some references are also given.

18 A note here on terminology: we use the term 'Pareto optimal' to refer to any situation such that no one can be made better off without someone being made worse off, whether in the context of a first-best economy, or a second-best economy. The concept of a Pareto optimum is much more general than the specific model in which it is being applied. Some authors seem to identify 'Pareto optimum' with 'first best', which in our view only leads to confusion.

19 For simplicity, these marginal costs are assumed constant. This means that shifts in demand curves do not cause price changes which cause further shifts in demand. . . .

20 In other words, as we would expect, the public enterprise price would not be used as an instrument of monopoly policy if in fact it does not affect the decision of the monopolist. This case is the so-called 'behavioural separability' case of Davis and Whinston (1965). Proposition (i) is really an application of the so-called 'general theorem of the second best' of Lipsey and Lancaster (1956/7). See chapter 6, where the general applicability of the theory of second best is further discussed.

21 This point is at the heart of the debate between MacManus (1967) and Bohm (1967), on the one hand, and Davis and Whinston (1967), on the other. Their disagreement was essentially concerned with the set of instruments a policy-maker has available, and the set of decision-takers in the economy he is able to influence directly.

chapter 4

1 Note that we are here assuming a competitive market for units of K. Recall the assumptions underlying the first-best economy, especially that of certain knowledge of future prices and technology; this clearly plays an important role in allowing us to regard the V_t as completely determined.

2 Note that this bears no relation to the accounting concept of the same name. The value δ_t

is an attempt to capture the idea that use of 1 unit of K in production reduces its market value or earning power. Accountants' depreciation provisions are essentially means of putting money by so as to be able to meet debts and replace assets, and are heavily influenced by taxation conventions. At the same time, in a real economy, as opposed to the first-best economy, δ_t may be very difficult to estimate, certainly as a single known number.

3 This assumption, together with the later assumption of no technological change, makes the 'vintage' of K, i.e. the year in which it was installed, irrelevant. All these assumptions could be relaxed at the cost of a good deal of complexity, which would not really further our present purpose.

4 In what follows, we shall assume that year 1 is the 'planning horizon' – no plans are formed for subsequent periods. This is equivalent to assuming no interdependence between the plans made at year 0 for year 1, and the plans made at year 1 for year 2, and so on. In practice, such interdependence almost invariably exists. Again, however, in the interests of simplicity, we ignore that here.

5 This requires it to set out the various technological possibilities of transforming inputs into outputs, given the knowledge it has at year 0, of the technology which will be available in year 1. Introducing input prices then allows it to choose the least cost process. The standard 'isoquant analysis' is one way of characterizing this procedure.

6 This assumes that 'depreciation', δ, does not depend on the rate of output actually produced within the year, i.e. on the rate of 'capacity utilization'. One unit of K 'depreciates' an amount δ over the year, however intensively it is used. This is not strictly realistic: some loss of value may occur simply with the passage of time, but some may also depend on intensity of use. Not a great deal of purpose would be served by introducing this distinction, however, and so we choose the simpler assumption.

7 Recall that the technology and input prices are those expected to prevail in year 1, and that in a first-best economy these are those which actually *will* prevail. Also, in the following analysis of the relation between year 0 and year 1 cost curves, an implicit assumption is that these input prices and technology are the same in each year. This is not a crucial assumption, and the consequences of its relaxation are considered at the end of this chapter.

8 See previous note.

9 This 'fixed cost' assumes, as was already stated, that δ is independent of q_0.

10 That is, minimizes cost for that output, given also optimal choice of L.

11 Note that by 'investment' is always meant *net* investment, the amount of K installed over and above that required simply for replacement. Also, since it is possible that $K_1^* < K_0$, if demand is declining, investment may be negative. In that case, we are implicitly assuming that it also takes one year to reduce installed K – by scrapping, selling on the K – 'second-hand' market, etc. In practice, the time it takes to reduce installed K may differ from the time taken to expand it, in which case we would define the 'year' differently for contracting as opposed to expanding enterprises.

12 Which, it should be recalled, are expressed in terms of *ratios* of quantities of two goods – marginal rates of substitution and transformation – to which *ratios* of prices are equal in a market equilibrium of the first-best economy. Marginal cost pricing of each good in the economy then emerges as a sufficient, although in some circumstances not necessary, condition for fulfilment of the equalities among these ratios.

13 Note that in the first-best economy, money plays no other role than that of a unit of account: there is no need for a store of value or medium of exchange. See Arrow and Hahn (1972).

14 Thus, from the necessary conditions for a utility maximum of a consumer, we have $MU_j/\lambda = p_j$, where MU_j is the marginal utility of good j, p_j is its price, and λ is the marginal utility of money. Note that permissible transformations of the utility function leave this equality unchanged, since MU_j and λ would be changed in the same proportion.

15 Thus, taking the two input case used so far in this chapter, we have that $C = nK + wL$, and therefore $dC/dq = ndK/dq + wdL/dq$. The input price w equals the value of the output which could be produced by a marginal increase in L in any other use; likewise n. The derivatives dK/dq and dL/dq measure the amounts of L and K which are absorbed (or could be released) by the marginal unit of output, when these amounts are chosen so as to minimize costs. Hence the marginal cost dC/dq is equal to the value of the outputs which could be produced elsewhere in the economy by the resources devoted to the marginal unit of output q.

16 It is sometimes postulated to be some form of consumer surplus measure, defined by integrating demand functions. The theoretical basis for this postulate is quite shaky, and since all that matters is actually the property in equation (4.6), it seems preferable to dispense with it. Cost-benefit analysts base their existence on the possibility of measuring some, presumably separable, part of this function, defined on a particular subset of the goods and services.

17 There are many expositions of investment appraisal procedures. The cheapest is probably Rees (1973a).

18 Note we assume that w, the price of L, is the same in each year.

19 Again, note that the production function f is assumed the same in each year.

20 This of course is the condition that, given K_1, L is set at the level at which its marginal value product equals its price in each year, or, equivalently, that price equals marginal cost, with K fixed, in each year. The condition is derived most directly by substituting from (4.13) into (4.12) and maximizing with respect to L_t only.

21 Thus, if A is the amount of an annuity in year $t = 1, 2, \ldots$, its NPV is $(A) = A(1+r)^{-1} + A(1+r)^{-2} + \ldots$, which can be written as $A\sum_{t=1}^{\infty}(1+r)^{-t}$. The summation represents the sum to infinity of a geometric series, which in this case is equal simply to $1/r$. For a fuller exposition see Rees (1973a).

22 In other words, we have found by algebra the solution $(p_1^* q_1^*)$ shown in figure 4.3(b). This conclusion uses the fact that marginal cost = input price ÷ marginal product at the optimal point. Equation (4.21) could also be rearranged to give the condition that optimal K_1 is set at the point at which the value of its marginal product in each year is equal to its price, rP.

23 See Turvey (1968b) and (1971) and Littlechild (1970), for examples of the more general analysis. The next chapter considers some problems arising from rigidities and indivisibilities in production.

24 Thus, suppose there are three inputs, L, K and R, with L immediately variable, K requiring one year to be varied, and R two years to be varied. The contention now is that marginal cost pricing is ambiguous. Extend the analysis of this chapter to show that it is not.

chapter 5

1   And private enterprises also; note that a profit-maximizing firm might well be faced with problems similar to those which will be looked at in this chapter. It could face the same difficulties of determining marginal costs in the presence of fixed capacity plant and indivisibilities, and might also find it profitable to practise peak–off-peak price differentiation. In analysing these problems in the public enterprise context, economists were in fact dealing with situations of much wider applicability. On the other hand, the actual pricing solutions will usually differ in the public case, because the maximand is social benefit, rather than profit.

2   In other words the marginal product of L is constant over the output range $O\bar{q}_0$. If it was assumed instead that the marginal product of L diminished over that output range, the segment ab of the C_0 curve would be convex from below; if the marginal product of L were assumed to increase, the curve would be concave from below. There would then be corresponding implications for the MC_0 curve in figure 5.2. The reader is invited to apply the subsequent analysis of this chapter to these cases, to show that nothing essential changes.

3   $\bar{q}_0$ is the output for which the fixed capacity K_0 minimizes cost. Given K_0, outputs $q_0 < \bar{q}_0$ are produced at non cost-minimizing input combinations, and so C_0 lies above C_1 over this range. See the discussion for the flexible plant case in the previous chapter. Note that again we are implicitly assuming unchanging input prices and technology between years 0 and 1.

4   For example, if one bus, working a specified route, can carry at most 10,000 passengers per year, and carries an annual interest and depreciation cost of £1,000, then the corresponding value of β is £0.10. If a transport undertaking has a fleet of 50 buses, capable of carrying 500,000 passengers per year, then its total capacity costs are 50 × £1,000 = £0.10 × 500,000 = £50,000 per year.

5   Using the previous note's example to illustrate these cost functions: given that its fleet is fixed, the total costs of the undertaking will be £50,000 + the running costs incurred in carrying some number of passengers, up to but not exceeding 500,000. When the size of the fleet is variable, then total cost is given by capacity costs plus running costs × the total number of passengers it is *planned* to carry.

6   A point on this vertical section of the curve does *not* show marginal cost at output $\bar{q}_0$, since this is undefined. The vertical section of the curve should be thought of as a diagrammatic device for helping us to analyse the pricing problem in the present case, rather than as showing the 'marginal cost' at some level of output.

7   In the case of electricity and gas, rationing would be carried out by supply interruptions on some basis of allocation determined by engineers; in transport systems it would probably be effected by queuing, so that those with lowest time valuations tend, other things being equal, to obtain relatively more of the good.

8   Assuming that rationing-by-price is part of this rule.

9   See previous note.

10   It has been pointed out that this problem is formally similar to that of joint production, which has been extensively analysed in economics – see Turvey (1971), and Littlechild (1970). Thus, just as putting inputs into raising sheep produces both mutton and wool, so installing electricity generating capacity produces both peak and off-peak electricity. The importance of the realization of this kind of analytical similarity is that techniques

and results established for one problem can then be directly applied to solve the other. The peak-load pricing problem had been solved before this similarity was first noted and exploited, however, and here we follow the 'traditional' approach.

11 The most general is that given by Mohring (1970). See also Takayama (1974) pp. 671–84, who analyses the continuous case.

12 The topic of 'transactions costs' is currently at the frontiers of theoretical work in economics.

13 See Craven (1971).

14 We have chosen the assumption, again for convenience, that the day is divided into two equal periods. It is possible to generalize by assuming, say, M periods, of lengths $l_1, l_2, \ldots,$ l_M, where none of these need be equal to any other. For an analysis of such a generalization, see Williamson (1966). Nothing of interest is added by such a generalization, and of course the second central problem, that of *determining* what these periods should be, is still ignored.

15 This 12-hourly interest rate r' is the solution to the equation: $£1(1 + r')(8760/12) = £1(1 + r)$. In other words, lending $£1$ for 1 year at r' compounded 12-hourly is equivalent to lending $£1$ for 1 year at r.

16 Drawing both demand curves on one figure saves space but may be misleading. There could be two figures, one relating to period 1, the other to period 2. The cost curves would be the same in each. One figure succeeds the other at 12-hourly intervals throughout the year. Daily outputs are given by the sum of the two values on the horizontal axes, and price fluctuates from period to period. Thus figure 5.6 takes advantage of the fact that the cost curves in each period are the same to save space, but the demand curves should be thought of as holding sequentially rather than simultaneously.

17 Thus, we have that peak and off-peak prices are the same, when marginal costs in the two periods are the same, as would be expected.

18 The problem just discussed can be set up and solved as follows. We wish to maximize the net social benefit function

$$S = B(q_1, q_2) - v'(q_1 + q_2) - 2\beta'q^0,$$

which was extensively discussed in chapter 4. We must impose the capacity constraints

$$q_1 \leq q^0 \quad \text{and} \quad q_2 \leq q^0.$$

In year 1, q^0 is variable and is to be determined, and so the variables with respect to which we maximize are q_1, q_2 and q^0. Necessary conditions for an optimum are:

$$p_1 - v' - \lambda_1 = 0 = p_2 - v' - \lambda_2,$$

$$-2\beta' + \lambda_1 + \lambda_2 = 0,$$

$$(q_1 - q^0) \leq 0 \; \lambda_1 \geq 0, \qquad \lambda_1(q_1 - q^0) = 0,$$

$$(q_2 - q^0) \leq 0 \; \lambda_2 \geq 0, \qquad \lambda_2(q_2 - q^0) = 0,$$

where λ_1 and λ_2 are Lagrangian multipliers. Note that we have used the property $\partial B/\partial q_i = p_i$, $i = 1, 2$, as discussed in the previous chapter. From these conditions we derive the two cases of most interest: (a) $q_1 < q_2 = q^0$ $\lambda_2 > 0$ and $\lambda_1 = 0$; then $p_1 = v'$

and $p_2 = v' + 2\beta'$; and (b) $q_1 = q^0$ and $q_2 = q^0$, $\lambda_1, \lambda_2 > 0$, then $(p_1 - v') + (p_2 - v') = 2\beta'$. Finally, note that there is a third possibility, in which $q_1 - q^0 = 0 = \lambda_1$, so that we still have $p_1 = v'$ and $p_2 = v' + 2\beta$. In terms of figure 5.8, this corresponds to the intersection of D_1'' with the line v' at output q_2^*. Therefore, although period 1 output equals capacity, this is not truly the 'shifting peak' case; in particular, the marginal value of additional capacity to period 1 consumers is zero at this point.

19 The problem was called this by Boiteux (1960), in his seminal work on marginal cost pricing, upon which this chapter has drawn heavily. Unlike many subsequent discussants, Boiteux clearly recognized the general nature of the peak-load pricing problem as one of dynamic optimization (see also Takayama, 1974), but chose the discrete period case both for realism and simplicity. He also discussed the question of load-curve decomposition, but far more succinctly than here.

20 This condition can be derived by solving the constrained maximization problem: max $B(q_1, q_1) - C_0(q_1) - C_0(q_2)$ subject to $p_1 = p_2$, given the demand functions $q_1 = D_1(p_1)$ and $q_2 = D_2(p_2)$. If we maximize with respect to p_1 and p_2, and then set $p_1 = p_2 = p^*$, the optimal uniform price, then condition (5.14) in the text is obtained.

21 We are here using the area under the demand curve as a measure of consumer welfare, which, although strictly speaking is erroneous, suffices for illustrative purposes.

22 Or, strictly speaking, the greatest optimal uniform price, since any price down to v' would suffice. If we are not indifferent to the extent of losses incurred by the enterprise, then the argument just set out would not apply, but this raises issues which are best analysed explicitly, as in chapter 7 below.

23 Thus, we now wish to maximize $B(q_1, \bar{q}_0) - v'(q_1 + \bar{q}_0) - R(q_2 - \bar{q}_0)$, subject to the uniform price constraint $p_1 = p_2$, and given the demand functions $q_1 = D_1(p_1)$ and $q_2 = D_2(p_2)$. This maximization gives condition (5.27) in the text. Note that in this maximization, *actual* consumption and output of q_2 must be taken as fixed at $\bar{q}_0$, the capacity output, and only *desired* demand can exceed $\bar{q}_0$. Hence, q_2 is treated as variable only in the rationing cost function, R. Also, we assume that the second-order conditions are satisfied.

24 This condition is derived by maximizing $B(q_1, q_2) - v'q_1 - (v' + 2\beta')q_2$ subject to the uniform pricing constraint $p_1 = p_2$, and given the demand functions $q_1 = D_1(p_1)$ and $q_1 = D_2(p_2)$.

25 These results are derived by solving the problem: max $B(q_1, \bar{q}_2) - v'q_1 - (v' + 2\beta')\bar{q}_2 - R(q_2 - \bar{q}_2)$, subject to the uniform price constraint $p_1 = p_2$. We maximize with respect to the *three* variables q_1, q_2 and $\bar{q}_2$, where $\bar{q}_2$ is capacity and actual consumption, while q_1 is desired demand.

26 For example, the optimal system requires knowledge of the slopes of demand curves which, in the absence of differentiated pricing, may not exist.

27 This analysis follows that of Williamson (1966).

28 For an analysis of this problem in the context of electricity supply see Turvey (1968b) and Boiteux and Stasi (1952).

chapter 6

1 See Lipsey and Lancaster (1956/7).

2 Especially that of Davis and Whinston (1965).

3   Though again, issues involved with the generation of revenue to the exchequer are lurking here, so this brief aside does not do full justice to the problem.

4   This appears to underly the approach to second-best problems of McManus (1957; 1967) and Turvey (1968b).

5   It also involves the assumption that monopoly policy continues to be ineffective (the reader should be warned that the view of monopoly policy as having been ineffective may not be universally accepted, although in the author's opinion it could be substantiated. An effective monopoly policy would of course remove much, though not all, of the force of second-best arguments.)

6   There is a similarity here with the 'targets-instruments approach' to macro-economic planning.

7   The general analytical framework for this section can be found in Rees (1968). Here, I shall be concerned with exposition and clarification rather than general validity of the results, and so a fairly informal partial equilibrium approach will be adopted.

8   The statement of this assumption tries to make as clear as possible two things: first, in discussing any second-best policy problem, we must specify the set of economic agents or decision-takers whose choices are controlled by the planner, and the nature of the policy instruments he has available – different specifications of these imply different problems with different solutions (see the debate between Bohm (1967) and McManus (1967) on the one hand, and Davis and Whinston (1967) on the other for an illustration of this); secondly, this piecemeal approach is very narrowly constrained in its policy options – unreasonably so perhaps, but see the discussion in the previous section.

9   Thus, the problem is to maximize net social benefit, $S = B(q_1, q_2) - C_1(q_1) - C_2(q_2)$, with respect to q_2 *alone*, but given the relation $q_1 = \beta_1(p_2)$, and the public enterprise demand function, $q_2 = D_2(p_1, p_2)$. The necessary condition for a maximum is given in (6.2), where we have used the property $\partial B / \partial q_i = p_i$, $i = 1, 2$.

10   This assumes that the tax is not an *optimal* one; if it is, then a different analysis applies. See the discussion of taxation in the following chapter.

11   This terminology reflects that used in defining partial and total derivatives, and indeed these are precisely what we have here.

12   Note that in general, each point on A refers to a different demand curve for q_2, since a change in price and output in market 2 causes a change in price and output in market 1, which in turn feeds back to change the demand in market 2. Thus, the curve A represents the value of the difference between price and marginal cost along a succession of demand curves for good 2.

13   Note, however, in adopting the policy, he must also adopt an appropriate redistribution policy if the change is *actually* to be Pareto preferred – see the discussion in chapter 3 on this point.

14   Which is equivalent to assuming that the function S is continuous on the interval $0 \le q_2 \le \bar{q}_2$ so that a maximum exists, and also that it is concave, so that condition (6.2) is satisfied as a true maximum.

15   If q_0 and q_1 have interdependent demands, then the β_i functions should be written: $\beta_0(p_1 p_2)$ and $\beta_1(p_0 p_2)$, which will affect the form of the necessary condition in (6.4), but not its essential meaning. Hence, we simplify by assuming demand independence between q_0 and q_1. This assumption is not innocuous as far as the stability and existence of an equilibrium solution for this model are concerned, but we do not analyse these here.

16 This condition is found by maximizing $B(q_0, q_1, q_2) - \sum_{i=0}^{2} C_i(q_i)$ given the functions $\beta_0(p_2)$ and $\beta_1(p_2)$, and the demand function for good 2.

17 These conditions are found by maximizing: $B(q_1, q_2, q_3) - \sum_{i=1}^{3} C_i(q_i)$ given the function $\beta(p_2, p_3)$ and demand functions for the public enterprise outputs. Note that we assume, for simplicity, demand independence between public enterprise outputs.

18 This was first pointed out to me by L. P. Foldes, in a comment on Rees (1968).

19 It is not hard to picture the sequence of newspaper reports to accompany this chain of events. The public enterprise first monopolizes the industry, and then on the one hand produces at enormous losses, or on the other raises prices anyway.

20 A mistaken application of our earlier analysis could also lead to a similar conclusion. The (false) argument might run as follows: 'since outputs are homogeneous, an increment of one unit of output by the public enterprise reduces that of the private enterprise also by one unit. Hence, in equation (6.2), $dq_1/dq_2 = -1$, and so the condition is $p_1 - MC_1 = p_2 - MC_2$. The appropriate second-best policy, therefore, is to accept the price increase.' The reader is invited to expose the fallacy in the argument.

21 In the case of cross-channel ferry services, British Rail appears to have joined the cartel (or perhaps even to be a leading member). In the case of the bulk energy market, prices are very close to marginal costs of the three major suppliers, coal, gas and oil. The above analysis does not purport to be a complete explanation of this difference.

22 Given by the price of the final good sold on the market, multiplied by the marginal physical product of q in producing this good.

23 See, for example, Turvey (1973), and the references given there.

24 Though this assumes a zero marginal disutility of labour to coal miners, which seems a very unrealistic assumption, given the nature of the work.

25 Even apart from any implications for macroeconomic policy it may have. Note that anyone who advocates that the government should not be concerned with public sector wage negotiations must implicitly support one of two further positions: (a) that a government should not be concerned with tax-expenditure policies; or (b) that public enterprise finances should be independent of the exchequer, which would be very close to denationalization.

26 Nor, regretfully, with the interesting approach of Mohring and Boyd (1971), which essentially transforms the treatment of externalities into a public enterprise pricing problem. However, the case analysed in this section brings out some elements of this approach.

27 Thus, we can write total cost, C_m, as $AC_m q_m$, where AC_m is a function of q_m. Therefore, $dC_m/dq_m = MC_m = d/dq_m[AC_m q_m] = AC_m + q_m \, dAC_m/dq_m$.

28 That is, the toll t^* would satisfy the necessary condition for a Pareto optimum. Our usual qualification applies here, however: if the initial equilibrium is at $\bar{q}_m$, imposition of the toll makes some people worse off, and so the *move* to the Pareto-optimal position is only justified on Paretian grounds if compensation is actually paid. On the other hand, this could well be done out of the proceeds of the tax, given by $t^* q_m^*$.

29 Note the similarity of this solution to the standard marginal cost pricing rule for a public enterprise. This gives a good illustration of the essence of the approach to externalities proposed by Mohring and Boyd (1971).

30 The condition is derived by maximizing $B(q_r \, q_m) - C_r(q_r) - C_m(q_m)$, given the demand functions $q_r = D_r(p_r, v_m)$, and $q_m = D_m(p_r, v_m)$. We make use of the properties of B, that

$\partial B/\partial q_r = p_r$, and $\partial B/\partial q_m = v_m$, and also that in the absence of a toll, we always have that $v_m = AC_m$.

chapter 7

1 In the previous chapter we looked at the consequences of this purely from the point of view of designing allocatively efficient policies for public enterprises, not themselves subject to taxation.

2 This is not peculiar to public enterprises: J. Hicks was speaking quite generally when he referred to the major benefit from monopoly power as a quiet life. On the other hand, the monopoly would not have to be an entrepreneurial, profit-maximizing one, but one in which the 'divorce of ownership from control' is complete.

3 In actual fact targets are expressed as rates of return on capital, which can under some circumstances lead to results which differ from those given in this section. That is, as Gravelle shows, a model in which the constraint is expressed as a rate of return on capital will generate different optimality conditions to one in which it is expressed as an absolute sum (see Gravelle, 1975). However, in my view, since financial targets are set by the policy-makers with the object of generating particular inflows into the exchequer, the expression of the target as an absolute sum is the more relevant form.

4 The analysis which follows is based on Rees (1968), in which is set out the general equilibrium analysis which validates the more informal partial equilibrium analysis given below. The paper by Boiteux (1956) is the seminal contribution in this area.

5 Note that the assumption of a 'break-even' profit target is easily generalized. If S is the target, then the revenue of the enterprise must equal $VC + S$, where VC is total variable cost. It follows that price (= average revenue) must equal $(VC + S)/q$, or $AVC + S/q$. Then, in the figure, we could imagine the curve AC as being derived from the average variable cost curve, by adding S/q at each output level. It has also been assumed that S is always such as to be greater than the surplus which would be generated by marginal cost pricing. The reader is invited to apply the above analysis to the case in which S is less than this.

6 Thus, the problem is to maximize the net social benefit function $B(q_1, q_2) - C_1(q_1) - C_2(q_2)$, subject to the profit constraint $p_1 q_1 + p_2 q_2 - C_1(q_1) - C_2(q_2) = S$. Then equation (7.1) is derived from the necessary conditions for a solution to this problem, given the property $\partial B/\partial q_i = p_i$, and the demand functions $p_i(q_i)$, $i = 1, 2$. λ is the Lagrangian multiplier associated with the profit constraint.

7 Recall that S is taken to be less than *maximum* profit, and so when S is satisfied, a reduction in output always increases profit, and an increase in ouput always reduces it.

8 Strictly speaking, these ratios should be negative, since $MR_i < MC_i$, $i = 1, 2$ by the assumption that S is for less than maximum profit.

9 See previous note.

10 Thus, $[-(1-\lambda)]/\lambda = -(1/\lambda) + 1$. Hence $\lim_{\lambda \to \lambda}[-(1/\lambda) + 1] = 1$. The effect of S approaching the profit maximum is to make λ tend to infinity.

11 As far as one can tell from the ambiguous statements about 'prices being reasonably related to costs at the margin', this is the system which seems to have been envisaged in Cmnd. 3437. Also, anomalies exist in practice: for example, the Bulk Supply Tariff, which determines the prices at which electricity is sold wholesale to the Area Boards by

the Central Electricity Generating Board, has two outputs priced at marginal cost, and the third bears the whole of the profit target. See Rees (1969) for a discussion of this.

12   The problem is formulated as before, but now the (inverse) demand functions are: $p_i = p_i(q_1, q_2)$. We denote the derivative $p_i + q_i(\mathrm{d}p_i/\mathrm{d}q_i)$ by MR_i, and $q_j(\mathrm{d}p_j/\mathrm{d}q_i)$ by MR_{ij}, $i, j = 1, 2, i \neq j$.

13   The problem now is to maximize over public enterprise outputs, the social welfare function: $B(q_1, q_2, \ldots) - C_1(q_1) - C_2(q_2) - \ldots$, subject to the n profit constraints

$$R_i - C_i = S_i, \qquad i = 1, 2, \ldots, n,$$

where R_i is the total revenue of the ith enterprise, and is a function in general of *all* outputs, and C_i is total cost of the ith enterprise, and is assumed additively separable in outputs of enterprise i alone. The λ_i are then the Lagrangian multipliers associated with the corresponding constraints.

14   That is, it can be shown that $\partial B^*/\partial S_i = \lambda_i$, where B^* is the value of net social benefit at the optimal point. This partial derivative then translates into the 'marginal welfare cost of the ith profit constraint'. This interpretation of the Lagrangian multipliers, or 'dual variables' as they are called in mathematical programming, is of great importance in economics. For a proof of the above equality, see Lancaster (1968).

15   There is a large literature in business economics concerned with the determination of transfer prices, which could very usefully be read in connection with the public enterprise sector, despite the fact that profit and not social benefit is taken to be the maximand. See, in particular, Hirshleifer (1956) and Arrow (1959).

16   There will also be a term in each condition which represents the welfare effect of the variations in E's outputs, in the markets supplied by A and B. Since the selling enterprise must meet its profit target, this does not so much affect the general level of its prices, as the relative contributions made to it by A and B. For details of the analysis, see Rees (1968).

17   Note the importance of the assumption of an otherwise first-best economy. If one of the inputs bought from the private sector is priced above marginal cost, then there is *already* a distortion, and in general this will require a deviation of price from marginal cost of the public sector input, along the lines discussed in the previous chapter. It is important to keep distinct the case in which only profit targets have to be met, from that in which private sector imperfections exist, to avoid confusion. The relation between them is explicitly discussed below.

18   The reader is invited to apply this discussion, and that earlier in this section, to show why (a) given that the Central Electricity Generating Board must meet a financial target, it is allocatively inefficient to load this entirely on one of its three outputs defined in the Bulk Supply Tariff; and (b) the imposition of a financial target on the CEGB is in any case allocatively inefficient. The answer to (a) is given in Rees (1969). The validity of (b) was my reason for saying there that the appropriate allocation of the target would make some, but not complete, sense of the Bulk Supply Tariff.

19   Reading the literature of criticism of public enterprise policies in the middle-to-late 1950s, one can make out a third strand of opinion. This was the feeling that low profitability implied both low efficiency and an *over-absorption of resources*, leading to a fat and inefficient public sector. But, as we have already observed, in non-competitive markets relatively high profits are consistent with low efficiency; while the problem of

determining the levels of public enterprise outputs and investment in a second-best world is approached by the kind of analysis carried out so far in this book, rather than a crude appeal to accounting rates of return. To make public enterprises 'as profitable as the private sector', whatever that may mean, has no obvious connection with efficient resource allocation, and sounds rather like a sublimation of the wish that no public enterprise existed.

20 In principle, the Consumers' Consultative Committees which are set up by each Nationalization Act to represent consumers' interests in the enterprise, could perform this task. They were not included in the discussion of the system of control in chapter 2, however, essentially because, with the possible exception of that in the steel industry, they are ineffectual. Their main purposes seem to be to fulfil a statutory requirement, and to rubber-stamp decisions agreed between board and department.

21 See Robson (1960).

22 A summary of parts of this work is given in Turvey (1971).

23 See Baumol and Bradford (1970), which gives a very clear statement of the optimal tax formula – together with an interesting discussion of its history – which included its rediscovery by various authors in various contexts. A more general treatment of the optimal taxation problem is given by Diamond and Mirrlees (1971). although, as Baumol and Bradford point out, their work was largely anticipated by Boiteux (1956).

24 Thus, given that

$$\frac{p_i - MC_i}{MR_i - MC_i} = \lambda,$$

and $MR_i = p_i(1 - 1/e_i)$, we can arrange to get

$$\frac{p_i - MC_i}{p_i} = \frac{\lambda}{(1 - \lambda)} \frac{x_i}{p_i} \frac{dp_i}{dx_i},$$

which, using the definitions of t_i and e_i, gives the result in (7.18).

25 A corollary of this is that the analysis in Rees (1968) is a solution to the problem of optimal taxation, when one sector of the economy is nontaxable and includes monopolies.

26 Boiteux (1956) used the term 'tolls'.

27 Thus, for example, although it appears to be the case that 'everybody' is prepared to pay the connection charge for electricity, for each consumer there exists a maximum charge, depending on his income, tastes and prices of substitutes, at which he would refuse to be connected.

28 The most general solution to this problem is by Mayston (1975) of whose work most of this section is a simplified presentation.

29 Note that if the indifference map is such that the curves do *not* have intercepts on the vertical axis, this is equivalent to assuming that *any* fixed charge, right up to the consumer's entire income, will be paid, to avoid forgoing consumption of good 1. We have already ruled this out as improbable.

30 This can easily be generalized. We assume the one-output case in order to focus on the interaction between fixed charge and price.

31 Note that we have assumed there to be no costs associated with n, the number of consumers. In practice, of course, there usually would be: where consumers have to be

connected to a supply network; equipment serviced; meters read and bills prepared, etc. However, it is not at all difficult to introduce a cost function defined on n in the analysis, and the optimality conditions change in an obvious way. Nothing essential is lost by this assumption, and simplicity is gained.

32 In fact, a rigorous treatment of this problem assumes a given continuous density function, which specifies how consumers are distributed over some consumer attribute variable. See, for example, Mayston (1975).

33 That is, capable of taking any fractional values. In the density function approach, n is simply defined as an integral over some specified domain. Note that these differentiability assumptions are important for the *kinds* of methods of analysis we wish to use, and not the essential nature of the results.

34 Thus, we maximize the net social benefit function $B(q_1) - C(q_1)$ with respect to p_1 and F, subject to the constraint in (7.19), and given the functions in (7.20) and (7.21). The discussion of these conditions is heuristic, and several shortcuts have been taken to simplify them, although they are essentially correct. For the general analysis see Mayston (1975).

35 Or more strictly speaking, the marginal revenue of price: $d/dp(pq) = q + p(dq/dp)$.

36 Needless to say, these assumptions are purely for ease of exposition, and more general analyses exist. The general approach is set out in Feldstein (1972a, b); Wilson (1974) makes a useful contribution to the operationalization of the concepts; and Mayston (1975) discusses distributional questions in connection with his analysis of the optimal two-part tariff.

37 Thus, recalling the earlier definitions, we have that:

$$\frac{\partial v^i}{\partial p_1} = \frac{\partial u^i}{\partial x_{i1}} \frac{\partial x_{i1}}{\partial p_1} + \frac{\partial u^i}{\partial x_{i2}} \frac{\partial x_{i2}}{\partial p_1}, \qquad i = 1, 2.$$

But from the conditions of consumer equilibrium, we have

$$\frac{\partial u^i}{\partial x_{i1}} = \lambda_i p_1 \qquad \frac{\partial u^i}{\partial x_{i2}} = \lambda_i p_2, \qquad i = 1, 2.$$

Also, given the budget constraints

$$p_1 x p_{i1} + p_2 x_{i2} = y_1, \qquad i = 1, 2,$$

we have, taking p_2 and y_1 as constant,

$$x_{i1} + p_1 \frac{\partial x_{i1}}{\partial p_1} + p_2 \frac{\partial x_{i2}}{\partial p_1} = 0, \qquad i = 1, 2.$$

Substituting for p_1 and p_2 gives

$$x_{i1} + \frac{1}{\lambda_i} \frac{\partial u^i}{\partial x_{i1}} \frac{\partial x_{i1}}{\partial p_1} + \frac{1}{\lambda_i} \frac{\partial u^i}{\partial x_{i2}} \frac{\partial x_{i2}}{\partial p_1} = 0, \qquad i = 1, 2.$$

Hence, rearranging gives

$$\frac{\partial v^i}{\partial p_1} = -\lambda_i x_{i1}, \qquad i = 1, 2,$$

and likewise for $\dfrac{\partial v^i}{\partial p_2}$.

38   This terminology was proposed by Feldstein (1972b).

39   Thus, recalling the definitions of the θ_{ij}, $i, j = 1, 2$, we can show that

$$D_1 - D_2 = (a_1\lambda_1 - a_2\lambda_2)(\theta_{11} - \theta_{12}) > 0,$$

on the assumptions made here.

40   Thus, the maximization gives as necessary conditions

$$\frac{\partial W}{\partial p_j} - \mu_j\frac{\partial x_j}{\partial p_j} - \beta\left[x_j + p_j\frac{\partial x_j}{\partial p_j}\right] = 0 \qquad j = 1, 2$$

$$\mu_j\frac{\partial f_j}{\partial z_j} + \beta w = 0 \qquad j = 1, 2$$

where the μ_j are the Lagrangian multipliers associated with the constraints in (7.35). The conditions in (7.37) then follow by rearranging, and noting that $MC_j = w\left|\frac{\delta f_j}{\delta z_j}\right.$. Note that considerable simplicity in these conditions results from assuming demand independence.

41   Note that here we have concentrated on the question of the optimal output pricing policies in the light of explicit distributional preferences. However an important case in practice is that in which the 'policy-maker' identifies households according to their input supply (coal-miners, steelworkers, etc.) and influences wage and employment policies in the attempt to re-distribute income towards certain groups. It is not difficult to extend the model of this section to that case, and the results are quite predictable – more of these inputs will be used at a higher price. For reasons of space, this case is not analysed here. One important conclusion which should be noted however is that, assuming substitutability of inputs in production and non-satiation of wants in the economy as a whole, it is not optimal to have overmanning, i.e. strictly surplus labour which could be removed without reducing output. The reason is of course that by employing such labour productively *everyone* can be made better off. The argument follows closely that of Diamond and Mirrlees (1971), in proving the optimality of technological efficiency under an optimal tax regime.

42   Examples of these are found in Rees (1968), which combined profitability and interdependence with 'deviant sectors'; Diamond and Mirrlees (1971), which combined taxation and income distribution; and Mayston (1975), which combined profitability, income distribution, and a two-part pricing system.

43   There is a large literature on the possibility of the existence of a social welfare function beginning with the fundamental work of Arrow (1963). An excellent exposition of this and later developments is given by Sen (1970). The problem is taken to be that of determining whether there can exist any set of rules or procedures, which may be called a *constitution*, capable of generating a social preference ordering over the alternative situations open to society, derived from the preference orderings of the individual members. The impact of Arrow's work was due to the demonstration that if it must meet

certain conditions of desirability, e.g. that no individual is allowed to be a 'dictator', then no such constitution can exist. I would not like to argue, however, that this implies that the present search for decentralized policies is doomed to fail. Somehow, despite Arrow's theorem, governments arrive at policies and sets of priorities which, as we saw in chapter 1, are manifested through choices. For our purposes the need is to make these 'revealed preferences' explicit. Arrow's work may raise important questions about the way in which these preferences are formulated, but for our present purposes that is not of direct interest. On the other hand, an attempt to understand the internal contradictions and lack of stability in implicit Government preference orderings may certainly be helped by the theorems on the possibility of social welfare functions (in Arrow's sense).

chapter 8

1 This is contained in the papers by Sandmo and Drèze (1971), Drèze (1974). I have also found the paper by my colleague Alf Vanags (1975) very helpful.

2 This assumption is not innocuous because the analysis has to change qualitatively, and the results are modified, when we move to n periods for the second-best models examined below. See Drèze (1974) and Vanags (1975), which explore this question. On the other hand, it *is* innocuous in the case of the first-best economy.

3 Maximize the utility function in (8.1) subject to the constraint in (8.4).

4 Thus, take the ratio of small finite changes in consumption, $\Delta x_1^i/\Delta x_0^i$. We can always find the number $\hat{\rho}_i$ which satisfies the equality $\Delta x_1^i/\Delta x_0^i = \hat{\rho}_i + 1$ by defining

$$\hat{\rho}_i = \frac{\Delta x_1^i - \Delta x_0^i}{\Delta x_0^i}$$

and $\hat{\rho}_i$ will be a pure number, just like an interest rate. Now,

$$\lim_{\Delta x_0^i \to 0} \frac{\Delta x_1^i}{\Delta x_0^i} = \frac{dx_1^i}{dx_0^i};$$

then, by defining $\lim_{\Delta x_0^i \to 0} \hat{\rho}_i = \rho_i$, we prove the equality in (8.6) (where, note, the sequence of Δx_0^i values, and corresponding Δx_1^i values, must always be such as to keep u_i at its constant value).

5 This identification of borrowing or lending with bondholding is a useful simplification: to borrow £1000 at fixed interest can be thought of as 'issuing' 1000 £1 bonds at that interest rate. No more than this is implied here.

6 In which consumption in each period is not an inferior good, and the indifference curves associated with the utility function in (8.1) have the usual convex-to-the-origin shape.

7 See, for example, Gravelle and Rees (1977) ch. 14.

8 Adapt the procedure for finding ρ in note 4.

9 This is effectively the macroeconomic national income equation; consumption plus investment = income.

10 This is obviously an exact replica of the argument for equality of consumers' marginal rates of substitution between pairs of goods in a one-period context.

11 This can be derived by maximizing the sum of year 1 outputs, $x_g + x_p$, subject to the constraint: $y_g + y_p = \bar{y}$, and given the 'investment production functions' in (8.11) and (8.12).

12 Which underlies the model in Sandmo and Drèze (1971).

13 Note that this specification of the taxable profit assumes that interest on capital invested is not deductible from taxable profit. To make it so would effectively restore the first-best economy. It could be argued that it is 'unrealistic' to make the assumption, but this misses the point. In reality, the overall effect of the tax system is to cause before and after-tax rates of return to diverge. The present model is capturing this divergence in the simplest way possible. It is the fact of this divergence which is of most importance, and not the precise way in which it is created.

14 The approach to the solution here is what is known as 'heuristic'. Though correct, the argument is developed in a fairly informal and non-rigorous way. This is partly to achieve the clearest possible insight into the solution, and partly because of the limitations on technique set for this book. For a fully rigorous derivation, see Sandmo and Drèze (1971).

15 That is, $x_1 = \sum x_1^i$, is total national income for year 1.

16 Where $x_0 = \sum_i x_0^i$ is total consumption (= national income *minus* investment) in year 0.

17 The simplest possible derivation of this is as follows: we wish to maximize a social welfare function $W(u_i(x_0^i, x_1^i))$, $i = 1, 2, \ldots, n$, subject to the constraints:

$$\sum_i x_0^i = x_0, \qquad \sum_i x_1^i = x_1, \qquad \phi(x_0, x_1) = 0,$$

where the third constraint represents the feasible combinations of total consumptions, given their underlying relations with y_{ij}. Then, necessary conditions for a maximum with respect to x_0^i, x_1^i, x_0, x_1, are

$$1 + \rho_i = \frac{\lambda_0}{\lambda_1} = \frac{\partial \phi}{\partial x} \bigg/ \frac{\partial \phi}{\partial x_1} = \frac{dx_1}{dx_0}\bigg|_{y_g},$$

where $1 + \rho_i$ is defined, as before, to be equal to the ratio of marginal utilities.

18 The reader should trace out the details of the argument, which are precisely those given in the previous section.

19 Since the maximization yields

$$\frac{dv_g}{dy_g} = \frac{dx_g}{dy_g}\frac{1}{1+r^*} - 1 = 0$$

implying $1 + m_g = 1 + r^*$.

20 This and other issues are discussed in Rees (1973), where also is presented an even more heuristic version of the analysis of the previous section, which is somewhat more general, however, since it has the public and private sectors producing different outputs.

21 This is because an enterprise forecasts demand and plans output on the basis of prices which are intended to cover *actual* interest and depreciation costs, plus the financial target, and then uses the TDR to determine the least-cost way of producing this output.

22 Which would be satisfied by the model set out earlier, if we add the assumption that the interest rate varies inversely with the excess of planned lending over planned borrowing.

23 This point is very similar to that made by Hirschleifer (1970), for the case in which borrowing and lending rates of interest are unequal in an imperfect capital market. A discounting procedure cannot be used to find the optimal solution, because the rate of interest with which to discount is not known until the solution has been found.

24   This is in fact very similar to the procedures actually in use in the public sector, except that the interest rate used in the detailed planning is probably inconsistent with the choice of aggregate investment totals. For further discussion, see Rees (1973).

25   See Feldstein (1972c) and Vanags (1975).

chapter 9

1   Described with great clarity in Berrie (1967).

2   More generally, an outcome may consist of values of a number of variables, for example profit *and* net social benefit. We would say in this case that the outcome is a *vector*. The formal theory is unaffected by this generalization, although of course computational problems may increase.

3   Taking the procedures described in Berrie (1967) as what in fact happens.

4   At least, this is how the Electricity Council's forecast is derived. The 'most probable demand' which is actually adopted may differ from this for a number of reasons, one of which is that there may be a conflicting forecast from the engineers of the Central Electricity Generating Board, who obtain this by an extrapolation of past trends. However, let us assume that the Electricity Council's forecast dominates.

5   This distribution is essentially a frequency distribution of *past* forecasting errors, which are treated as random or serially uncorrelated. There are several objections to this procedure which could be made on statistical grounds, one of which is that the forecasting errors actually *are* serially correlated. A different approach was adopted in Rees and Rees (1972), where the distribution of prediction errors from the regression equation used in forecasting, provided the distribution of future demands. This seems a more coherent procedure.

6   To say *the* problem may be misleading: there is also the problem of optimizing the plant mix, once the capacity level is determined. This problem is not treated in this book, since it is somewhat specialized (while the 'capacity margin problem' is in fact common to most investment decisions under uncertainty, as we shall see). For good expositions of the plant mix problem, see Berrie (1967) and Turvey (1968).

7   Thus, unlike many other commodities, the 'rationing' of electricity supply cannot be achieved by dividing up available output so that everyone gets something: some consumers get all they want and others get nothing. If there is deficient supply over a lengthy period, of course, disconnections can be varied among consumers on some equitable rotating basis, as is done in the event of protracted strikes which affect power supply. We do not take this as the typical *planning* situation, however. In addition, it is possible to reduce voltage without disconnecting consumers, for small amounts of excess demand, but we ignore that here.

8    $F(\hat{q})$ is found as

$$F(\hat{q}) = \tfrac{1}{2} - \int_{\bar{q}}^{\hat{q}} f(q)\mathrm{d}q, \qquad \hat{q} \geq \bar{q}.$$

9   The word 'roughly' conceals an important point: in general it is not the expected monetary value of costs and profits but the expected *utility* of these money values which

matters. To introduce utility theory at this stage would require too great a digression, however, and the reader is asked to tolerate the deliberate vagueness at this point.

10   There is a partial offset: the investment undertaken in year t, to bring capacity in year $t + 6$ up to the level K^*, will be in new, more efficient plant than the oldest currently in production. Thus, the greater the capacity margin, the greater the total cost saving arising from displacment of old plant, so that the actual cost of the plant margin is less than the straightforward capital cost. In effect, the margin will be supplied by a range of older plants, which would otherwise have been scrapped, and which will impose lower capital costs than the new plant. On the other hand, the greater the capacity margin, the smaller the *marginal* cost saving: the total cost saving increases but at a diminishing rate. See Berrie (1967) for details.

11   See Berrie (1967). The loss of consumption of electricity due to a power cut at peak demand is a very small proportion of total annual consumption, and so implies a negligible loss of revenue.

12   In Rees and Rees (1972), it was possible to show that in the case of water supply, the planners' solution was very likely to be very far from this optimum. This was due to the technical aspects of their forecasting and treatment of uncertainty, however, rather than any over-valuation of the benefits of reduced risk of supply shortages.

13   Looked at generally, what matters is choice $\hat{q}^*$ and K^* in our earlier notation; the fact that this can be expressed as $\hat{q}^* = \bar{q} + M^*$ is not strictly important. This implies that in its most general form, we should allow the possibility of negative as well as positive capacity margins. It could perhaps be argued that the question: how big should the capacity margin be? implicitly biases capacity choices upward, since negative values seem to be ruled out *a priori*. We cannot yet say, however, whether this bias leads away from or towards the optimal result.

14   This model is close to, but not identical with, that of Brown and Johnson (1969). It could also be looked on as a partial equilibrium version of the more general analysis in Rees (1973b).

15   The two-state assumption is purely for simplicity; an infinite number of states could be assumed, implying a lot more mathematics and no real change in results. See Brown and Johnson (1969) who took the general case.

16   Brown and Johnson (1969) assumed that price was chosen simultaneously with capacity, which seems to be quite unrealistic. On the other hand, the assumptions they made about rationing procedures effectively make their model equivalent to the present one, as far as capacity choice is concerned.

17   Thus Berrie (1967) shows that the average forecasting error for peak demands one year ahead was -0.6 per cent, with a standard deviation of 3.1 per cent. Thus, 95 per cent of the time, forecasts fall within ± 6.0 per cent of the actual outcome, assuming the distribution of forecasting errors is normal. However, this relates to the 'weather-corrected' figures: uncertainty about weather conditions, which cannot really be known until shortly before systems peak, still exists. Nevertheless, the degree of uncertainty is obviously a great deal less for pricing than for investment decisions.

18   Though, because of the equiprobability assumption, *not* the most probable demand. It would not be difficult, however, to construct an example which made state 3 the most probable state, and $\bar{q}_3$ the most probable demand. Again, this somewhat complicates the exposition while adding nothing of principle.

19   We exclude those states not in S_1 from this expression, because for these $p_s(\tilde{q}) \leq v$, and so their inclusion would make the condition inaccurate. An alternative formulation of it would be

$$\sum_{s \in S} \pi_s [p_s(\tilde{q}) - v] < \beta, \qquad [p_s(\tilde{q}) - v](q_s - \tilde{q}) = 0.$$

20   He may refer to the 'well-known tendency' of economists to do this, as reflected in the famous joke about the economist shipwrecked on a desert island, with one can of beer but no can opener. How did he avoid dying of thirst? He *assumed* that the can was open, and drank it.

21   Another version of the joke in the previous note has a mathematician and an engineer writing down in the sand all the equations they know, in a vain attempt to solve the problem of opening the can without a can opener, before the economist takes over.

22   Brown and Johnson (1969) obtained the result that the optimal uniform price should be set equal to v. This followed from their assumption that, in effect, there were no costs associated with non-price rationing of excess demands: an example of opening cans without openers for which they were justly reproached by Turvey (1970).

23   Thus, as in the case of electricity, there are essentially only two possibilities, power cut or not, which here have probabilities π and $1 - \pi$. This could obviously be generalized, in that there might be a whole probability distribution of output availabilities. The nature of the results of this generalization will be obvious from what follows, however.

24   For an exposition of these, see for example Borch (1968), Hirschleifer (1970), or Gravelle and Rees (1976).

25   In other words, we assume that the consumer's response to unavailability of good n does not affect market prices and income. Although a strong restriction, on empirical grounds it is reasonable. Note also that many theoretical niceties in the following analysis are not observed, and in particular all q_j^s and Lagrangian multipliers are assumed non-zero at the optimum, except q_n^x in state $1a$. Finally, note that in the analysis, the possible occurrence of state $1a$ has no effect on consumption on other states. This would not be true where, for example, consumption of good n in each state depended on a consumer investment decision which would be influenced by the *risk* of non-availability in state 1. This seems an empirically important and interesting case to analyse, but space limitations preclude that here.

26   Here we have to make explicit an implicit assumption of this section. We ignore the intertemporal aspects of the problem, for simplicity, so that we do not adopt the more natural definition, as the amount which the consumer would pay in year 0 to reduce the probability of supply withdrawal in year 1. This is not a worrying simplification, as long as we ignore time-discounting. It is not difficult to extend the analysis to include this, however.

27   Thus, assuming suitable continuity properties for the utility functions, we can apply the Mean Value Theorem to write

$$\hat{v} = \tfrac{1}{2}[\hat{\pi}(v^{\alpha}(y_1) - \lambda_{\alpha}\hat{P}) + (1 - \hat{\pi})(v^{\beta}(y_1) - \lambda_{\beta}\hat{P}) + v^2(y_2) - \lambda_2\hat{P})]$$

where the marginal utilities λ_{α}, λ_{β}, and λ_2 are evaluated at appropriate points. Writing: $\Delta\pi = \pi - \hat{\pi}$, we have

$$\bar{v} - \hat{v} = \Delta\pi[v^{\alpha}(y_1) - v^{\beta}(y_1)] + \hat{P}[\lambda_{\alpha}\hat{\pi} + (1 - \hat{\pi})\lambda_{\beta} + \lambda_2]$$

$$= 0 \text{ (by definition of } P).$$

Rearranging gives

$$\frac{\hat{P}}{\Delta\pi} = \frac{-[v^{\alpha}(y_1) - v^{\beta}(y_1)]}{\lambda_{\alpha}\hat{\pi} + (1 - \hat{\pi})\lambda_{\beta} + \lambda_2}$$

And so:

$\lim_{\Delta\pi \to 0} \hat{P}/\Delta\pi = \hat{P}^*/d\pi$ and gives the expression in equation (9.39), since $\lim_{\Delta\pi \to 0} \hat{\pi} = \pi$, and

$\lim_{\Delta\pi \to 0} \hat{P} = \hat{P}^*.$

references

ARROW KJ *Social Choice and Individual Values* (revised edition) 1963.

ARROW KJ 'Optimization, Decentralization, and Internal Pricing in Business Firms' in *Contributions to Scientific Research in Management* Los Angeles 1959.

ARROW KJ and HAHN FH *General Competitive Analysis* Oliver & Boyd Edinburgh 1971.

BAUMOL WJ *Economic Theory and Operations Analysis* Prentice Hall 1965.

BAUMOL WJ 'On Taxation and the Control of Externalities' *American Economic Review* 1972.

BAUMOL WJ and BRADFORD DF 'Optimal Departures from Marginal Cost Pricing' *American Economic Review* 1970.

BERRIE TW 'The Economics of System Planning in Bulk Electricity Supply' in Turvey (1968a) 1967.

BOHM P 'On the Theory of "Second Best" ' *Review of Economic Studies* 1967.

BOITEUX M 'Sur la Gestion des Monopoles Publics astreint à l'Équilibre Budgetaire' *Econometrica* 1956; translated and republished as 'On the Management of Public Monopolies subject to Budget Constraints' *Journal of Economic Theory* 1971.

BOITEUX M 'Peak-Load Pricing' *Journal of Business* reprinted in Nelson (1964) 1960.

BOITEUX M and STASI P 'The Determination of Costs of Expansion of an Interconnected System of Production and Distribution of Electricity' in Nelson (1964) 1952.

BORCH K *The Economics of Uncertainty* Princeton NJ 1968.

BROWN G and JOHNSON MB 'Public Utility Pricing and Output under Risk' *American Economic Review* 1969.

COOMBES D *State Enterprise* Allen & Unwin London 1971.

CRAVEN J 'On the Choice of Optimal Time Periods for a Surplus Maximizing Utility subject to Fluctuating Demand' *The Bell Journal of Economics and Management Science* 1971.

DAVIES OA and WHINSTON AB 'Welfare Economics and the Theory of the Second Best' *Review of Economic Studies* 1965.

DAVIES OA and WHINSTON AB 'Piecemeal Policy in the Theory of Second Best' *Review of Economic Studies* 1967.

DEBREU G *Theory of Value* Wiley New York 1959.

DIAMOND PA and MIRRLEES JA 'Optimal Taxation and Public Production' *American Economic Review* 1971.

DRÈZE JH 'Discount Rates and Public Investment: Post-Scriptum' *Economica* 1974.

FELDSTEIN M 'Equity and Efficiency in Public Sector Pricing: The Optimal Two-Part Tariff' *Quarterly Journal of Economics* 1972(a).

FELDSTEIN M 'Distributional Equity and the Optimal Structure of Public Prices' *American Economic Review* 1972(b).

FELDSTEIN M 'The Inadequacy of Weighted Discount Rates' in Layard (1972) 1972(c).

FERGUSON CE *Microeconomic Theory* Homewood Illinois 1972.

FOSTER CD *Politics, Finance, and the Role of Economics* Allen & Unwin London 1971.

FRIEDMAN M *Essays in Positive Economics* Chicago 1953.

GRAVELLE HSE 'Public Enterprises under Rate of Return Financial Targets' *Manchester School* 1976.

HIRSHLEIFER J 'On the Economics of Transfer Pricing' *Journal of Business* 1956.

HIRSHLEIFER J *Investment, Interest, and Capital* Englewood Cliffs NJ 1970.

LANCASTER K *Mathematical Economics* Macmillan London 1968.

LAYARD RG *Cost Benefit Analysis* Penguin Harmondsworth 1972.

LIPSEY RG and LANCASTER K 'The General Theory of the Second Best' *Review of Economic Studies* 1956/7.

LITTLECHILD S 'Marginal Cost Pricing with Joint Costs' *The Economic Journal* 1970.

MACMANUS M 'Comments on the General Theory of Second Best' *Review of Economic Studies* 1959.

MACMANUS M 'Private and Social Costs in the Theory of Second Best' *Review of Economic Studies* 1967.

MALINVAUD E *Lectures on Microeconomic Theory* North-Holland London 1972.

MAYSTON DJ 'Optimal Licensing in Public Sector Tariff Structures' in M. Parkin and AR Nobay (eds) *Contemporary Issues in Economics* Manchester University Press 1975.

MISHAN EJ 'A Survey of Welfare Economics' *Economic Journal* 1960.

MOHRING H 'The Peak Load Problem with Increasing Returns and Pricing Constraints' *American Economic Review* 1970.

MOHRING H and BOYD JH 'Analyzing "Externalities": "Direct Interaction" vs. "Asset Utilization" Frameworks' *Economica* 1971.

NELSON JR *Marginal Cost Pricing in Practice* Prentice-Hall Englewood Cliffs NJ 1964.

PRYKE R *Public Enterprise in Practice* MacGibbon & Kee London 1971.

REES JA and REES R 'Demand Forecasts and Planning Margins for Water in South-East England' *Journal of Regional Studies* 1972.

REES R 'Second Best Rules for Public Enterprise Pricing' *Economica* 1968.

REES R 'The New Bulk Supply Tariff: Comment' *Economic Journal* 1969.

REES R *The Economics of Investment Analysis* CSD Paper 18 HMSO London 1973(a).

REES R 'Public Sector Resource Allocation under Conditions of Risk' in M. Parkin (ed.) *Essays in Modern Economics* Longman 1973(b).

REES R and GRAVELLE HSE *Microeconomic Theory* Longman London 1977.

REID GL and ALLEN K *Nationalized Industries* Penguin Harmondsworth 1970.

REID GL and HARRIS DJ *The Nationalized Fuel Industries* Heinemann Educational Books London 1973.

ROBBINS L *Essay on the Nature and Significance of Economic Science* Macmillan London 1932.

ROBSON WA *Nationalized Industry and Public Ownership* Allen & Unwin London 1960.

SANDMO A and DRÈZE J 'Discount Rates for Public Investment in Open and Closed Economies' *Economica* 1971.

SEN A *'Collective Choice and Social Welfare'* Holden–Day San Francisco 1970.

STIGLER GJ *Price Theory* New York 1966.

TAKAYAMA A *Mathematical Economics* Dryden Press Illinois 1974.

THOMSON AWJ and HUNTER LC *The Nationalized Transport Industries* Heinemann Educational Books London 1973.

TURVEY R *Public Enterprise Economics* Penguin Harmondsworth 1968(a).

TURVEY R *Optimal Pricing and Investment in Electricity Supply* Allen & Unwin London 1968(b).

TURVEY R 'Public Utility Pricing and Output under Risk: Comment *American Economic Review* 1970.

TURVEY R *Economic Analysis and Public Enterprises* Allen & Unwin London 1971.

VANAGS A 'A Reappraisal of Public Investment Rules' in M. Parkin and A. R. Nobay (eds) *Contemporary Issues in Economics* Manchester University Press 1975.

VINER J *Cost Curves and Supply Curves*, reprinted in AEA *Readings in Price Theory* 1952.

WILLIAMSON OE 'Peak Load Pricing and Optimal Capacity under Indivisibility Constraints' *American Economic Review* 1966.

WILSON LS 'Some Work on the Distributional Effects of Nationalized and Regulated Industry Pricing Policies' PhD Thesis University of Essex (unpublished) 1974.

index

DATE DUE